THE ARCHER'S CRAFT

Some useful addresses:

The Archery Centre,
Highgate Hill, Hawkhurst, Kent, TN18 4LG.
Tel. 01580 752808.

British Longbow Society,
29, Batley Court, Oldland, S. Glos., BS15 5YZ.
Tel. 01179 323276.

Grand National Archery Society,
7th Street, National Agricultural Centre,
Stoneleigh, Kenilworth, Warwickshire.

Welsh Archery Federation,
Mrs S. Mayers, 16, Miskin Green, Llanyrafon, Cwmbran, Gwent,
NP44 8TF.

English Archery Federation.
Mr. A. D. Logan, 25 Alexandra Avenue, Droitwich, Worcestershire,
WR9 4DG.

Welsh Archery Specialists,
Crick Manor, Crick, Near Chepstow, Gwent.

Quicks Archery Specialist, 18/22 Stokes Hill Rd.,
Waterlooville, Portsmouth, Hants, PO7 7JF.
Tel. 01705 254114.

The Bow (magazine),
Bowhouse, The Dale, Wooton Wawen, Solihull, W. Midlands,
B95 6AZ.

The Glade (magazine),
62 Hook Rise North, Tolworth, Surrey,
KT6 7JY.

Craft Supplies Limited (suppliers of wood for bow staves),
The Mill, Millers Dale, Buxton, Derbyshire.

Disclaimer: Llanerch Publishers have no vested commercial interest
in any of the above. Their addresses have been included for the benef
of isolated readers. There may be other firms or organizations providin
similar services.

THE
ARCHER'S CRAFT

A Sheaf of Notes
on certain Matters concerning Archers and Archery,
the Making of Archers' Tackle
and the Art of Hunting with the Bow

written and illustrated by

ADRIAN ELIOT HODGKIN
O.B.E., M.C., M.A.

First Published in 1951.
Copyright © Faber and Faber.
Reprinted 1995
by Llanerch Publishers,
Felinfach.

ISBN 1 897853 80 7

First published in mcmli
by Faber and Faber Limited
*24 Russell Square London W.C.*1

PUBLISHER'S NOTE

Reference to Part Three: *The Art Of Hunting With The Bow And Arrow*
It is now **illegal** in the British Isles to hunt with a bow and arrow, and
this chapter has been printed for historical purposes only.

To
B.N.H.

CONTENTS

CONTENTS

Appendices

ILLUSTRATIONS

PLATES

9

ILLUSTRATIONS

DIAGRAMS

ACKNOWLEDGEMENT

Apart from acknowledgements made in the text, I wish to record my indebtedness to Dr. G. M. Trevelyan's *History of England* and *English Social History* for much background material and for pointers for further study in the preparation of the historical notes; to the Clarendon Press for permission to use certain quotations from the *Oxford Dictionary of English Proverbs* by Wm. George Smith; to the Director and staff of the British Museum for facilities afforded and help given me in photographing *Toxophilus* and other volumes; to Mr. C. B. Edwards, Hon. Secretary of the Grand National Archery Society, for his trouble in reading my MS. and for his kindly criticism and advice; to Major S. B. Carter, of Shire End, Wickhamford, for his generosity in providing me with a piece of authentic Warwickshire speech; and finally to my son John Eliot for his skill in the taking of some of the photographic illustrations and for his patience in posing as subject in many others.

FOREWORD

'*So long as the new moon returns in heaven a bent, beautiful bow, so long will the fascination of archery keep hold of the hearts of men.*'
MAURICE THOMPSON, *The Witchery of Archery* (1878)

It all began in a second-hand bookshop, where I was browsing in the basement, dreaming of places where the air is large and freedom a reality. There my eye lit on a book with an engaging title. A dull-looking book; sombre dark blue-green covers, and rather faded gold lettering. For seven shillings it became mine; and I remember thinking that it was a little expensive.

If needs must, you can take all my small library, always excepting one or two particular treasures, but you shall not have this book, this dull-looking book, which has given such pleasure and entertainment to me and others of my immediate tribe. It is called *Hunting with the Bow and Arrow*, and is by Dr. Saxton Pope, late of the University of California.[1]

Once, also in the same shop, I had an opportunity of buying the sequel, *The Adventurous Bowmen*. I did not buy it, and have regretted it ever since. Never have I seen another copy.

Dr. Pope, who, most irreplaceably, has passed on to happier hunting grounds, is therefore my spiritual father in all that follows here. How many besides myself he has set on the path of so much that is delightful I cannot guess; but however many our company may be, should these notes of mine add but one to the number then I might feel that my debt had been repaid in some small part. Pope's book tells in simple language how to make bows and arrows, and how to shoot with them practically, in the field. And it started me on making my first bow and my first arrows, from which I have had unending delight ever since. Why? I cannot say. Atavism, I suppose; and a burning desire to escape, even for a little while, from our drab, mechanized, penny-in-the-slot modern world, and get back to something which at any rate savours of a simpler way of life.

[1] G. P. Putnam's Sons, New York, 1925.

FOREWORD

It is four hundred years now since the bow was a practical everyday thing in England. From the middle of the sixteenth century, perhaps from even a little before that, its rapid decline began. It is now apparently forgotten by all except a few enthusiasts who have been shown, or maybe discovered for themselves, what good sport there is still to be had with it.

I say 'apparently' forgotten; for it is curious to watch the reactions of an ordinary Englishman when confronted with a bow. I have yet to meet one, young or old, particularly if he be a countryman, who, when shown this peculiar thing which had never come his way before, has not displayed the greatest interest, even sometimes to the point of fascination. They all know, of course, what a bow is; every right-minded child has made one out of a stick at some time or other. But they have never seen a real one. So, if you merely talk to them about bows and arrows, it is their childhood's image that will be in their mind's eye, and you will find yourself regarded as not quite right in the head, as a child babbling about his toys. If you do not just talk, but show them a bow, a real hunting bow with its formidable arrows, the scene is transformed. It seems as if they had at last found an old friend; as is, I believe, indeed the case. So marked is this interest, and so unique, that I cannot help thinking it springs from a source deeper than that of mere novelty or curiosity. I am sure that the longbow lives in us yet, did we but know it; and that our ancient skill lies just skin-deep waiting for another turn of Time's wheel. Whether this be a day-dream or not, certainly there is no doubt that the bow still lives in our speech, although perhaps only an archer may perceive the fact, and be aware that these sayings have so old and distinguished an origin.

The longbow is not a thing which should evoke a smile. It is an efficient and terrible weapon, capable of piercing body-armour (although there are few opportunities for proving that nowadays) and of slaying almost everything on this earth. With heavy arrows, it has an extreme range of about two hundred yards; and an effective range, within which a man may reasonably expect to hit his mark according to his skill, of eighty to one hundred yards. It is a great deal more dangerous than the shotgun; it can be more accurate than the pistol at long distances. Certainly it is no toy.

Then why do people dismiss it as of no account, if indeed they ever think of it at all? Partly, I think, because it is old-fashioned and for that alone to be condemned; partly because it is no longer a familiar object in men's hands; and partly, I have no doubt at all, from some dim recollection of Victorian archery; the crinolines, the side-whiskers, and all the rest. 'So elegant, my dear Amelia; Charles has become a toxophilite!'

FOREWORD

Target archery, useful and indispensable as it is, can never be anything but the means to an end. It is not the end itself. To engage in target practice only is equivalent to having a gun and confining your shooting to clay pigeons; or to keeping a horse and only riding him in the school. The end is the practical use of one's weapon, in the field, hunting game as our forebears did.

This work (if such a hotch-potch may be so called) has been written in the hope that, in reading it, some may have their eyes opened, as mine were opened by Dr. Pope, and so discover what good fun can be had with the bow, both in the making and in its use.

Our friends across the Atlantic have already found this out; and in their country, just before the war, the bow was again really beginning a new lease of life. With that came a host of books, from which I pick out particularly Pope's volumes and *The New Archery* by Paul H. Gordon[1].

So far as I know there is no comprehensive modern English book on archery, certainly none which tells the would-be bowyer how to set about making a bow, or the fletcher an arrow, or the archer how to use them when made. So, having enjoyed myself to such a degree in learning about this craft and sport; knowing that, what with wars and suchlike, it is not easy to obtain copies of existing books on the subject; and having a desire to record in some permanent form the trials and successes of a new-born archer; I have ventured into print on my own account.

Roger Ascham, the Elizabethan don, who is the 'father-in-archery' of us all, wrote a book which he called *Toxophilus*, of which much more later. As soon, however, as I had read what he has to say (and very delightfully he says it), it was obvious that here was a gold-mine which had never been properly worked, a storehouse of archery lore crying out to be made public.

So I have done so, using for the most part Bennet's edition of 1761.

There are four good reasons for quoting as freely from Ascham as I have done. The principal is that his practical advice on the bow is as sound now as when it was written; and is, perhaps, the original source of all our knowledge of the subject. The three others which weigh with me are: first, that his views on matters other than archery shed light on his character, besides being interesting in themselves as a commentary on the thought and manners of the sixteenth century; second, that his writing is so simple and direct (if, at times, amusing also to modern ears or eyes) that it serves now, as it did and was intended to do in 1545, as a wholesome reminder that English properly used is a beautiful and expressive language; and third and last, that what he wrote is not now generally accessible.

[1] New Appleton-Century Co., New York, 1939.

FOREWORD

Apart from the note dealing with Ascham's life, there are, at the end of almost every section in the second part of this book, extracts from *Toxophilus* which give Ascham's own views on the matter. Read these: they are the groundwork of archery.

I make no apology at all for using Ascham in this way. I am sure he would be pleased and flattered himself, and for your part you will profit greatly by it. It is well to drink from the springhead when you can.

One thing led to another, after reading Ascham; and the historical part of this notebook is the result.

As to the practical parts, I have set down as faithfully and as clearly as I could my own experiences in the making of archery tackle, and in its use. I do not claim to be original, since there can be little originality in a craft so old, notwithstanding certain modern developments. If there be any merit at all in these practical notes, it is that they contain nothing, unless specifically indicated, which I have not done myself and found good.

On the other hand, let me be quite clear on one point. I began from the very beginning, as I hope you will, guided at first by Pope, and then, much later, by Gordon; and I developed as a result a certain facility in making what I wanted. Even so, no one realizes better than I do that the skill and knowledge of a professional bowyer (a real bowyer, not the mechanic who turns out machine-made bows by the hundred), are things which only come after long and hard experience, and I lay no claim to either.

Anyone can, I suppose, make a violin if he has time and some skill with tools, yet the odds are heavily against it being of the quality of a Stradivarius. His instrument may play sweetly, but it will not be superb. So with bows. Those that I have made have been serviceable in all respects, and so will yours be. But whether either of us will ever make a masterpiece is a thing which need not trouble us. Let us hope we shall; but let us not be dissatisfied or discouraged if we only achieve the essentials. The great thing is to make a bow, even if it should turn out a poor one for a start. When once you have made a bow you will be hopelessly ensnared for life, and I shall have accomplished what I set out to do. But, you may say, such a thing is beyond you. Believe me, it is not, if you have any skill at all in your fingers and patience in your make-up. Listen to this.

Not so many years ago my younger son began to cast longing eyes on my bows, and clearly thought it was unreasonable that I should have so many while he had none. So, for discipline's sake and the right upbringing of the young, I promised him the weakest, the first bow I had ever made, provided —and here I employed some cunning and stratagem—that he would make first six arrows, unaided. Just what this means you will appreciate better when you have made your first half-dozen!

So for a space he retired, armed with the requisite raw material. After a considerable season he emerged, and with him were six arrows, neat and practical, with vermilion shafts feathered with white turkey. He got his bow, and Archer No. 1 was born.

That was too much for John, my first-born. If Dick could do that so could he: would I give him a stave to make a bow with. No, I would not; until, again, he had made six arrows. Now John had never to my knowledge made anything in his life, and was indeed at that time disinclined to use his hands at all, until the idea of the bow occurred to him. So I expected much tribulation and little result. However, the Little Gods of the Outdoors were on his side, and in due course forth he came with six arrows, feathered with white turkey and with vermilion shafts, very neat and practical. So Archer No. 2 was born. And the bow? Yes, he made it, and its string; and it turned out very well.

So be encouraged by this. The craft is not difficult, and the pleasure finally achieved is out of all proportion to the trials endured.

I will not say it is easy to learn to shoot; it is not. Therein lies, I think, some of the attraction. Good archers do not grow on every bush.

As to 'game', are there not rabbits everywhere, and perhaps hares; birds, including wildfowl, also, if you are prodigal of arrows? Deer, even, if you know where to go and have the freedom of the place; much more widely distributed than might be thought. And, of course, if you travel and go abroad into the really wild places, all nature is open to you; and if you have the courage of Pope you can shoot lions, as he and the old kings of Assyria did.

To get the full pleasure from archery you must, however, enter into the spirit of the thing.

If you are one of those who like organized 'shoots' where everything is done for you except the final act of pointing your gun and pulling the trigger; if you like beaters, and noise and trampling in the woods; if you enjoy a sense of competition: if you are content to take little part in finding and rousing the game and in bringing it to the appointed place; if, in short, it is for you only the adroit handling of your gun and the size of the bag which counts; then the bow is not your weapon. The bow will not produce you big bags; you will go solitary, and in silence, and upon your own skill and patience alone will depend such sport as you may get.

Nor is it enough merely to be able to shoot well. With that accomplishment must go a high degree of woodcraft and knowledge of the habits of your game. You will, even with your utmost skill, miss much more than you hit, and it will be a great day when you come home heavy-laden. But I'll warrant you'll have more satisfaction in having stalked and missed a roebuck at fifty yards with an arrow than in killing him at two hundred with a rifle, or plastering the poor beast with small shot point-blank in a drive.

If you do not feel this way do not take up archery; or, if you do feel like this but have no facilities for hunting, take to shooting at inanimate targets. There are many clubs in the British Isles, and in the Commonwealth, which concern themselves with target shooting. Some of them have Field Courses, and that is, at any rate, looking in the direction of hunting. The governing body for archery in the United Kingdom is the Grand National Archery Society, which has its headquarters at the club house of the Royal Toxophilite Society, 1 Albion Mews, London, W.2.

To be an archer is one thing; to be a writer is quite another. Just as I do not offer to compare myself with the professional bowyers and fletchers (although I am rash enough to think that their criticism of my tackle might not be altogether unkind), so I am more than conscious of the shortcomings of my literary craftsmanship. I ask, therefore, that you consider more the substance of what I have attempted to say than the manner in which it is said.

For a final word let me give you Roger Ascham's own *apologia* for what he wrote. It will serve much better than anything I could have said myself; and I would not wish to alter any of it:

'I truste no man will be offended with this little booke, excepte it be some fletchers and bowiers, thinking hereby that manye that loue shootygne shall be taughte to refuse suche noughtie wares as they woulde vtter. Honest fletchers and bowyers do not so, and they that be vnhonest, oughte rather to amende themselues for doinge ill, than be angrie with me for sayinge wel. . . . And this lytle booke I truste, shall please and profite both partes: for good bowes and shaftes shall be better knowen to the commoditie of all shoters, and good shotynge may perchaunce be the more occupied to the profite of all bowyers and fletchers. And thus I pray God that all fletchers getting theyr lyuyng truly, and al archers vsynge shootynge honestly, and all maner of men that fauour artillery, may lyue continuallye in healthe and merinesse, obeying theyr Prince as they shulde, and louing God as they oughte, to whom for al thinges be al honour and glorye for euer. Amen.'

Cobham, Surrey   A.E.H.

Part One

HISTORICAL

THE OLD ENGLISH ARCHER

'These were they that in times past made all France afraid. And albeit they be not called Master as gentlemen are, or Sir as to Knights apperteineth, but onlie John and Thomas &c: yet haue they beene found to haue done verie good seruice.'

W. HARRISON, *Description of England.*

According to Ascham, who had it from Sir Thomas Eliot, who in turn got it from 'an exceedinge olde chronicle', the bow came into England in the days of Vortigern, about A.D. 449. This Vortigern was a rather dubious Prince of Kent who, fearing an attack from the Picts and Scots, called over the Saxons Hengist and Horsa to his aid, and bade Horsa to be sure to bring his beautiful daughter Rowena as well. The Saxons came, bringing their shortbows with them, and stayed; while, at the instigation of some saint, Vortigern was eventually destroyed by fire from heaven along with his numerous wives. So runs the tale. Modern authorities will not have it, and declare, as is indeed much more probable, that the bow came over with the Danes in their expeditions against this island.

It is impossible, from lack of material, to write a coherent history of the bow in England from the earliest times. In the days when the bow was really a live thing men did not write about it. Indeed they could not; and few could read anyway. The notes that follow are therefore necessarily brief, and leave untouched many things that one would like to know; but they may, I hope, serve to shed a little light on the position of the old English archer both in war and peace.

In peace, there is really very little that can be said at all. The bow was the natural weapon of the mediaeval and later hunter of the lower sort—the yeoman, the poacher, the outlaw; and deer was the principal game. The ancient nobility despised the bow as unsporting, since it killed at a distance and the hunter was rarely in personal danger. They hunted according to set form, with spear, sword, and hound. The archer was well enough in war to slay Frenchmen and Scots, but not, if you please, at the hunt to kill the King's deer—at all events, not until much later on in Tudor times. So the archer in peace (as indeed in war too) was a common man, and is personified for us in Robin Hood, in William of Cloudesley, Clym of the Clough, and others. To this day it is a matter of controversy whether Robin was a real person or not. Even as late as 1944 a most circumstantial account was published in *Archery News*, in which Robin is represented as having been born at Wakefield between the years 1285 and 1295, the son of a forester in the employ of Earl Warrenne; that he married and lived at Wakefield; and that he owed his outlawry to having fought against Edward II at the battle of Boroughbridge. Robin is then said to have gone to live in the Forest of Barnsdale (not Sherwood) and there to have performed the exploits which are so familiar to us in the story-books. Eventually, having made his peace with the King, Robin took service under him; but left it again after a short while and returned to Barnsdale. There he is said to have died in 1347 in the arms of Little John, and to have been buried just without the consecrated ground of the Priory of Kirklees, between Mirfield and Brighouse, where the remains of his tomb can still be seen.

Well, it may be so. But is it not equally likely that, in an age of illiteracy, of rigid privilege, and of perpetual social unrest, the story of Robin Hood grew out of the mind of the common people, and that Robin himself is no more than a convenient peg upon which to hang all the tales and legends of outlawry and of common rough justice? Learned opinion seems to incline to this view. At all events, it matters little now. Robin's exploits are lively tales, and his alleged feats of archery are entertaining if impossible. But the old ballads and stories do give us some insight into the life of those far-off days; and there we may leave them.

It is unfortunate that only two books on archery written by Englishmen have come down to us from the time when the bow was in general use. The first, the *Master of Game*, was written by Edward Duke of York about 1410, and is a shameless plagiarism on the *Livre de Chasse* of the Frenchman, Gaston de Foix, of whom more later. This treats of archery as incidental to certain forms of hunting. The other is Ascham's famous *Toxophilus*, published in 1545, a discursive treatise on the bow (and much else) as an instrument of recreation and pleasure. It is, however, a mine of information, and is probably the most celebrated book on archery that now exists. The only other publications relating to peace-time archery are the various Forest Charters, issued to regulate the conduct of the King's Forests. These deal voluminously with the subject of poachers, and poachers are, of course, archers. The Charters are long and complicated; and we need merely note that anyone found in the

Forest (not just any forest, but those tracts of land specifically designated as the preserves of the King) with a bow and arrows, or with a hound, shall be arrested and imprisoned after trial if he be found in one of the four following positions: 'Stablestand', that is, standing with a bow ready bent or with a hound ready to loose; 'Dogdraw', that is, trailing a wounded beast with a hound; 'Backbeare', that is, carrying game; and 'Bloodyhand', which sufficiently explains itself. The preservation of the King's game may have been carried to a high degree, and enforced with a high hand; but it is certain that without these laws, which go back at least as far as Canute, there would be no game in England to-day.

That is the full tale of old archery literature. It is little enough, in all conscience. For the rest we must draw upon our imagination as to what men did with the bow when they were not fighting with it. It should not be difficult since the bow has not changed much, if at all. It is still the primitive thing it always was; while the deer and the forests have not changed at all, save that the latter have shrunk to a fraction of their former grandeur. While it is easy enough to reconstruct in imagination the actions and equipment of the old archer hunting his dinner, 'clad in cote and hode of grene, a shefe of pecocke arrowes bryghte and shene under his belt', it is not so easy to visualize the compulsory week-end archery practices which took place (or not) according to law through a long span of years. For the English, contrary perhaps to some of our preconceived notions, had to be driven to practise with the bow. For them, in those days as in our own, 'unlawful gammes' were much more congenial than the dull round of fitting themselves for military service; and there was besides the continual attraction of the much easier but less effective crossbow. In edict after edict the successive kings of England compelled their subjects to practise archery in their leisure hours; but of these practices, their organization and equipment, there is no account, nor any trace of the weapons themselves until we come to the comparatively late times of the Tudors. We know simply that they shot at long range, and that their mark might be either a circle or a rag on the ground to be hit by an arrow shot high up into the air and falling almost vertically (clout shooting), or a vertical stick planted in the ground which had to be split by the arrow, or a plain target with a white mark on it (prick shooting). But we know nothing of their accuracy, nor of their methods of training; we know only that they shot far and hard. It is a pity, for the gap can now never be filled. That we have fragmentary accounts of archery meetings in the time of Henry VIII, and of that monarch's own prowess with the bow, and even a list of his wagers when shooting with his friends, is well enough even though the bow was then long past its prime; but it helps not at all to dispel our ignorance of how Edward III trained those archers who became a terror and a byword in all Christendom. That book is closed for ever.

Halfway between peace and war comes private vengeance. Thus:

'Supposing I were in yonder sloping wood opposite, and in my hand a bow of red yew ready bent, with a tough, tight string, and a straight round shaft with a well-rounded nock, having long slender feathers of a green silk fastening, and a sharp-edged steel head, heavy and thick, and an inch wide, of a green-blue temper, that would draw blood out of a weathercock. And with my foot to a hillock, and my back to an oak, and the wind to my back, and the sun towards my side; and the girl I love best, hard by, looking at me; and I conscious of her being there; I would shoot him such a shot, so strong and far-drawn, so low and sharp, that it would be no better there were between him and me a breastplate and a Milan hauberk, than a wisp of fern, a kiln rug, or a herring-net!'

That is from a fifteenth-century MS., the 'Tale of Iolo Goch', bard to Owen Glendower; and is quoted in Hansard's *Book of Archery*, 1841. Is it not magnificent? Can you not see the archer, tense and drawn like his own bowstring, his fingers itching to loose that shaft that would draw blood out of a weathercock? What a passage! Only an archer could have written it.

So we pass from peace to war; and here inquiry is better rewarded. Let us accept that the bow, the shortbow that is, came in with the two-handed battleaxe of the Danes, and that later on it was exchanged, as we shall see, in preference for the Welsh longbow. What of it? Is this a significant historical event? Was the old English archer as important as that, and did he, as some think, lay the foundations of England's greatness? Was he the backbone of our military system some hundreds of years ago? If so, when, how, and for how long? Has his place in the order of things been exalted too high, by time and ballad-monger alike, or was he really the paragon that we like to think? Some of these questions can be answered with fair assurance. But let us take a look at some of the facts first, and then try to draw conclusions.

From the Danes to the invasion of Duke William of Normandy is not a very far cry. The Norman nobility, mail-clad and with sword, shield and spear, rode their heavy chargers; the unarmoured archers came on foot, carrying their shortbows. There is no conjecture about this; you can see it all in the Bayeux Tapestry. Only one English archer is shown, and he has a shortbow too. They found Harold and his men entrenched and on the defensive behind stakes driven into the ground, armed with axes. Both sides had learned of the bow from the Danes, but only the Normans had persevered with it. The Duke ordered some of his archers to shoot straight forward and others to direct their arrows upwards, to get at the English behind their palisade. William lured the English out of their strongpoint with a feigned retreat, and in the confused fighting which followed Harold was killed by an arrow in the brain. So cavalry with 'artillery' beat infantry with hand-weapons only, and England was won by a single arrow.

After so notable a victory, it is not surprising that we hear nothing about archery for a long time. Duke William was busy subduing and despoiling his new kingdom, defending himself against local risings, and giving us a system of law and order for much of which we still have cause to be grateful; while Rufus carried on his father's policy with all his ruthlessness but none of his wit until an arrow (whether aimed or not we shall never know) took his life in his New Forest. It is not till we come to the time of the somewhat milder Henry I, when, a generation and more after the Conquest, the sharp division between conquerors and conquered was beginning to lose its harsher asperities, that there is anything to record about the bow. Henry decreed that no man practising archery should be held for murder or manslaughter if he killed anyone in the process. Whether this was more for the benefit of Norman or Englishman it is hard to say; but the odds are on the former. At any rate, archery had reached the Statute Book for the first time in England, and the first of many milestones was set up thereby.

A hundred years after Hastings, Dermot McMorrogh, King of Leinster, asked the English for aid against Roderic, King of Connaught; which was brought by Richard de Clare, Earl of Pembroke, nicknamed Strongbow, and resulted in the conquest of all Ireland. In the tale of each body of troops sent over archers are prominent and outnumber greatly both knights and esquires. The Irish had no bows; and so again the lesson of Hastings is repeated.

While the Irish were in this plight, it was otherwise with the Welsh. Giraldus Cambrensis notes (about the year 1200) that the Welsh had bows not of horn or yew but of wych-elm; that they were not particularly well made or comely; but that they were strong and designed to deliver a heavy blow in close fighting. They could even shoot through oaken church doors, or pin an armoured man to his saddle. Later on the English were to experience the prowess of these Welsh archers, and to profit greatly from it.

In 1252, Henry III held his celebrated Assize of Arms; and decreed that all who were physically capable of bearing arms should do so, and keep them by them. The bow is prominently mentioned, and even the poorest was to have one of these. Only, if a man dwelt in one of the royal forests, then his arrows were to be blunt. So, Defence of the Realm or not, he was to be rendered incapable of killing the king's deer!

Thus far, in some two hundred years, the Danish bow has conquered first England and then Ireland; and now all Englishmen are to have bows by order. What for? For the 'Defence of the Realm', or for the conquest of Wales and Scotland, and maybe for adventures in France as well? There is not long to wait. In 1276, the capable and strong-willed Edward I, competent son of an incompetent father, made his invasion of Wales; succeeding, not by any particular prowess in arms, but by starvation of the Welsh in their own mountains. It was, nevertheless, on this expedition that due note was taken of the length and strength of the Welsh longbow. Trevelyan, in his *History of England* (1926), says that it was between the upper waters of the Wye and the Bristol Channel that this remarkable weapon first became famous. It was adopted by the English as their standard infantry weapon, but it did not become really firmly established as the national weapon until the fourteenth century.

After Wales, Scotland. Wallace, the battle of Falkirk; Bruce, and the defeat of Bannockburn. At Falkirk, the Scottish archers were chased off the field by their English counterparts, who then broke the entrenched ranks of the pikemen with arrows. Longbow or shortbow? I do not know; but there had been full twenty years since the Welsh adventure, and that should have given time enough for the important change to have been made. Bannockburn was lost by Edward II partly through Bruce's cunning, but more through his own inability to control the deployment of his cavalry and archers. The result, as all the world knows, was utter disaster.

It is as well, if we are to assess the position of the archer, to try to visualize what these battles were like. In Anglo-Saxon times archers and other fighting men were used indiscriminately; and many had horses to convey them to the scene of the fight, much as people use cars nowadays to take them to the Meet. This was a thing learned from the Danes. The horses were then led away and held out of the zone of the fighting. Duke William had quite different ideas. In the feudal armies which he and his immediate successors led (I will, deliberately, not say 'commanded') the horse was no longer a simple conveyance from one place to another, but had become an integral part of the battle, a fighting-platform for his rider. The fully-armed knight, that heavy, unwieldy, one-man tank, encased at first in mail and later in plate, lumbered into battle on his Great Horse, and from that highly-trained creature's immense back hacked away at his opposite number. To fall, or be thrust off, was practically a death sentence. Cumbered with his armour, hampered by its weight and unable to move quickly, he could be set about on all sides by the foot-soldiers, hangers-on, and all the riff-raff waiting to take him prisoner for ransom or cut his throat for loot. Truly a fall was 'a hawful thing'. Nevertheless, the assault of the heavy cavalry had become the main thing in military tactics, and the side with the greater weight had a good expectation of winning the day. Among the heavy armour fought the archers on foot, lightly clad, dangerous, waspish, and individual, for the feudal battle was in no sense an ordered whole. The feudal array—the king with his immediate followers; the barons with their own group of knights; each knight with his own private retainers, men-at-arms, and archers—did not make for any sort of concerted action or discipline. The groups were surely jealous of each other, intent on individual and striking feats of arms, and were uncontrollable in any real sense. The battle was a confused mêlée of semi-private fights without central direction. No planned action against the enemy, except perhaps in the very beginning, could be expected in such conditions. The archer, therefore, was not yet properly employed *en masse*; such success as he had was more or less fortuitous, dependent on quick opportunism and lucky shooting. It took the genius of Edward III to organize and use him properly.

Two earlier developments had paved the way for Edward's innovations directed towards a better control of operations. The one, begun by Henry II with his Assize of Arms, that the shires had been ordered to keep up a sort of local militia (on the old Saxon principle and quite separate from the prevailing feudal system) in which each man should have certain specified arms and be called up for such service as the king might require; the other, that certain feudal nobles themselves, desiring more adventure than normally came their way, had formed 'companies' which they were willing and even anxious to hire out, with themselves as leaders, to the king or anyone else who would take them where there was a chance of pay, fighting, and spoil. Based on this militia and on these companies, directly responsible to himself and depending for their pay upon the satisfaction they gave him, Edward was able to transform an important part of his forces from a rabble to an organized formation, and it became possible to give orders with a reasonable anticipation of their being obeyed. We must assume, I think, that whatever the great barons might have thought of this at first they eventually came to see that it was a sensible thing that the king should be a commander in fact as well as a leader in name, since it is clear from early accounts of the battles of this and later periods that discipline really had improved.

Edward's main tactic was simple. Mounted nobility formed the main striking force of the enemy. A dismounted man in armour was, for all practical purposes, incapable of advancing to the attack, but could very well stand on the defensive and give a good account of himself there, as had been learned at some cost in Scotland. Clearly, then, if the enemy's chivalry could be un-horsed before they reached our position, we should then only have to deal with an encumbered and shaken mob making their way to the encounter as best they could; while, supposing our horsemen had already dismounted voluntarily, and were drawn up in formation, such of the enemy as arrived, hot and breathless, to do battle with them would be at a grave disadvantage. For the execution of this simple plan the archer was indispensable. He was to be stationed among our dismounted knights. On the advance of the enemy, and not before, he would shoot into the colourful and glittering mass; and he would shoot, not at the armoured riders, but at their horses. No horse could stand the torture of the arrow; the gallant beasts would either be killed out-right or become uncontrollable and throw their riders. If this preliminary was successful, then the odds (which were on so many occasions against us) would have been evened up or perhaps turned in our favour, and the battle could proceed as circumstances might require. If, however, the enemy still came on, though disordered somewhat from the effect of the arrows, the archers would discard their bows and take to their other weapons; and the enemy would find himself faced with a calm, steady, and well-ordered front of dismounted men in armour and archers turned infantrymen. The set battle, at all events in the French campaigns, thus became a defensive one of mixed heavy and light infantry against heavy feudal cavalry, in which the archers played a double part. In this way were Crecy, Poitiers, and Agincourt won. Other tasks, of course, the archers had; to soften up strongpoints in the enemy's dispositions; to lay ambushes; to protect flanks; and other things for which a lightly-armed, highly mobile artillery could be used. But his main task was, and remained, the demoralization and neutralization of the heavy cavalry. Instances of all these uses can be found in the accounts of the fighting in France, with Crecy as the classical example of the main idea.

Of the archer himself we can construct a fairly authentic picture. He was of low degree, a man of the people, landless and poor, in the service of some knight or noble. He would be dressed in homespun cloth; a tunic reaching to his knees, his legs and feet encased in cloth 'chausses', with pointed cloth shoes or leather ones if he was lucky. Ragged and barefoot he must often have gone after a little campaigning. Over his head and shoulders would be the 'capu-chon', the medieval hood, with its long point hanging down behind, its wide upper end forming a serviceable cape, and his face sticking out of the hole in the middle. On his broad leather belt were a sword, a knife or dagger, and a wallet holding his spare gear and his own small personal possessions; if he had a maul, that too would be hung on it. Between his belt and his body were his regulation sheaf of arrows; possibly he may have carried a quiver as well. It is unlikely at this time that he had any sort of protection for his body, though later on he was better equipped with a steel cap and a partly-armoured jerkin. Standing in line with a fully-armoured knight on each side of him, he must have felt singularly defenceless in the mêlée—but never do we hear that he shirked his duty. His bow would be full his height, or more; of yew, made by a country bowyer, 'weighing' perhaps 75 lb. or heavier, plain and without horn tips. The string, thick heavy flax or hemp, well waxed and served. A 'tab', to protect his fingers; or, more likely, his fingers were hard enough without. And the arrows under his belt? Long heavy shafts, of birch probably, though the lighter aspen is often mentioned; shafts long enough to draw to the ear, feathered with goose, and armed, not with the conventional broadhead, but with that dreadful thing the bodkin point—a small sharp-ended cold-chisel, some two inches long, of square or diamond section, and carrying four small barbs—the terror of all Europe.

Such were our archers; plain men plainly, even meanly, equipped; individually of no account, collectively the masters of the finest chivalry that could be brought against them.

It is reasonable to assume that Edward first tried out his new ideas in the Scottish war; since at Halidon Hill the archers managed to discomfit the Scottish horsemen even though they, clearly expecting something, had taken the precaution of dismounting before the advance. Froissart's account of this battle may or may not be reliable; but, assuming that it is, then we have a clear example of what the new discipline accomplished. Thirty thousand Scots dead; while the English lost only one knight, one esquire, and thirteen foot-soldiers—'an inequality almost incredible', as the chronicler most truly says; and a fine example of the power of the bodkin-head arrow to penetrate chain mail.

As on land, so at sea; for sea fighting was not yet any affair of naval skill other than that the masters were required to lay their ships alongside the enemy's, and grapple thereto 'with great hokes and grapers of yron'. At Sluys, Edward 'set all his shyppes in order, the grettest before, well furnysshed with archers, and euer bytwene two shyppes of archers; he had one shypp with men of armes, and than he made another batell to ly alofe with archers, to confort euer them that wer moost wery, yf nede were.' The French ships were manned with Genoese crossbowmen, who, as on so many occasions, found their weapon no match for the longbow. Froissart says that this battle was 'right fierse and terryble; for the batayls on the see are more dangerous and fierser, than the batayls by lande; for on the see ther is no reculying nor fleyng, ther is no remedy but to fight, and to abyde fortune, and euery man to shewe his prowes'—which last is most strangely reminiscent of Nelson's signal before Trafalgar.

The pinnacle of English military archery is reached at Crecy in 1346. Edward had drawn up his army in three lines, on slightly rising ground, the archers disposed thinly on a wide front ('in maner of a herse'), and the flanks protected by entrenchments. All the baggage had been sent to the rear, and also was covered by earthworks. Here, in accordance with his set plan, he addressed his troops and awaited the French. This 'idiotic feudal array', as Trevelyan calls it, arrived in disorder and out of hand, 120,000 men all told, with some 15,000 Genoese crossbowmen in the van. The total English force amounted to 2,300 men at arms and 5,200 archers. Let us now have Froissart's account of the opening phase of the battle, translated into early seventeenth-century English by Berners:

'Thenglysshmen who were in the batayls, lyeing on the grounde to rest them, assone as they saw the frenchmen approche, they rose upon their fete, fayre and easely, without any hast, and aranged their batayls: the first, which was the princes batell, the archers there stode in maner of a herse, and the men at armes in the botome of the batayle. . . . Whan the french kyng sawe the englysshmen, his blode chaunged, and sayd to his marshals, make the genowayes go on before, and beginne the batayle in the name of god and saynt Denyse; ther were of the genowayes crossbowes, about a fiftene thousand. . . . Also the same season there fell a great rayne, and a clyps, with a ter-ryble thonder, and before the rayne, ther came fleyng ouer bothe batayls, a great nombre of crowes, for fears of the tempest commynge. Than anone the eyre beganne to waxe clere, and the sonne to shyne fayre and bright, the which was right in the frenchmens eyen, and on the englysshmens backes. Whan the genowayes were assembled toguyder, and beganne to approche, they made a great leape and crye, to abasshe thenglysshmen, but they stode styll, and styrrede nat for all that; thanne the genowayes againe the seconde time made another leape, and a fell crye, and stepped forward a lytell, and thenglysshmen remeued nat one fote; thirdly againe they leapt and cryed, and went forthe tyll they came within shotte: than they shotte feersly with their crossbowes; than thenglysshe archers stept forthe one pase, and lette fly their arrowes so holly, and so thycke, that it semed snowe: when the genowayes felte the arowes persynge through heedes, armes, and brestes, many of them cast down their crossbowes, and dyde cutte their strynges, and retourned

30

dysconfited ... and euer styll the englysshmen shot where as they saw thyckest preace: the sharpe arrowes ranne into the men of armes, and into their horses, and many fell, horse and men. . . . This saturday, the englysshmen neuer departed fro their batayls for chasynge of any man, but kept styll the felde, and euer defended themself agaynst all such as came to assayle them: this batayle ended aboute euynsong tyme.'

The demoralization produced by the fine discipline and good shooting of the English archers was such that all the Genoese turned tail and were cut up by their own side as a punishment, while the masses of French cavalry were so confused that the Black Prince, then scarcely more than a boy, led an impetuous attack on them which for a time got him into serious difficulties. The French never recovered from their initial reverse, and were routed with immense slaughter. Thus discipline and what is now called 'fire control' triumphed over an outworn technique, at odds of 17 to 1. The archers' steadiness had enabled Edward to get out of a tight corner, and was the direct cause of his most celebrated victory.

It is curious, and rather melancholy, to reflect that on the field of Crecy it is probable that cannon were used for the first time in European history. Anyone who has had to do at all with the English soldier will have no difficulty in imagining the surprise and delight, the cat-calls and the ribald jokes, with which the foot-soldiers doubtless greeted the first appearance of these engines; but little could the archers then have believed that these crude, slow, and uncertain monsters (and in particular their lesser progeny) would, in a distressingly short space of time, render their own devastating skill of no avail, relegating them first to a secondary place, and finally ousting them altogether. Yet so it proved; and we may well, even now, regret that it was so.

Ten years later, the Black Prince fought the battle of Poitiers. Whereas Crecy was an example of the set defensive battle, in which there would have been no encounter at all had not the French been stupid enough to attack the apparently forlorn little force of English, Poitiers is a good example of the opportunist use of archers during the combat. One William Douglas, a Scot, had persuaded John, King of France, to order his army to fight on foot as did the Scots and English, and so avoid the awful confusion that invariably followed the arrival of the arrow-storm among the horses. While John had reluctantly agreed to this, he had also, with a perversity amounting almost to imbecility, set apart five hundred horsemen whose sole duty was to be to ride down the English archers! The dismounted warriors then began their advance, during which they had to pass through a narrow lane bordered with high hedges. It seems to have occurred to nobody that there would be anything behind the hedges—to feudal nobility hedges had no significance in the art of war; one saw one's enemy afar off, in the open, in any decently conducted affair. But to English archers hedges proved very convenient, particularly if they could lie behind them well-hidden in trenches. And so they rose up at the proper time and shot down the French at leisure. Meanwhile, the five hundred horsemen had been sent against the main body of archers, who, being forewarned, had been stationed on a patch of soft ground. When the French arrived, and were presumably getting themselves into difficulties in the marsh, the Earl of Oxford whipped up the archers and hurried them away to a flank, when they shot up the horses as usual. By this time John had grown desperate, had gathered up what forces were left to him, and had launched a fierce and final attack against the Prince. Whereupon a certain de la Buche took nine foot-soldiers and one hundred archers by leave of the Prince and 'marched a compasse about' until he arrived in the rear of the French army. There he suddenly showed himself, displaying the ensign of St. George as a signal. The Prince, redoubling his efforts, nobly aided by de la Buche pouring in arrows in the rear of the unhappy French, had so much success that 'the forme of the bataille was quite spoiled' as Stow quaintly says, 'neither could they put themselues in order of array any more . . . at length God having so disposed, the Prince preaseth forward on his enemies, and like a fierce lion beating downe the proud, hee came to the yeelding uppe of the French King'.

So the French found that even fighting on foot did not do them much good. Had they even wanted to imitate the organization and tactics of the English they could not have done it; for they had no militia and no 'companies'. France was still bogged firmly in the old feudal idea. However, something obviously had to be done; and so, in desperation, we may assume, their foot-soldiers were given 'pavesses', heavy wooden shields upon which to catch the arrows; and by this means they overcame the archers at Nogent in 1359. They tried it again at Auray, five years later; but it was no longer a surprise, and, although the pavesses certainly did neutralize the arrows, the Englishmen cared little for that and, running in among the French, the archers took their own weapons from them 'wherwith they fought after ryght handely'. Later still, the French forsook chain mail for plate-armour; but what they may have gained in protection they certainly lost in mobility—and they found after all that a bodkin-head would penetrate even plate if it struck fair and square.

So the Hundred Years' War dragged on, inconclusive, interminable. Fine adventure, no doubt, for king and baron, but possibly not so good for the common man. He would much rather have been at home in peace, in his spare time playing football, quoits, dice, and 'casting of the stone', instead of the everlasting archery practice and the chance of being called up for service again at any moment.

Richard II had to take some notice of this war-weariness, to keep the reserve of archers up to scratch, even though he himself undertook no expeditions to France. He ordained that no servant or labourer should have any arms other than a bow and arrows; that he was to practise with them on Sundays and holidays; and that he was to stop playing his favourite games. It is the first of many later Statutes of the same kind.

Henry IV had trouble with his arrowsmiths, who were 'to the great jeopardy and deceit of the people' making arrowheads of inferior metal. The fraudulent army contractor is of ancient lineage.

Both the above measures are signs of the times. The practice of archery had become as burdensome as the war itself, and even the makers of tackle could no longer be trusted. We are now in the fifteenth century, and but for Agincourt there is little left to say of the old English archer. The longbow had begun its long losing fight against hand firearms and the crossbow, although for some centuries yet it was to remain a better weapon than either.

Agincourt is the last outstanding occasion on which the defensive tactics of Edward III gained the day for England. Henry V had, as was usual with our kings in their French adventures, got himself into a tight corner; his small army, making its way to the port of Calais and home, found itself confronted with four times as many of the flower of France, barring all chance of escape. Henry was desperately short of supplies, and sickness was rife among his men. Seeing no way out but to fight, he drew up his army on a narrow front, the flanks being protected by two belts of trees. Each man had fixed in the ground before him a sharp-pointed stake. There, true to the old idea, he waited for the French to attack.

The French, true equally to their old idea and having learnt nothing whatever from their previous experiences, advanced. Had they only sat quietly in their tents, Henry would have had to capitulate to starvation and disease. But as on each and every previous occasion of the kind the English tactics provoked the French to rash action. Their nobility were so confident, and so stupid, that they advanced alone on horseback, leaving their esquires and men-at-arms in the rear. They came on in two sharp-pointed triangular bodies, intending to crash right through the English lines. The ground was wet, slippery clay. In a matter of minutes the field was a shambles. The archers threw down their bows and with the men-at-arms went in among the kicking, struggling mass to hew and kill with sword and axe. 'Thus after a long and cruell batell, by the demerits of their great pride there approched no man of the French to batell, but to death. . . .' It is incredible that after more than fifty years' experience of English archery and tactics the French leaders should have learned so little. That there were some, like Bertrand du Guesclin, who were more adaptable and therefore more successful in their enterprises, seems to have made no impression. Would the longbow have been so effective against good generalship? It is a hard question to answer.

In attempting to form a correct impression of the value and position of archers in these battles of the fourteenth and early fifteenth centuries, we should note three things: that the archers were usually only employed at the very beginning; that they carried no more than one sheaf of twenty-four arrows ('Every English archer carries 24 Scots under his belt'), and could get no more unless they went and picked up those they had already shot; and that, when they were out of arrows, and sometimes before, they discarded their bows and became ordinary foot-soldiers.

It is the second of these points which gives, I think, the key to the whole matter. That each archer should have only twenty-four arrows is an extraordinary circumstance considered by itself; and particularly if we also take into account the rapidity with which these could be discharged. When these were expended, there were no more. There was no sort of ammunition column. If more were required later on, they had to be gathered from the ground. So the archer did not shoot and shoot until he was tired. A few brief moments while the air sang with shafts; a struggling mass of men and horses; and then the bow was cast away and the archer took to his sword and maul and became an ordinary foot-soldier. It was quite logical that, when he had shot his arrows and unhorsed the enemy, he should take to cold steel; since, although his arrows would on occasion pierce plate armour and would always kill horses, they would not be so satisfactory against dismounted armour. The arrow-storm was normally a deadly and effective preliminary, but not the main battle. That would be fought out after the archers had done, ding-dong, steel on steel, man to man. The armoured nobility, and the man-at-arms, were the hard core of the fight, not the lightly armed archer. Sword and lance, mace and axe, would determine the issue after the archers had done the preliminary 'softening up'. The archer's task was to sow alarm, despondency, and finally confusion in the ranks of the enemy before he had a chance to retaliate. That done, his work, *qua* archer, was over. Then as now, neither artillery nor any other auxiliary arm could win battles alone; the decision lay,

34

as it still does, with the infantry who alone can drive the enemy from the field and remain in possession of it.

The archer was the light artillery of that day, and came to be so called. Battles could indeed be fought without him, but it was much more profitable, and more comforting, to have him present.

There is one other curious circumstance that deserves notice. How was it that the longbow became to all intents and purposes an English monopoly?

We know that the weapon came from Wales; yet we hear little of Welsh archers in these wars. We fought the Scots and French on and off for a hundred years, but neither nation copied our methods. The French (or more usually their Italian mercenaries) persisted in using the easy but ineffective crossbow; while as for the Scots, 'neyther the love of theyr countrye, the feare of theyr enemyes, the avoydinge of punishment, nor the receyving of any profite that might come by it, could make them to be good archers: which be unapte and unfitte thereunto by God's providence and nature.'

I have not succeeded in discovering anything specific which can throw light on this remarkable aptitude of the English; and it is even harder to understand if one remembers that all the best bowstaves came from the Continent. It is unlikely that it had anything to do with physique, since Englishmen had no monopoly of bodily strength. Nor is it easy to believe that it had anything to do with the way the bow was drawn, or with some knack preserved by miraculous means for the inhabitants of this island alone. The ingenious theory that Englishmen did not draw their bows with their left hand extended, but held the undrawn bow with the string against the ear or jaw and then pushed the stave forward with the left hand, would neither give any mechanical advantage in the force of the shot, nor be practicable. Let anyone take a moderately light bow, say of 60 lb., and try to 'draw' it this way. It is impossible; Samson himself could not do it. No—this idea will not serve to explain the meaning of 'to lay one's body in the bow'. If there is any explanation at all, it lies surely in the constant practice which was enforced on all fit Englishmen by their successive kings. The longbow is exhausting to draw, and difficult to shoot accurately with. It requires bodily fitness and unremitting practice for its proper management. When it has been mastered, it is a magnificent weapon of astounding force. Just as the discipline of the English troops far exceeded that of their enemies, so it is fair to assume that they gave to their chosen weapon the attention that it required for efficiency, while the French and others did not. No other explanation seems reasonable or necessary.

We are nearing the end. Let us break off while the archer is still invincible. We have answered some of the questions with which we began, but not all.

That the longbow outdid the shortbow and the crossbow there is no doubt at all. We have seen the archer in his prime, and we need now no ballads to tell us of his prowess. He was a great and redoubtable figure; but he was not the whole story. He reached the pinnacle of his fame in the fourteenth century, and his decline thereafter, in the face of firearms, was rapid. As to whether we English of to-day owe him anything of our position in the world, we must, perhaps with some feeling of sentimental regret, confess that we do not, if, that is, we consider only material things. When Henry of Anjou came to the throne of England, he was master of very much more of France than the king of that country himself. By the time of Henry VI we had been clean driven from France. Yet in the interval the longbow had reached its zenith. The archers had helped successive sovereigns to invade Ireland and Wales; to fight endlessly with the Scots; and to harry the French. The net result was our expulsion from the Continent, and little peace at home. England did not become a Power at all until long after the day of the longbow.

Is there then nothing left? Of course there is! The tradition of the English archer is indestructible. His courage and steadfastness, his willingness to fight against impossible odds, his versatility, the respect accorded him by his adversaries; are not all these still characteristic of the English race when it goes to war? It is a fine inheritance.

So let us take our leave of that tough, common man, our friend the old English archer. See him now as he sits in his little shelter of boughs in a Norman field after the battle. He is humming a little song (something about 'Owre Kynge . . .' it seems) as he fits a new bowstring and watches his supper cooking. Camp fires twinkle all around, and from them come, now and again, snatches of talk and gusts of laughter. The night is very quiet, and all the stars are out. Far away, beyond the firelight, some of his friends lie oddly twisted and very still on the ground, face down. He nods, and is soon asleep. Will his dreams take him backwards, up the long ladder of history to the days of Duke William and beyond to the Danes and Saxons; or forwards some five or six hundred years so that he sees Englishmen once again in Normandy? Who knows? But, if it be the latter, be sure that he has found himself among friends. A little strangeness of tongue, perhaps, and unfamiliar new hand guns; but the same ideas, the old rough humour, the same courage and endurance. Then will he turn in his sleep, and settle himself more comfortably, knowing that faith has been kept.

36

To the moste gracioufe, and our moft dred Soueraigne lord,
Kyng Henrie the .viii, by the grace of God, kyng
of Englande, Fraunce and Irelande. Defen
der of the faythe, and of the churche
of Englande & alfo of Irelande
in earth fupreme head, next Vn
der Chrift, be al health
victorie, and fes
licitie.

HAT tyme as, mofte graci-
ous Prince, your highnes this
laft year paft, tooke that your
mooft honorable and victori-
ous iourney into Fraunce, accompanied vvith fuch a porte
of the Nobilitie and yeomanrie of Englande,
as neyther hath bene lyke knovven by experience, nor yet red of in Hiftorie: accompanied
alfo vvith the daylie prayer's, good hartes, and
vvilles of all and euery one your graces fub-
iectes, lefte behinde you here at home in Englande: the fame tyme, I beinge at my booke
in Cambrige, forie that my litle habilitie could
ftretche out no better, to helpe forvvard fo no
ble an enterprice, yet vvith my good vvylle,
prayer, and harte, nothinge behynde hym that
vvas formofte of all, conceyued a vvonderful

A. delyre

1. Toxophilus
Beginning of Ascham's dedication to King Henry Viii
slightly reduced

TOXOPHILVS,

The schole of shootinge
conteyned in tvvo
bookes.

To all Gentlemen and yomen of Englande,
pleasaunte for theyr pastyme to rede,
and profitable for theyr use
to folow, both in war
and peace.

The contentes of the first booke.

2. Title page of *Toxophilus*
slightly reduced

ROGER ASCHAM

'Rather would I have cast ten thousand pounds into the sea than have lost my Ascham'—so Queen Elizabeth is reputed to have said on hearing of his death. And if Gloriana was so moved, can we not be sure that her Ascham was a man of uncommon character?

And yet, poor Roger! How little of him is generally known to those who in fact owe him so much. A few desultory quotations; a brief and uninformative note, as if we knew all about it already, that he wrote a book on archery; and his name commemorated, if you please, in a case or cupboard for the storage of tackle. That is all. 'Roger Ascham? Yes, of course. He wrote *Toxophilus* didn't he?' and so we leave him.

How much we lose by this lack of interest; of archery lore, of history, of scholarship, of humour, and of pathos.

Roger was an accomplished but impecunious university don, to whom fate gave high place, but never means enough to sustain it without anxiety. Life in the sixteenth century had at least this much in common with our own age, that the struggle for ordinary folk to make ends meet was just as great then as now. From his letters of which a great number survive, Roger seems always to have been in difficulty. Added to this was some infirmity of body; so that his later life, particularly after his marriage, must have been one of constant care and anxiety.

Yet this quiet, sick, and, it must be confessed, somewhat improvident scholar has left a permanent mark not only as an authority on archery, and doubtless the father of us all in that respect, but also as a writer of fine direct English prose.

As befits an archer, he came of yeoman stock, his father, John, being a steward to Lord Scrope, of Bolton. Roger was born in 1515, the third son, at Kirby Wiske in Yorkshire, at a time when the bow was beginning to feel seriously the competition of gunpowder; not so much in respect of efficiency (since at that time there was no question which was the more potent weapon of war), as of novelty and of the prestige which potentates no doubt gained by the display of the new and terrifying inventions of their armourers.

Be that as it may, the bow was, for good or ill, in the first stages of its permanent decline when Roger came into this world.

He was educated in the first instance by his father, whom he calls affectionately 'the wisest of men', and secondly by Sir Humphrey Wingfield, a lawyer who afterwards became a Member of Parliament and Speaker of the House of Commons; into whose house he was, in accordance with the odd and patriarchal custom of the time, received to be taught along with Sir Humphrey's own family and other children.

For this good man Roger seems to have conceived a lasting affection. Hear what he says:

'This . . . maketh me remember the right worshipful, and my singular good maister, *Sir Humphreye Wingfielde*, to whom, next God, I ought to referre, for his manifold benefits bestowed on me, the pore talent of learninge which God hath lent me: and for his sake do I owe my service to all other of the name and noble house of the *Wingfieldes*, both in worde and deede.

'This worshipful man hath ever loved and used to have many children brought up in learninge in his house, amonges whom I myselfe was one. For whom at terme-times he would bring down from London both bowe and shaftes, and, when they should playe, he would go with them himselfe into the fielde, and see them shoote, and he that shotte fayrest, shoulde have the best bowe and shaftes, and he that shotte ill favouredly, should be mocked of his fellowes, till he shot better.'

Good Sir Humphrey! He is back from town, and has taken off his fine clothes. He has put on his long black gown, with its interminable row of little buttons all down the front, and its long fur edging and stole; his plain, small white collar, open at the neck; his round black cap like a tea-cake; and his square-toed leather shoes. Here he comes, through a side door, gravely striding out on to the grass where the children are at play. Behind him comes the old retainer, his arms full of the new bows and arrows.

The children stand hushed, expectant: for in those days, as until recently, one's elders were persons to be held in awe and reverence. The shooting begins. Squeaks of delight for the good shots; howls of derision for the bad. When time is up the winner comes forward for his prize, and the worst shot, poor little chap, gets his dose of 'mockery'. The play is at an end. But not until Sir Humphrey is gone will the chattering break out, and eager (and envious) comparisons be made. One wonders how often the young Roger won the best bow; how often he was mocked. There is nothing to guide us, but I think he must have been at least moderately proficient, or he would not have persevered in later life.

His stay with the Wingfields was not long. In 1530, at the age of fifteen, Sir Humphrey sent him to St. John's college, Cambridge, at his own expense. Here Roger, who clearly must already have had a notably good grounding in the Classics, showed a special leaning towards Greek and Latin, besides a proficiency in mathematics, music, and, strangely enough, fine penmanship. So good was the latter that he was appointed to write official letters for the university. And all this at an age when, nowadays, he would have been an irresponsible schoolboy.

At nineteen he took his B.A. and was elected a Fellow of his College. So he begins what was really, in spite of some interruption, his life work, that of a university don. His election was made notwithstanding the fact that he had already, rather rashly for his age and prospects, declared himself in favour of the reformed religion. England was still a Catholic country, and Henry VIII, in spite of his zeal in challenging the authority of the Pope and suppressing the monasteries, was no Protestant. This attitude to religion he maintained throughout his life, even during the reign of 'Bloody Mary'; it was evidently not just a young man's enthusiasm, but a deep conviction, and we must grant that he had the courage of it.

In 1537 he took his M.A., occupying himself with a number of pupils, among whom, fortunately as it turned out later, was one William Grindal who became tutor to the young Princess Elizabeth.

The years 1540 to 1542 he spent at home in Yorkshire, ill with recurrent fever. On his return to Cambridge after this there broke out in the university a prolonged and sharp controversy as to the proper way of pronouncing the Greek language. A new method had been put forward by Thomas Smyth, of Queen's, afterwards a knight, and Principal Secretary to Edward VI and Elizabeth. That such a matter should provoke the acrimony that it did sounds strange nowadays; but it affected Ascham to such a degree, keen Classic that he was, that he contemplated leaving Cambridge altogether, and applied for incorporation at Oxford, a step which affords some measure of Ascham's depth of feeling. Nothing, however, seems to have come of the idea, and he remained at Cambridge.

Almost immediately afterwards he began to write *Toxophilus*, in English; or as he says himself, he wrote this English matter in the English tongue for English men, since what the best of the realm thought it honest to use he ought not to suppose it vile for him to write. On the straightforward simplicity of his prose all later writers have commented.

Dr. Johnson, in Thomas Bennet's edition of Ascham's works, published in 1761, has this to say about it:

'However great was his learning, he was not always immured in his chamber: but being valetudinary, and weak of body, thought it necessary to spend many hours in such exercises as might best relieve him after the fatigue of study. His favourite amusement was archery, in which he spent, or, in the opinion of others, lost so much time, that those whom either his faults or virtues made his enemies, and perhaps some whose kindness wished him always worthily employed, did not scruple to censure his practice, as unsuitable to a man professing learning, and perhaps of bad example in a place of education. To free himself from this censure was one of the reasons for which he published, in 1544, his *Toxophilus*, or the "Schole or Partitions of Shooting", in which he joins the praise with the precepts of archery. He delighted not only to teach the art of shooting, but to give an example of diction more natural and more truly English than was used by the common writers of that age, whom he censures for mingling exotick terms with their native language, and of whom he complains that they were made authours not by skill or education, but by arrogance and temerity.'

By 1545 the book was through the press and published. Ascham personally presented a copy to Henry VIII at Greenwich. Henry 'did so well like and allow it as he gave me a living for it', amounting to £10 a year, equivalent nowadays to perhaps £300 or so.

Roger's little plot had, indeed, been a brilliant success! The reasons given by the ponderous Dr. Johnson for the writing of the book do not convince me in the least. Ascham knew perfectly well that Henry was keen on archery and that he had started and encouraged a shooting club, as we should say now, called the Fraternity of St. George. Moreover, had there not been recently issued, on Henry's orders, a long and detailed Act complaining of the decline of archery, and compelling, therefore, all men to keep and use longbows? Was this not a heaven-sent opportunity for an impecunious don, who was also an archer, to please the king and achieve thereby a little much-needed publicity and, perhaps, some advancement also?

No doubt the book did provide as well a convenient vehicle for explaining to his fellow dons that archery was not a waste of time, nor unsuitable for learned men to practise; but I cannot bring myself to believe that Ascham would have gone to all the trouble and expense of writing and publishing just for that. I am the more persuaded to this view by the fact that he began to write in the year in which the celebrated Act was put out.

And are we to ignore the skilful timing of its presentation, when Henry, pleased with himself and all the world, was just back from his useless but popular gallivanting on the Continent, which had yielded him the town of Boulogne? I think not. Roger was both strategist and tactician in this matter of his book.

However, this may be, Ascham got a yearly income for his pains, which he kept, with some vicissitudes, for the rest of his life. This pension was his financial sheet-anchor; and his agitation lest it should not be renewed on Henry's death, and again when Mary came to the throne, was extreme.

Toxophilus is a slim, elegant little volume, which would slip easily into your pocket; not at all the big quarto which I had expected. Evidently Ascham had not much to spend on his publication. The best copy in the British Museum has a page 7½ x 5⅜ in., and is about ⅜ in. thick. This copy has, of course, been rebound, but there is still a considerable part of the original binding left; finely-tooled dark-brown leather.

It starts not with a title-page, but with an engraving of the Royal Arms (Leopards of England and Lilies of France), with a Crown over and scrolls at the sides. Underneath is this breath-taking piece of doggerel:

> *Reioyce Englande, be gladde and merie,*
> *TROTHE ouercommeth thyne enemyes all,*
> *The Scot, the Frencheman, the Pope, and heresie,*
> *OVERCOMMED by Trothe, have had a fall,*
> *Sticke to the Trothe, and euermore thou shall*
> *Through Christ, King Henry, the Boke and the Bowe*
> *All maner of enemies, quite ouerthrowe.*

The whole page is unworthy of the rest of the book, and might with advantage have been left out.

On the back of this, set in beautiful italics, is a tribute to Ascham, in Latin, by Walter Hadden, of King's College.

Opposite, there begins the author's dedication of the book to Henry VIII, printed in fine, bold Roman type. This is followed by Ascham's foreword, entitled

'TO ALL GENTLE MEN AND YEOMEN OF ENGLANDE'

for which a very crabbed Roman character has been chosen.

At last we come to what, I suppose, is the title-page proper, and once more the invitation:

> 'To all Gentlemen and Yomen of Englande, pleasaunte for
> theyr pastyme to rede, and profitable for theyr use to folow,
> both in war and peace.'

The main body of the text is printed in an exquisite and clear modification of the Black Letter; at least, that is how I, being no expert, should describe it. It is a well-bred, delightful little book, in spite of the poor paper and worse craftsmanship used by Edw. Whytchurch, the London printer who made it.

It is a curious work, in two parts, written in the form of a dialogue between TOXOPHILUS (Ascham) and PHILOLOGUS (a Greek tutor), probably his old friend Sir John Cheke, also a Fellow of St. John's.

The first part contains nothing of any practical use, unless you count moralizing so. I think Ascham must have found (perhaps like certain other writers on the subject!) that a plain account of how to use and shoot the bow would make only a very slender volume, which might not attract the desired attention.

It begins with a defence of shooting as an honest pastime, introducing Claudian's idea of the invention of the art, ascribed to 'the Porpentine, which doth shote his prickes, and will hit any thinge that fightes with it. . . .' Shooting is proclaimed a fit occupation for princes, great men, scholars, and students; and obviously includes Ascham's own case. Then, for some inscrutable reason, he launches into a long tirade against music and learning to play instruments; but brings himself back on an even keel again by praising the art of singing and lamenting its decay. Perhaps his college chapel choir was poor, since he says:

'But when a man is alwaye in one tune, lyke an Humble bee, or els nowe up in the top of the churche, now downe that no man knoweth where to have him: or piping lyke a reede, or roring lyke a bull, as some lawyers do, whiche thinke they do best when they crye loudest, these shall never greatly moove, as I have knowen many wel learned, have done, bicause theyr voyce was not stayed afore, with learnyng to synge.'

Being now thoroughly warmed up, he lashes out, at great length, against 'unlawfull gammes, and namely cardes and dise', and contrasts their vices with the virtues of archery: 'For whatsoever is the one, the clean contrarye is the other.'

At long last we get a little nearer the bow, and reach his appreciation of it as a weapon of war, with a catalogue of all the ancient kingdoms founded upon it, and the battles won by the English archers—Crecy, Poitiers, Agincourt, and Flodden. As he had read many of the old manuscripts relating to this historical matter in Cheke's room, he takes the unseasonable occasion to introduce a long and affectionate tribute to him, on his leaving Cambridge to become Prince Edward's tutor. Then he gets back to what is really his main theme, both here and elsewhere: good shooting, good singing, good anything else, can only be learnt by good teaching; and he deplores the lack of competent instructors. Finally, he discusses perfection in art and craft, and gives us this piece of advice:

'In learnyng any thyng, a man must covete to be best, or els he shall never attayne to be meane.'

Admirable! But how glad one is that the first part is now over! Somewhere in the mêlée he vents his wrath on one Textor, Rector of the University of Paris, who had dared to say that the Scots were good archers. Of this unenlightened wretch he says:

'And here I must needes remember a certaine *Frenchman*, called *Textor*, that writeth a book which he nameth *Officina*, wherein he weaveth up many broken ended matters, and settes out much riff-raffe, pelfery, trumpery, baggage, and beggary ware, clamparde up of one that would seem to be fitter for a shoppe indede than to wryte anye booke. And amonges all other ill packed up matters, he thrustes uppe in a heepe together all the good shooters that ever hath been in the worlde. . . .'

Well, I do not want to criticize the excellent Roger, but if anything was ever 'clamparde up', it is the first part of his own book. And, in view of his well-known partiality for cock-fighting, and (some say) even dicing, I cannot help wondering, wondering just ever so little, whether he had his tongue in his cheek now and then.

We turn with some relief to the second part, of which, as has already been said, I have reproduced a good deal of the more practical advice for our mutual benefit. So I shall say no more here, except that, although not entirely free from discursiveness, it is carefully worked out and written to a plan; and that it does not deal at all with the making of tackle, the author being afraid of offending the Guilds, the trade unions of the day. Perhaps, in this respect only, this present notebook may serve as a complement to Ascham's work.

After this *tour de force*, which not only restored to some extent his unstable financial condition but also gave him a sure place in our affections, Ascham was chosen Public Orator, in which office he continued, managing much of the public work of the university, until an event occurred which was to rouse him from what we may properly conceive to have become a somewhat humdrum and sterile existence in college, enlivened only by petty intrigue and academic controversy.

In 1548 his old friend and pupil, Wm. Grindal, died, and the Princess Elizabeth was left without a tutor. It seems that he was already acquainted with Elizabeth, no doubt through Grindal; and on the strength of this he wrote to her commiserating with her on her loss, and hinting broadly that he would like the post himself. After that he wrote to Cheke, 'most accomplished Cheke':

'That illustrious lady is thinking of having me in the place of Grindal . . . she signified to me her pleasure, and I did not try to make any bargain for my own advantage, but at once declared that I was ready to obey her orders.

It is a pity that this is not in his own language; but he wrote it in Latin, and the translation is that of the Rev. Dr. Giles (*Works of Roger Ascham*, 1865).

Ascham was not, however, the only candidate; the influence of the great Sir Wm. Cecil had to be brought to bear before the scales turned in his favour. His connection with Cecil is not very clear, save that the latter had intervened to extricate him from an awkward, and perhaps dangerous, position in which he found himself as a result of some rash words spoken in a disputation at Cambridge respecting the Mass.

At this time the Princess Elizabeth was living at Cheshunt. Lest one should rate too highly Ascham's position as her tutor, it is well to note that on his arrival he was put to share not only a room, but also a bed, with one John Whitney, a young gentleman of the court! Ascham must have been a most enthusiastic teacher; for he forced this young bedfellow of his, who surely must have been interested in much lighter matters, to learn Latin. One must conclude that the effort of learning a foreign language tucked up in bed with his taskmaster was too much for him; for certain it is that he died soon after, to Ascham's great regret.

Ascham kept his post for about two years. He had the highest opinion of his pupil. In a letter to his friend Sturm, Master of the Grammar School at Strasburg, he writes, in Latin, in 1550:

'There are many honourable ladies now who surpass Thomas More's daughters in all kinds of learning; but among all of them the brightest star is my illustrious Lady Elizabeth, the King's sister. . . . It is difficult to say whether the gifts of nature or of fortune are most to be admired in that illustrious lady.

'The praise which Aristotle gives wholly centres in her—beauty, stature, prudence, and industry. She has just passed her sixteenth birthday, and shows such dignity and gentleness as are wonderful at her age and in her rank.

'Her study of true religion and of learning is most energetic. Her mind has no womanly weakness, her perseverance is equal to that of a man, and her memory long keeps what it quickly picks up.

'She talks French and Italian as well as English; she has often talked to me readily and well in Latin, and moderately so in Greek. When she writes

TOXOPHILVS,[1]

A,

The first boke of the schole of shoting.

Philologus.   Toxophilus.

PHILOLOGVS. You studie to sore Toxophile.
TOX. I wil not hurt my self
ouermoche I warraũt you.
PHI. Take hede you do not,
for we Physicions saye, that
it is nether good for the eyes
in so cleare a Sunne, nor yet
holsome for þ bodie, so soone
after meate, to looke vpon a
mans boke. TOX. In eatinge and studyinge I will
neuer folowe anye Physike, for yf I dyd, I am sure
I shoulde haue small pleasure in the one, and lesse
courage in the other. But what newes draue you
hyther I praye you. PHI. Small newes trulie, but
that as I came on walkynge, I fortuned to come w̃
thre or foure that went to shote at the prickes: And
when I sawe not you amonges them, but at the last
espyed you lokynge on your booke here so sadlye, I
thought to come and holde you with some commu-
nicacion, lest your boke shoulde runne awaye with
you. For me thought by your wauerynge pace & earnest lokyng, your boke led you, not you it. TOX. In
dede as it chaunced, my mynde went faster then my
                                      I   feet

3. Opening page of the first part of *Toxophilus*
slightly reduced

Full size

4. *Toxophilus*

Ascham's celebrated passage on the wind and the weather. This illustrates admirably his discursive style. About one-third size.

Greek and Latin, nothing is more beautiful than her handwriting. She is as much delighted with music, as she is skilful in the art.

'In adornment she is elegant rather than showy. . . . She read with me almost all Cicero, and great part of Titus Livius; for she drew all her knowledge of Latin from those two authors. . . .

'Whatever she reads she at once perceives any word that has a doubtful or curious meaning. . . . She likes a style that grows out of the subject; chaste because it is suitable, and beautiful because it is clear. . . . Her ears are so well practised in discriminating all these things, and her judgment is so good, that in all Greek, Latin, and English composition, there is nothing so loose on the one hand or so concise on the other, which she does not immediately attend to, and either reject with disgust or receive with pleasure, as the case may be.

'I am not inventing anything, my dear Sturm; it is all true. . . .'

A fine tribute: both to Elizabeth's mental powers and discernment, and, perhaps not altogether unconsciously, to Ascham's relentless drive as a teacher. But, poor child! What a way to spend one's youth! And what an ill-assorted couple they must have been, the young, masterful girl, daughter of the formidable King Harry, and destined to be herself the Queen of England; and the pedantic, disputatious don, dependant for his uncertain livelihood on chance and the favour of his superiors. Still, as we know already, Ascham left his mark, and Elizabeth seems to have liked him.

This state of affairs was not to last long. Ascham took offence at some slight offered him by the Princess's steward, left in a hurry, and returned to Cambridge in 1549 or 1550.

His sojourn in high places seems to have developed in him a *wanderlust*, and made him unwilling to return to his narrow life in college. Through his friend Cheke (he seems to have been highly skilled at getting his friends to use their influence on his behalf), he was appointed secretary to Sir Richard Morysin, who was to go as English ambassador to the Emperor Charles V. He has recorded his experiences in what he calls his 'Report and Discourse'.

It is an account, very personal in places, of some of the princes of Europe, and of the troubles of the Emperor Charles V. Ascham sees everywhere 'the foule vice of ambition', and writes: 'O Lord! how many worthy men hath this one vice beareft from our good common weales. . . .' The centuries do not seem to alter man's nature much.

One of his Latin letters written at this time has a familiar sound: 'For how can I keep up, I will not say a court, but even a city life, a whole year on twenty pounds, when, living closely and sparingly, I have spent forty within the last five months.' I sympathize with him; translating into modern values, six hundred a year, or thereabouts, was not a great deal with which to keep up the position of Secretary to an Ambassador to the greatest prince in Europe.

The death of Edward VI in 1553 put an end to the mission, and Ascham returned to England, tired of adventure. The Reformation came to an abrupt end with the accession of Mary, and there might have seemed to have been trouble ahead for the Protestant Roger. However, it did not turn out this way and Mary not only left him alone, but actually increased his income.

His appointment as Latin Secretary to the late king, procured for him by his friends while he was still in Germany, of course lapsed; but he still had his Fellowship and Public Oratorship at Cambridge. As usual, his connections came to the rescue, Bishop Gardiner and Sir William Paget getting him made Latin Secretary to the new queen with forty marks a year as well as his pension, now doubled to twenty pounds.

The story of how it came to be doubled is amusing. The Patent had, of course, to be written out afresh for the new appointment, and the scribe (who surely was Ascham himself) had left too big a space for the small word *decem*. Here is the letter he wrote to Gardiner:

'In writing out my patent I have left a vacant place for your wisdom to value the sum; wherein I trust to find further favour; for I have both good cause to ask it, and better hope to obtain it, partly in consideration of my unrewarded pains and undischarged costs in teaching King Edward's person, partly for my three years' service in the Emperor's court, but chiefly of all when King Henry first gave it me at Greenwich, your lordship in the gallery there asking me what the King had given me, and knowing the truth, your lordship said it was too little, and most gently offered me to speak to the King for me. But then I most happily desired your lordship to reserve that goodness to another time, which time God hath granted even to these days, when your lordship may now perform by favour as much as then you wished by goodwill, being as easy to obtain the one as to ask the other. And I beseech your lordship see what good is offered me in writing the patent: the space which is left by chance doth seem to crave by good luck some words of length, as *viginti* or *triginta*, yea, with the help of a little dash *quadraginta* would serve best of all. But sure as for *decem* it is somewhat with the shortest: nevertheless I for my part shall be no less contented with the one than glad with the other, and for either of both more than bound to your lordship. And thus God prosper your lordship.

'Your lordship's most bounden to serve you,   'R. ASKAM.'
'To the Rt. Reverend Father in God
'My Lord Bishop of Winchester his Grace, these.'

46

Evidently the good bishop had a sense of humour, for, as we know already, the letter had the desired result, even though *quadraginta* was found to be too long a word after all.

Presumably Ascham (who evidently pronounced his name as if it had a 'k' in the middle) was now fairly well off as a bachelor, and all might have been well had he not fallen in love with one Margaret Howe, daughter of a good family and much younger than himself, and married her in 1554.

By the laws of the university he had to give up his Fellowship and his Oratorship; and from then on his money troubles lay heavily on him.

'God, I thank him, hath given me such an one as the less she seeth I do for her, the more loving in all causes she is to me, when I again have rather wished her well than done her good, and therefore the more glad she is to bear my future with me, the more sorry am I that hitherto she hath found rather a loving than a lucky husband unto her. I did choose her to live withal, not hers to live upon, and if my choice were to choose again, I would even do as I did, so that the comfort I take because I have so good a wife is the only cause of my care, because she hath so poor a husband.

'For my own self, I could measure my mind to live as meanly as ever I did at Cambridge, but now duty and love drive me to further desire. . . .'

A year later he resumed his old job of tutor to the Princess Elizabeth; and on her becoming Queen was confirmed in his Latin Secretaryship as well as continuing her private education. Elizabeth does not seem to have been very generous to him; but she did, very surprisingly, appoint him, a layman, to the prebend of Wetwang in York; and had, in consequence, some high words with the outraged archbishop!

Court life, however, did not suit him, as he had already found out in Germany. He made few friends, and, so far as one can make out, was never really well. In 1562 he writes to his old friend Sturm:

'I have had such constant fevers during these few years, that, before one has left me, I have caught another. My strength has been so broken down that my whole body suffers from a continual hectic fever, which the physicians can sometimes perhaps soothe but not cure for good.'

In 1563, as the result of a discussion at dinner at Sir Wm. Cecil's on the strange news that 'divers scholars of Eaton be run away from the schole for fear of beating', he was asked by Sir Richard Sackville to write a book and system for the instruction of his son; and offered to pay for the education of Ascham's own boy, Giles, as well, if he would do so. The result was *The Scholemaster* for which Ascham is probably better remembered now than for *Toxophilus*, although opinions differ sharply as to its practical merits.

Its title goes:

The Schole Master

Or plaine and perfite Way of teaching Children, to understand, write, and speake the LATIN TONGE, but specially
purposed for the private bringing up of Youth in Jentlemen
and Noblemens Houses, and commodious also for all such
as have forgot the LATIN TONGE and would, by themselves, without a Scholemaster, in short Tyme, and with
small Paines, recover a sufficient Habilitie, to understand,
write and speake LATIN.

1571

To the Honourable Sir WILLIAM CECILL,
Knight, principal Secretary to the Quenes Most
Excellent Majesty.

Just as before, he apparently found it necessary to defend himself:

'And some also will nedes busie them selves in merveling, and adding
thereunto unfriendlie taulke, why I, a man of good yeares, and of no ill
place, I thanke God and my Prince, do make choise to spend such tyme in
writyng of trifles, as the schole of shoting, the Cockpitte, and this booke of
the first Principles of Grammar, rather, than to take some weightie matter in
hand, either of Religion, or Civill discipline.'

To which he says that great ships are expensive and difficult to manage,
whereas little boats 'cary many tymes, as good and costlie ware, as greater
vessels do'; and, perhaps one might add, are sometimes more entertaining.

It is surprising to learn that, after all his thunder against 'unlawful gammes',
and the rest, he was still human enough (for those times) to like cock-fighting.
The *Cockpitte* seems to have been lost. What a pity! It would have been
interesting to see what moral principles he adduced in support of this pastime.

Ascham never lived to see the publication of his last work. Sitting up late
one night, to finish a New Year's poem to the Queen, and suffering greatly
from insomnia, he was stricken down with a chill, and died on 30th December
1568.

Behind him he left his wife, who published *The Scholemaster* in 1571; and
his son Giles, who presently was to take his place at Cambridge. His younger
son, Sturm, had died in infancy.

And now, what of Roger Ascham, the man? It is difficult to draw a satisfactory picture. On the one hand, he was religious, learned, and an ardent
teacher; kind and affectionate, but restless and, perhaps, importunate. On the

other hand, materially, he was of humble birth, poor (according to his own ideas, at any rate), indifferently well for most of his life, but fond of archery, cock-fighting, dicing (if Camden is to be believed), and roasted chestnuts. We may also conclude, from *Toxophilus*, that he liked his glass of wine or beer. I think this is a very human catalogue. It cannot be said that Ascham was a great man; there was no grandeur in him. Circumstances, also, were against him. He, the clever poor boy, of humble birth in a day when these distinctions were very real, was carried by his brain into a society where he could barely manage to support himself. His work, not very profound, however much affection it may inspire in us, was never, in his view, properly rewarded; although one might have thought that a life-pension in return for writing one small book was no ill recompense. Had he been possessed of greater riches perhaps he might have become a great man of letters; his learning and his style would have provided a foundation. That, however, was not to be; he had to take, or procure through the influence of his friends, such work as he could get in order that he might live at all. So he remained all his life the poor teacher, scholar, and scribe, dependent on his betters for his daily bread, and, I think we may properly infer, despising both this way of life and himself for living it. He found himself, by force of circumstance, 'above his station', and paid the penalty in an attitude of defence and mild complaint, a little man struggling to keep his head above water in a sea too big for him.

I hope this is a just judgment. Life was no easier then than now, and are not most of us in similar condition? We need not have less affection for a man because he is not, by the common standard, 'successful'; rather the contrary, perhaps. And how many of us will accomplish anything that will still command attention four hundred years from now?

Ascham was buried in the chapel of St. Stephen Harding, in St. Sepulchre's Church, London. Whether he lies there still no man can say. There is neither tomb nor tablet to commemorate him, unless we count a very doubtful niche in the wall. Nor is any contemporary portrait of him known.

No matter, *Toxophilus* is his monument . . . and there are still archers in England.

THE DECLINE OF ARCHERY

'O what cause of reproche shall the decaye of archers be to us now livynge? Yet what irrecuperable damage either to us or to them, in whose time nede of semblable defence shall happen? Whiche decaye, though we all redy perceive, fear, and lament, and for restaurying thereof cesse nat to make ordynaunces, good lawes, and statutes, yet who effectuelly puttethe his hand to continual execution of the same lawes and provisions? Or beholdyng them daily broken: wynketh nat at the offendours?

SIR THOMAS ELYOT, *The Governour* (1531)

The Wars of the Roses did little to encourage archery. It was one thing to fight the Scot, who had never taken wholeheartedly to the bow; or the French, who relied for the most part on hired crossbowmen who could always be outranged; but quite another to be confronted with one's own kinsmen from the next shire, armed with the same longbow and just as well able to use it.

One cannot, however, assert that it was that which caused the decline of the longbow, a decline which set in with ever increasing momentum from the time that Richmond, afterwards Henry VII, won the battle at Bosworth and finished the long civil war. The real enemies of the bow were much more formidable than ever could be the dislike of using it against one's own countrymen. Laziness and the restless invention of men's minds were the twin causes of the abandonment of the old weapon which had done such outstanding service. Laziness took the familiar form of the crossbow. Here was a weapon of Continental origin, of inferior fire-power, and proven unreliability in battle, which nevertheless came to be used increasingly for war and sport. Apart from certain huge Spanish examples, it was a feeble thing by comparison with the old longbow; it shot smaller arrows, called bolts or quarrels, and it did not shoot them so far or so hard. But, probably, within its range, it was easier to use and more accurate. It did not require a man to be strong and

50

tough, so that he could draw his heavy bow without effort, and hold steady for the instant of the smooth release; any little creature could use the crossbow, winding up the string with a crank, or pulling it back with both hands, fixing the bolt in place, and then pointing it craftily at the mark as occasion might serve. So very much less trouble and effort!

One may conjecture, also, that it was easier to become a good shot with the crossbow. The long, interminable hours of statutory practice with the longbow could, therefore, be reduced—and this gave more time for the enjoyment of 'unlawful gammes', tennis, bowls, clash, and so on, of which contemporary writers complain. So much so, that Henry VII was sufficiently disturbed to cause the issue of a Statute forbidding the use of the crossbow to all except lords and freeholders of more than 200 marks annual value. The Statute was not, however, entirely disinterested in its concern for the defence of the realm; for, after a cursory mention of the fact that the longbow was being neglected, it is the great and increasing destruction of the king's deer in his forests and parks which emerges as the principle reason for its appearance. It is also good evidence that the crossbow was the more accurate weapon.

Apart from this and three or four minor Statutes, the kings between Henry V and Henry VIII do not seem to have interested themselves overmuch in archery.

Invention manifested itself in the increasing perfection of the hand-gun. These were neither formidable nor reliable in the fifteenth century; but undoubtedly the introduction of firearms which could be carried and used by an individual, with whatever element of danger to himself, was an attractive new fashion; which, coupled with the flash, noise and smoke, might be calculated with some confidence to strike awe into the hearts of the enemy even if the leaden balls did not carry so far or so truly.

There is no need to labour the point. It must have been evident to anyone who reflected upon the matter that the doom of the longbow, and indeed of the crossbow too, was at hand. Just how many years would be required before the bow was laid aside for good would depend only upon the gunmakers' ingenuity and craftsmanship. In point of fact, it took over one hundred years after Henry VIII came to the throne, although the last fifty years of this period are not of much account. But we are getting ahead of the story.

Henry VIII did much for archery, and was in his youth a notable archer himself, practising with his companions and betting with them on the results. 'Item, 20th March 1531—Paid to George Coton, for vii shott lost by the King's grace unto him at Totthill, at 6s. 8d. the shotte, xlvjs. viijd.'

He had not been three years on the throne before he issued a Statute concerning archery, because 'archerie and shotynge in longbowes is ryght lytell used but daily mynessheth decayth and abateth more and more'. By this, every fit man up to sixty years of age, with certain exceptions, and every boy of seven years upwards, were to have and use a bow and shafts; every bowyer was to make two bows of some common wood for every one of yew; and butts were to be set up in every city and town according to ancient usage. There is a certain flavour of the present day in the provision that Justices of the Peace were given powers to distribute bowyers as their services might be required, and to compel them to reside in designated localities for the benefit of the inhabitants thereof.

In 1510, Henry ordered 10,000 bows from the bowyers of London, and 40,000 more to be imported from Venice. Three years later, on his first French expedition, he took 12,000 archers with him; and in the same year the longbow contributed notably to the success of the English arms at Flodden.

One might, therefore, assume that the longbow was still unchallenged, were it not for the repeated orders against the use of crossbows which Henry found it necessary to make. Evidently he found these unavailing, and thought it wise to trim his sails a little from time to time. In no other way can his shilly-shallying between condemnation of the crossbow, and his giving permission for its use, be reasonably explained. There is no doubt at all that he himself favoured the longbow, and could use it skilfully. Otherwise he would never have ventured to give a personal display before the King of France and the Court on the Field of the Cloth of Gold. But neither his personal example nor his orders could halt the clock. By 1531 the longbow was well on its way out, and Sir Thomas Elyot had been moved to write the lament which heads this chapter. The king might order, but who was there to enforce his commands? He might, and did, dress up his own bodyguard archers in fine uniforms of red and blue, with steel caps and jerkins armoured with little plates of steel; and give them five-foot mauls with leaden heads, a dagger, and two stakes; but of what use was that if people had begun to realize that firearms were the weapons of the future, and to some extent of the present also?

More Statutes, following one another in quick succession because 'men in general nowe of late have layde aparte the goode and laudable exercise of the longe bow, whiche alwaye heretofore hathe bene the suertie savegarde and contynuall defence of this Realme of Englande, and an inestimable dread and terror to the Enemyes of the same'. And finally, since bowyers and fletchers for lack of work have gone to Scotland, and others are unemployed, comes the last Statute of Henry's reign on this subject, in much the same terms as before, and with much the same result. The 'crossbowes and little shorte handguns and little hagbuttes' are winning, and one cannot help being sorry for the king who loved his longbow so much.

And now a new portent. A young Cambridge don, one Ascham, writes a book on the practice of archery, dedicates it to the king, and receives a life pension for his pains. Archery has become a game or sport. No longer the grim genius of the pitched battle, the old longbow has been 'let down', weakened, and refined, to be a pastime for college tutors. Time moves fast. Ascham is, however, worried about the parlous conditions of military archery, and that is to his credit. He has a notable passage on the matter:

'. . . As a good ground, well tylled and well husbanded, bringeth out great plenty of byg eared corne, and good to the saule: so if the youth of Englande being apte of itself to shoote, were taught and learned howe to shoote, the archers should not be onely a great deal ranker, and mo than they be; but also a good deal bigger and stronger archers than they be. This commodity should follow also, if the youthe of Englande were taught to shoote, that even as the plowinge of a goode grounde for wheate, doth not only make it mete for the seede, but also ryveth and plucketh up by the rootes, all thistles, brambles, and weeds, which grow of their own accorde, to the destruction of both corne and grounde: Even so should the teaching of youthe to shoote, not only make them shoote well, but also pluck away by the rootes all other desyre to naughtye pastimes, as dysinge, cardinge, and boulinge, which, without any teaching, are used every where, to the great harm of the youth of this realme.'

Ascham had published his book just in time, for the old king's life was nearly done. With his death in 1547 there was removed perhaps the last real buttress of the old longbow. From then onwards his children, three of whom reigned in succession, could not, either from youth or the circumstance of their sex, give much support to the bow, even supposing that their personal example could have had the least influence in retarding the development of firearms. There was, nevertheless, to be one more occasion for the use of the longbow in battle, and this was perhaps the last notable appearance of the kind.

On the accession of the young Edward VI, the Lord Protector Somerset marched to Scotland and fought the battle of Pinkie, near the seaboard south of Edinburgh. Here the Scots were defeated; but, however much this encounter may be cited as an archers' battle, the bow was in competition with the arquebus handled by both horse and foot, and with great guns both military and naval. No doubt the archers were as formidable as ever, but it cannot be more clear that they were now only one arm of several, and probably not the predominant one at that.

Hard on this came the remarkable sermon preached by Bishop Latimer before the King and his principal officers of state. It seems an odd thing to have done, but perhaps there was more behind it than we now know; or it may simply have been that the good man, an archer from his youth up, could not bear to see the old weapon falling into disuse in the face of the modern new-fangled guns. For a modern parallel we should have to start with the fact that the rifle-shooting of the army is not what it used to be, and imagine a prelate getting up in St. Paul's before the King and Cabinet to advocate, passionately, that we return to the training and standards of 1914-18. Scraps of this celebrated discourse have been given in various archery books, but it deserves to be quoted more *in extenso*. Here it is:

'The arte of shutynge hath ben in tymes past much estemed in this realme, it is a gyft of God, that he hath geven us to excell all other nacions wythall. It hath bene Goddes instrumente, whereby he hath gyven us manye victories agaynste oure enemyes. But now we have taken up horynge in townes, insteede of shutynge in the fyeldes. A wonderous thynge, that so excelente a gyft of God shoulde be so lyttle esteemed. I desire you, my lordes, even as you love honoure, and glorye of God, and intende to remove his indignacion, let there be sent fourth some proclimacion, to the Justices of Peace, for they do not thyr dutye. Justices now be no Justices; ther be many good actes made for thys matter already. Charge them upon their allegiance, that thys singular benefit of God may be practised; and that it be not turned into bollyng, and glossyng, and horing, wythin the townes; for they be negligente in executying these lawes of shutynge. In my tyme, my poore father was as diligent to teach me to shute, as to learne any other thynge; and so I think other menne dyd thyr children. He taught me howe to drawe, howe to lay my bodye in my Bowe, and not to drawe wyth strength of armes, as other nacions do, but wyth strength of bodye. I had my Bowes brought me according to my age and strength, as I encreased in them; so my Bowes were made bigger and bigger; for men shall never shute well, excepte they be brought up in it. It is a goodly arte, a holesome kynde of exercise, and much commended in phisicke.... In the reverence of God, let it be continued. Let a proclamacion go forth, Charging the Justices of Peace, that they see such actes and statutes kept as were made for thys purpose.'

No notable result is traceable to this outburst. If Great Harry could not get his archers to practise, there was little hope for the young Edward. One Justice, however, seems to have been roused to action of a sort a few years later. At Malling, in Kent, this good man received a general complaint that a certain archer shot so well, and won so many wagers at the butts, that it was quite evident that he had enlisted the aid of black magic. He was therefore haled before the Justice and severely punished 'to the great encouragement of archers, and to the wise example of Justices; but especially to the overthrow of witchcraft.'

Mary could not be expected to do much in defence of the bow; she had none of the athletic tendencies of her half-sister Elizabeth. Still, she did issue one of the customary statutes, in which the relative number of 'hacquebuts' and bows to be kept by the people at large is laid down. It is interesting to see that in Cheshire, Lancashire, and Wales guns may be dispensed with altogether provided an equivalent number of bows is kept instead; from which it is a reasonable inference that all parts of the kingdom were not alike in their neglect of archery, and that the bow was still holding its own in its old place of origin and the adjacent territories. Further evidence of the same sort is provided by the report, written in 1557, of Giovanni Michiel, emissary of the Venetian Senate:

'Above all, their proper and natural weapons are the bow and arrows . . . in which the English place all their strength and all their hope, they to say the truth being most expert archers . . . and such is their opinion of archery and their esteem for it, that they prefer it to all sorts of arms and to harquebusses, in which they trust less, feeling more sure of their bows and arrows.' But, he adds, this confidence in the bow is not shared by the military opinion of other nations. It is difficult to believe that his account was really accurate; firearms had most certainly established themselves at the time he wrote, or Harrison, Holinshed's collaborator, would never have had occasion to write his scathing and celebrated passage:

'In times past the cheefe force of England consisted in their long bowes. But now we have in manner generallie given over that kind of artillerie, and for long bowes in deed doo practise to shoot compasse for our pastime: which kind of shooting can never yield anie smart stroke, nor beat downe our enimies, as our countrie men were woont to doo at euerie time of need. Certes the Frenchmen and Rutters deriding our new archerie in respect of their corslets, will not let in open skirmish, if anie leisure serue, to turne up their tailes and crie: Shoote English, and all bicause our strong shooting is decaied and laid in bed. But if some of our Englishmen now lived that serued King Edward the Third in his warres with France, the breech of such a varlet should have been nailed to his bum with one arrow, and an other fethered in his bowels, before he should have turned about to see who shot the first. But as our shooting is thus in manner utterlie decaied among us one waie, so our countrie men were skilfull in sundrie other points, as in shooting in small peeces, the caliuer, and handling of the pike, in the seuerall uses whereof they are become verie expert.'

Elizabeth liked hunting and shooting, but it is more than probable that the crossbow was her weapon even though she had had Ascham for her tutor. She does not appear to have interested herself directly in the military use of the bow; but one can imagine without difficulty the arguments that must have taken place in public and private between the champions of the old and new weapons respectively. Considering the power of the bow and the inefficiency and cumbrous bulk of the firearms of the time, it is a remarkable thing that the latter should have gained upon the former at the rate they did. It has been said somewhere that even the musket used at Waterloo had not the accuracy and range of the old longbow; and Hansard, in his *Book of Archery* (1841), has a passage which bears this out. 'During the month of August 1792, a match was decided at Pacton Green, Cumberland, between the gun and the bow, at one hundred yards. Victory fell to the latter, which put sixteen arrows into the target; the former only twelve balls. During the same year, a similar contest took place at Chalk Farm between Mr. Glynn of the Toxophilite Society, and Dr. Higgins of Greek Street, Soho; distance also one hundred yards. The result was, that out of twenty-one shots each at a four-foot target, the former gentleman scored fifteen, the latter only twelve.'

The relative values of bow and firearm in the sixteenth century have been summarized for us by Sir John Smythe, in his *Certain Discourses* (1590). Sir John was an out-and-out partisan of the older weapon. The three big advantages that he claims for the bow are that it is weatherproof; that it will kill or wound·over any part of the arrow's flight (though this is also true of a ball); and that the noise of the arrows in the air, and the sight of them, is a very terrifying thing. Undoubtedly he was right. A missile that can be seen as it approaches will cause, at least, apprehension where an invisible one would not; but when such missiles come by thousands at a time, singing and whistling in the air, the effect must be unnerving to a degree. Sir John says even the horses (or perhaps he meant particularly the horses) were frightened. A flight of heavy war-arrows striking a mass of lightly-armoured men must have wrought untold havoc both physical and mental. Not so the arquebus or musket, of which Sir John is very scornful. After two or three encounters, when the noise, flash, and smoke have ceased to terrify by their novelty; and when it is realized that for many thousands of shots there are not twenty men slain or hurt; then both man and horse lose any fear they might have had, while retaining their respect for cold steel, and for the destructive arrow which, in a whole mass of horsemen or footmen, will scarcely leave one unwounded. Sir John's conclusion is characteristically (one may think) downright: 'For my part I will neuer doubt to aduenture my life, or many liues (if I had them) amongst eight thousand Archers complet, well chosen and appointed, and there withall prouided and furnished with great store of sheafs of arrowes, as also with a good ouerplus of Bowes and Bowstrings, against twentie thousand of the best Harquebusiers and Mosquettiers, that are in Christendome.'

He is also an advocate of the use of mounted archers. He would mount them on quiet horses, give them steel caps, an armoured jerkin, a short broad sword and a dagger, with 'bowes of yeugh, long and well nocked and backed, and all their strings well whipt, with sheafes of foure and twentie arrowes apeece, with shooting gloves and bracers after the manner of our Archers in times past.'

'In times past. . . .' Just so; and not even Sir John's advocacy could recall the old archers of England.

He is echoed by Sir John Hayward a few years later. Within a reasonable distance, says this new Sir John, the bow has greater force and accuracy than the gun. It can be discharged with more rapidity. More men can shoot simultaneously, since only the front rank of the musketeers can shoot. Moreover, owing to its flat trajectory, the ball will only wound the front rank of the enemy; whereas the high curved flight of the arrow can cause it to land anywhere within the mass of the enemy, and do damage from the head to the very nailing of the feet to the ground according to the angle at which it strikes. And the fact that men are now very lightly armoured increased the danger.

True enough. Then why was the bow given up? To this there seems to be no answer that does not run counter to reason. Here was an ancient proven weapon of the simplest construction and maintenance, cheap to make, light in weight, weatherproof, easy to use sufficiently well for battle purposes provided only that one were fit and strong, capable of rapid fire, and of devastating effect. The firearm of the day was, on the contrary, heavy, clumsy, inaccurate, unusable in wet weather, complicated and costly, and of no more (if as much) power than the weapon it was so rapidly displacing. On the assumption that men were going to fight at one hundred yards range or less, as they did pretty much until the invention of the modern rifle, what advantages did the firearm have over the bow? None are apparent. The reason for the change must therefore lie, not in the relative merits of the two weapons, but elsewhere, probably in the circumstances in which military forces then took the field.

As yet there was no standing army, and hence no central authority to lay down the law on armament. The king went to war with what he could scrape up from the countryside; and although he might issue statutes enjoining the use of the longbow, and the proportion of bows to firearms that he would like to see, it by no means followed that when the troops assembled they would be armed accordingly. On the one hand, statutory archery practice had always been unpopular and would be dropped the moment there was no effective authority to enforce it; and on the other, the common man would always prefer the crossbow for his private poaching expeditions, and would have this as his personal weapon when called up for service. The early Tudors had broken the power of the old nobility, and with that had gone also the private armies and the companies of skilled archer-retainers. There was, then, no armed force in the kingdom other than the county and city militias, inexperienced, undisciplined, and haphazardly armed. It is, nevertheless, reasonable to suppose that the counties, or their newly-appointed lords-lieutenant, would vie with each other (as would certainly do the individual parishes whence came a few armed men each) in making as brave a show as possible, and so it would be natural that the latest inventions of the gunsmith would find as prominent a place in the array as expense would permit. Devon would not be outdone by Somerset, nor York by Chester. In plain language, it was Fashion, not Reason, that threw away the bow. What other explanation is there? Even as late as 1776, Benjamin Franklin wrote to General Lee: 'I still wish, with you, that pikes could be introduced, and I would add bows and arrows; these were good weapons not wisely laid aside.'

James I faced both ways. He caused the butts in and around the City of London to be restored to the condition they were in during the time of Henry VIII, but he also repealed the arms provisions of the ancient Statute of Winton. Right at the end of his reign there was published *The Double Armed Man*, an illustrated drill book by one William Neade professing to teach the combined use of bow and pike. It gained some little attention at the time, but nothing came of it; it was too late.

Charles II was more forthright than his grandfather. In his *Act for ordering the Forces in the several Counties of the Kingdom* (1662) the prescribed weapons are swords, pistols, muskets, and pikes. There is no mention of bows of any kind.

Thus ends finally the long and glorious military history of the longbow, and silence descends until the last quarter of the eighteenth century.

THE DECLINE OF ARCHERY

And of all the thousand upon thousand of bows which went to make up the tale, not one, not one single solitary complete bow, remains. A couple of rough staves in the Tower, and rumours of others elsewhere; but of the old-English longbow not one finished example. Tudor furniture we still have, clothes, books, glass, silver, and paintings—all perishable, but still with us. But of bows, not one. Where are they?

SCENE: *A little cottage in Warwickshire, in the early eighteenth century.* JOHN, *a farm worker, has just come in, and waits while* MARY, *his wife, gets his supper. Hard frost outside.*

' 'Tees main cold to-night, Mary.'

'Ah, 'tees John, an there b'aint no 'ood fer I to cook wee' or fer we to warm oor sels wee'. Why do'int 'ee bring a few stickes whom wee 'ee?'

'T'aint soa asy as that, Missus. 'Is Lardship be in a swivvy if us do go into 'is 'oods an that there bailiff chap be wuss. I baint no sort a feller to 'ave ought from the sawpit.'

'I do'int reckon as 'ow thee cares much, John. 'Tis me as ought to get the 'ood in, but I be getting a bit long in the tooth and I got the screws an me lags do ache proper. I can't abide to 'unt the 'ood an if I find a bit I canna heft it on me old back. I baint afeared o' that there bailiff chap even if thee be'ist, John. Damn is eyes, says I, stapping we old 'uns 'aving a bit o' firing to kep we vittly loike. But there 'tis an it 'unt be no tiser. If thee want thy vittles you'm best fetch that there old faggot o' sticks what 'ave bin in the tallet this unnerd years a more. They be nawthing but ole bean sticks an best burnt.'

'Does thee mane Granddad's bows, Mary?'

'Bows, John, bows do 'ee say? I never minded them was that. Think o' that, bows! That do mind 'ee of ole times do'int it loike. Fetch 'em down, John. Bows be no good to we naow.'

'I do'int rightly fancy it, Mary. Granddad did set store on they bows. Some on 'em were 'is Granddad's loikely as not. I do'int reckon as 'ow us ought to burn 'em.'

'Well, John, 'tis the bows or an empty belly and cold to bed. Get along naow an' fetch 'em. What good be bows to we?'

'Well, 'ooman, I reckon us 'ull 'ave to burn 'em, but 'tain't praper loike; makes I feel loike I were doin' summot wrong loike. Makes I feel funny loike, I dunno why. Olright! oll right! I fetch 'em.'

Following Roger Ascham's lead, nearly one hundred years before, Peacham, in his *Compleat Gentleman* (1622), had said that shooting with the

59

bow was a very healthful and commendable recreation for gentlemen. Even as late as 1776 there were still bowyers; and one of them, Waring, introduced the game of target-shooting to Sir Ashton Lever, who derived great benefit from it in the matter of an 'oppression upon his chest'. This trifle (historically speaking, and with no lack of sympathy for the good Sir Ashton) led to the formation, in 1780, of a Society 'under the title of Toxophilites'.

It is no part of these notes to recount the history and exploits of this and other famous English archery societies. It is enough to say that the bow being dead began to live again through them; and that they kept alive the tradition until once more the bow found work to do, not this time for war but for hunting.

And now, oddly enough to English susceptibilities, we cross the Atlantic. The American Civil War produced, as a by-product, two most accomplished archers, Maurice and Will Thompson. These brothers from the Southern States had lost everything in the war, and were besides forbidden the use of firearms. They retired to the Florida Everglades, where they lived for some years almost entirely by the bow. Maurice's book, *The Witchery of Archery* (1878), is celebrated. Later, Saxton Pope took up the bow seriously for hunting, feeling that modern firearms were not fair to the game. His book, mentioned at the beginning of these notes, is also famous, and is no doubt the foundation upon which rests the present numerous and enthusiastic company of American hunters with the bow.

So our old longbow has become, temporarily let us hope, an American citizen, rubbing shoulders with the short flat bow of the Indian. Perhaps it is a good thing. In England 'unlawful games' abound, and there is no statute to restrain them. The bow is a simple, beautiful, difficult thing, unsuited to the temperament and opportunity of a crowded, mechanized, urban society. But there will always be some who will take to the bow precisely because of its virtues of simplicity and difficulty, and some maybe from sentiment also. They will keep the old tradition alive here; and in time, perhaps through adversity, we shall revert to a saner way of life. Then the bow will return to its old home, and the long shafts will sing again.

Part Two

PRACTICAL—THE MAKING OF ARCHER'S TACKLE

TOOLS AND MATERIALS

'A good workman will not complain of his tools.'

It is not necessary to have an elaborately-fitted workshop. True, I have a place called 'the workshop', but it is full of mowing-machines, potatoes, apples in season, and a vast quantity of junk. Still, it has an old work-bench in it, and some few tools inherited when I was a boy. There are no mechanical contrivances of any kind, unless a small hand grinding-wheel can be so called: nor are any necessary or desirable. Bowmaking is not, emphatically not, an affair of precision and engineering accuracy; rather is it an art, dependent far more upon the eye and touch than upon measurement. A bowyer is a bowyer, not a cabinet maker.

The tools required are very few and simple. Indeed, if one reflects for a moment, what did primitive man make his bows with? An axe, a stone axe most likely, and a piece of sandstone for smoothing. So did Ishi, the Yana Indian in Dr. Pope's book, make his weapons; and we are told that his handicraft was the best in all North America. So confront me with a suitable yew tree and give me a light *axe* and I will make you a bow. It will be a tiresome and ·tedious business, wasteful of much good timber and time: but I will make you the bow none the less. 'Axe?' you say. Yes, axe; the most useful tool of all. Not the ugly blunt cumbersome thing, used for breaking coal and striking nails, that is to be found in most households: but a proper small-size woodsman's axe with an edge like a razor. I find it convenient to have two sizes: one weighs, with its helve, $3\frac{1}{4}$ lb. and is for the rougher work at the beginning; the other, one of the Marble make, weighs 20 oz. complete, and with this midget practically the whole work of shaping the bow can be done. But the edges must be thin and really sharp. Once brought to this condition with file and stone, never never lend your axe to anybody!

A *plane* saves a lot of time; and I find an iron plane, with finely-adjustable blade, the most convenient. It is 10 inches long and can easily be worked with one hand.

63

PRACTICAL

Get a *shoemaker's rasp*; with this and the little axe one might almost dispense with the plane if strict economy is necessary. It is a little thing, 7 inches long; on one side it has a flat, fairly coarse file, and on the other one flat and one half-round rasp. The rasp eats off wood like magic, while the file smooths it in the twinkling of an eye. On no account buy a heavy cumbersome carpenters' rasp; you will ruin your work.

Of *saws* you will want two. A fairly big rip-saw for getting-out bow staves if for any reason splitting the log is not advisable; and a hacksaw, for all sorts of little jobs. A tenon-saw is also nice to have but not essential, unless you are going to make jointed bows.

Files are five in number. You have already got one on your shoemakers' rasp. You will want another finer flat cross-cut file about 9 ninches long, with one edge smooth; a small, thin warding file for making nocks in arrows; and two sizes of rat-tail files, one about ¼ in. thick for filing nocks at the bow-ends, and one about ⅛ in. thick for rounding the bases of arrow nocks.

If you like you can have a *spokeshave*; but I prefer to use the rasp. The spokeshave does nice clean work, but the bow has to be held in a vice or clamp so that both hands can be free to work the tool. I like to hold the bow in one hand and work with the other. Nor is the rasp given to making sudden and violently deep cuts as is the spokeshave if one is not wholly its master.

A steel *scraper* is nice to do the ultimate finishing with, followed by steel-wool. But a good man-size pocket knife is just as good.

A *drill* of the Miller's Falls type is wanted for arrowheads, with ¼ in. and ⅛ in. twist drills to go with it.

A small pair of *cutting pliers* for cutting rivets.

A small *riveting hammer* for fastening arrowheads.

A *wooden mallet* if you propose to make 'carriage' bows.

A *sledge-hammer* and two *steel wedges*, for splitting yew logs.

And, of course, you want a *bench* of some sort. If this is fitted with an old-fashioned carpenters' vice (the clumsy thing which works with a great wooden screw) it will perhaps be better than the modern kind made of steel which may bruise your work.

You can make arrowheads entirely in the hand, but it is hard on the fingers. It is much more comfortable to have a small engineers' *vice*.

Scales of sorts are indispensable. The first, to help determine the 'weight' of the bow, should be a spring balance reading up to 80 or 100 lb.; actually this can be dispensed with by using a little ingenuity, as will be seen farther on. The other should be a little apothecary's scales, or something of the kind for weighing arrows and arrowheads. If it can take 2 oz. as a maximum that will be sufficient, but it must be sensitive.

An *oilstone* of course.

So is completed a very modest list. There yet remain certain indispensables which you cannot purchase. These are hands which will do the brain's bidding, and a straight eye: gifts of God both. The former can be trained, and those which have never been really used can have their latent skill developed; but the eye, the power of seeing straight and true, of judging the essential fitness of the work through all its stages, that is something with which, I think, one is either blessed or not. And if one is not so blessed then bowyers' and fletchers' work is not for him be his hands never so nimble.

MATERIALS

As in the case of tools, no great outlay is required for materials. Here is the list.

Wood—for the bow itself, and for arrows. For particulars, see 'The Bow' and 'Arrows' respectively.

Linen Thread—for bowstrings. Shoemakers' thread of about 5 lb. breaking-strain is best.

Waste Vellum Strips—for 'backing' bows. This can be got from makers of vellum and parchment.

Leather or Whipcord—for covering the handgrip of the bow. Leather, preferably horsehide, is also wanted for 'tabs'.

Feathers—for arrows. The strong primaries of turkeys or geese are the only ones worth bothering about.

Scissors and Safety-Razor Blades (perhaps these are tools rather than materials) —for cutting and trimming feathers.

Strong Linen Carpet-Thread—a reel of any colour.

Sewing Cotton—a reel of any colour.

Thin Silk Tape—about ⅛ in. wide, for binding ends of feathers to arrow shafts. Not indispensable; thread will do.

Paint and Brushes—for painting arrows and decorating bows. I find the 'synthetic finishes' give a very fine, hard surface; and the best of them can be obtained in very small and convenient tins.

Celluloid Varnish—just a little for waterproofing the binding of the feathers on your arrows.

Glue—any kind you like. Casein glue is wonderfully strong, easy to use, and will withstand the wet in moderation, an important consideration when arrows are lost and found again perhaps after some days in the open.

PRACTICAL

Celluloid glue has its advantages for bamboo arrows. Certain newer synthetic resin glues are good, and are completely waterproof.

Steel Strip—for arrowheads. Mild steel for rabbit-points; spring-steel for broadheads. See 'Arrowheads'.

Steel Rod—⅛ in. diameter, for locking-pins on 'carriage' bows.

Bullet-Jackets—for heads of practice arrows. Can probably be got from a gunmaker if you pester him enough. The right size is that of the German service rifle, 7·9 mm. or ·311 in.

Wire Nails—about ⅛ in. diameter, for making rivets for arrowheads.

Beeswax and Rosin—melted together in the proportion of 3 of wax to 1 of rosin. The surest way to get real beeswax, and to avoid the many substitutes which you will be offered, is to buy honey in the comb and separate out the wax yourself. The tip is to warm the whole thing up so that the honey will run freely from the mashed-up comb, and then filter it through a piece of muslin. It is a messy business at best.

Cobbler's Wax (or any other good adhesive compound)—for securing arrowheads.

Boiled Linseed Oil—for the final finish to the bow.

Soft Leather or Canvas—for a quiver. Canvas is very noisy in the woods.

Vulcanized Fibre—a few small scraps, red or black, and $\frac{1}{32}$ in. thick, for arrowplates.

Surgical Gauze Bandages—four 2 in. wide, for use while backing bows and covering the handgrip.

That's all.

It may be useful to you to know of two places from where you can obtain at least some of the essential materials. These are Messrs. John Jaques & Son, of Thornton Heath, Surrey, and, in the United States (among scores of others, but this is where I got my first batch of raw materials) Stemmler Archery, Manorville, L.I., New York. With neither have I any connection except as a satisfied customer.

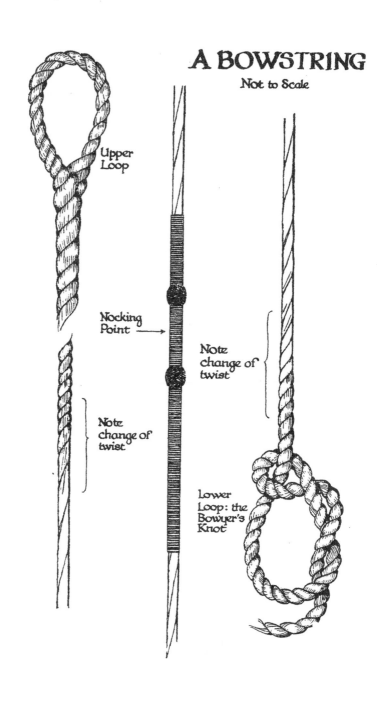

A BOWSTRING

Not to Scale

Upper
Loop

Nocking
Point →

Note
change of
twist

Note
change of
twist

Lower
Loop: the
Bowyer's
Knot

BOWSTRINGS

'As unto the bow the cord is,
So unto the man is woman;
Though she bends him, she obeys him,
Though she draws him, yet she follows,
Useless each without the other.'

LONGFELLOW, *Hiawatha.*

aking a bowstring is a jolly business. It has all the fascination of a good conjuring trick without the necessity for laborious practice. You will make a success of even your first.

The things you make it with are linen thread, wax, two nails, and your hands; nothing else. Linen is not, of course, the only possible material; you can use hemp, silk, and other fibres, but, as this is not an encyclopedia, and as flax is inexpensive and entirely satisfactory, let us leave it at that. The method I use is that described by Dr. Pope, easy and practical. Later on, if you like, you can try to make one of the solid Flemish kind, spun straight off the distaff without the intermediate production of thread; but I cannot tell you how you are to set about this.

The shoemaker's thread which you must use is thin and rather woolly-looking, not glazed at all. It should break at a pull of about 5 lb. weight. If you can't get that, use any other size available, increasing or decreasing the number of threads in the bowstring accordingly. But don't use too thick a variety or your string will be lumpy and weak; and don't use ordinary glazed thread which cannot properly take up the wax. The kind I have usually managed to get is called 'Finlayson, Bousfield & Co.'s No. 9 Patent Shoe Thread 16's', which you should be able to get from any shop which stocks leather-workers' materials. Of this, I use not less than sixty strands.

A bowstring is made up of a number of threads laid side by side, and twisted together with a loop at one end. The ends, both of them, are thicker than the middle and are twisted differently.

The strength of the string must be related to the 'weight' of the bow. Not only that, but there must be a large margin of strength to take care of the tremendous momentary strain to which the string is subjected as the bow snaps back at the instant when the arrow leaves it. Allow, therefore, a factor of about 5; that is, make a string which will only break when subjected to a tension in pounds weight of five times the 'weight' of the bow.

Thus, for a 60 lb. bow, the string should just be capable of supporting a trifle under 300 lb. Since each strand of linen breaks at 5 lb. weight, sixty strands will be about right; and, indeed, this makes a string of very convenient thickness to take the nock cut in an arrow of $\frac{5}{16}$ in. diameter. For weaker or stronger bows the calculation is simple. But, although the thinner the string the faster the bow is said to cast, do not make it too thin. A broken string usually means a broken bow; and anyway you are making hunting gear, which should be robust and reliable. So, if in doubt, err on the thick side.

Let us suppose, then, that we are going to make a string of sixty strands. First, measure your bow from nock to nock, and add sixteen inches to this length. Drive two nails into the floor, or a wall, at that distance apart. Take your spool of linen, fasten the end to one nail, and wind round the other back and forth until you have twenty strands altogether. Slip or cut them off the nails, cut any loops that remain at the point where they went round the nails, and lay the whole bunch aside. Do this three times. Thus you will have three skeins of twenty strands each, in length equal to that of your bow plus sixteen inches.

Now alter the distance between your nails to six feet. Wind another skein of twenty strands, cut it off, and lay it aside as before. One only of this length is required. Cut it into six pieces, each 12 in. long. These will be used to reinforce the ends of the string, where the chafe of the nock comes. You may do without them if you like to take a chance; but, if so, then see that the part that encircles the nocks is well bound and protected with leather or string serving. But it is not good to take chances when hunting.

Now comes a little job which sometimes proves simpler to describe than to do. Both ends of each of your nine skeins, long and short, must be tapered. To do this, pick up a skein and hold it between the thumb and forefinger of the right hand at about one inch from the end. Pull out the individual threads so that each is about $\frac{3}{8}$ in. (accuracy doesn't matter) in advance of the other; the length of the tapered part will then be about 6 to 7 in. Occasionally, while you are doing this, look inside your right hand to see what sort of infernal tangle is building up there; and if you find the makings of a good birds' nest stroke out the threads in the direction away from the end you are working on. Easier said than done! When finally you have got the end tapered (the other end of course tapers automatically), spend quite a little time seeing that the threads are as straight as possible and all at equal tension when you stretch the skein out straight. You will find that it has twisted somewhat, and it is a great help in equalizing the tension to untwist as far as you can. Do this for all nine skeins.

Some folk will avoid all this by laying the skeins down on a table and scraping the ends with a sharp knife till they taper after a fashion. I recommend you to do the thing properly if you do it at all.

Then take your lump of beeswax and rosin, and wax each skein thoroughly and liberally, working from the centre to the ends so as not to tangle up the tapered parts. These preliminaries are rather tedious, and they hold one back from the really nice work which follows.

Take your three long skeins, and roll each up from one end until 18 in. only is left unrolled. Squeeze the roll, and it will stick together. Along the last foot of each of the unrolled parts lay one of your short skeins. Wax each pair together, working from the middle to the ends of the short skeins in each case. You now have three long skeins rolled up and thickened at the free end with a short one. Now lay all three in front of you with their free ends pointing to your left and the rolled-up parts to your right, all three parallel and close together. Light your pipe, grip them together eight inches from the free ends with your thumb and finger of the left hand, and settle yourself in your easy chair.

Three skeins of threads, ending in the rolled-up parts, will be dangling in front of you. Unroll a little more so that you have about a foot to work with in each case. Seize the skein that seems to be farthest away from you with the thumb and forefinger of the right hand, quite close up to the left thumb. Give it a twist away from you, hard, until you feel it all tight in your fingers. Then draw it down towards you over the other two skeins and tuck it away under your left thumb, still tightening the twist as you do so. Do this for each skein in turn; and continue thus, always taking the skein that seems farthest away from you and keeping to the proper order. A little sleight-of-hand with the left forefinger will keep the skeins sticking out straight to your right; they have a tendency to point in towards your body otherwise. Go on doing this for a little, and resist for the moment the temptation to see what is happening under your left thumb. Twist hard and take the skeins in rotation.

When you have twisted a couple of inches or so in this way open your left hand (it's all right, the wax will hold everything tight) and see what you have done. Nice, isn't it? Now go on until you have three inches of your little rope. Then look at it carefully. The thickest part should be in the middle. If it isn't, reverse the whole thing in your hand and twist just a little of the tapered ends until the rope is symmetrical.

Now unroll another foot or so of your skeins. Bend your little rope into a loop so that its two ends are level and grip it just on the loop side of that point with your left thumb and forefinger. You now have three long parts and three short parts sticking out of your hand. Separate them and arrange them so that each long part has one short part lying close to and parallel with it. Wax these pairs together. After this 'marrying' you will clearly be left with three thickened skeins only. Strictly speaking a short end should not be married to its own long end, and you can overcome this by tieing pieces of different coloured silks to each skein before you begin; but I don't think this is really material in practice and I have never troubled to do it.

Now continue your twisting in exactly the same way as you made your little rope, taking care that all is tight and firm at the base of the loop. Go on until you come to the end of the thickened parts of the skeins, do another half-inch, and then stop. Now admire the beautiful thing you have made; a loop, twice as thick as your string will be merging into a considerably thicker neck which itself tapers away gracefully into what will be the string itself. No ends will be visible, nor join, nor splice.

When you have done looking at it hang it up on a hook or nail on the wall, unroll all the rest of the three skeins and pull them straight. Take it down again, put it on the table, and taking the skeins one by one roll them back and forth on the table with the flat of your two hands until they are as round as you can get them. Take trouble over this.

Now you still have three short skeins which you have tapered and waxed. Take these and wax them to the ends of your long skeins so that the ends are level. When all is firm put your loop on the hook again, grasp all three parts together just above the point where the short skeins end and arrange them so that they run straight from end to end and do not twine round each other. Equalize the tension on all three parts as carefully as you can, and then start twisting the free ends exactly as before, making a second little rope at the bottom of the string. Continue until you come to the very end; and there tie a knot, a wall-and-crown knot if you are nautically minded, otherwise an ordinary overhand knot. Put your string back on the hook if it is not already there, twist the whole thing from left to right to straighten out the middle e bit, and give it a good stretch. Then twist from right to left until it makes ona complete turn on itself for every inch or so of its length.

Is the top of your right forefinger rather sore? It ought to be if you have done your twisting faithfully. You have nearly done now, but not quite.

The little Axe

Roughing out a Bow

5. *The Axe*

String-making on a hot afternoon

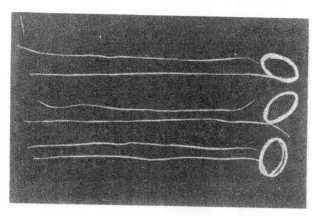

The Beginning. Three long skeins, and three short skeins (thickeners)

6. *String-making I*

Sometimes at this stage I like to soak the middle part of the string, that is excluding the thickened parts at each end, in melted beeswax. This ensures that all threads are properly waxed, and makes a rounder string. It is not really necessary, and if you are in a hurry to get on you can omit it. But do it with your next string and see if you think this worth the trouble. The way to do it is to melt a little beeswax in a shallow bowl, get it really hot, and then coil the middle part of the string up and immerse it. Holding the end of the uppermost coil in your left hand draw the string out slowly through a thick rag (the wax will burn you if your rag is only thin) held in your right hand. This wipes away the surplus wax.

Now put your string on the bow. To do this slip the loop over the end of the upper limb and let it slide down until it is about four inches from the nock. Then in the other end tie a bowyer's knot, slip it into the lower nock and pull tight. Then brace your bow. Adjust the length of the string until the bow is braced fully to 'fistmele'. Now take a piece of thickish leather in your hand, doubled up so that it will embrace the string, and with it rub the string up and down vigorously until it is as round and smooth as you can get it. Mark now on the string the exact point where the arrow nock will come. In doing this remember that the arrow must stand accurately at right-angles to the string and must rest on the arrow-plate immediately above the hand-grip.

Above this point mark two others, one $\frac{1}{4}$ in. and one $1\frac{1}{4}$ in. up the string; and below mark one $\frac{1}{4}$ in. and one 3 in. down the string. Let us call these points, starting from the uppermost, A, B, C, D, E, respectively. All this part has to be bound or served with thread, carpet thread for choice, to preserve the string from being chafed by the arrow and fingers. You can get a little gadget to help you with this; but for so short a piece of work it is not really necessary. Plain fingers can do just as good a job. The serving is done while the string is still taut on the bow. Sit down and lay your bow over your knees, upper limb to the left and string away from you.

Start your serving at point A. Do not wax your thread and do not cut it off the reel. Hold the reel in your right hand so that the thread unrolls from its lower side, unroll a little thread and lay the end along the string pointing towards the right. Make your first turn over this end at point A, and continue for half a dozen turns; then pull the end tight and cut it off. Continue serving, as tightly as you can and holding all firm with your left forefinger as you go, until you reach point B. Now wind back for $\frac{1}{8}$ in. and then forward again. This will make a little lump in the serving. Continue to $\frac{1}{8}$ in. below point D, wind back again to that point and then forward again. This makes another little lump; the two will be ½ in. apart and will enable you to find at once, even in the dark, the point where the arrow nock goes.

Go on now till you reach a point about ¼ in. above point E. Then take a round pencil and lay it along the string so that its end is ½ in. below point E. Grip both string and pencil together with the left hand and continue your winding (but loosely this time) over both. When you have wound down to point E withdraw the pencil. This will leave a row of loops of thread standing up. Now cut off your thread from the reel, pass the end through these loops from right to left and hold it down to the string with your left forefinger at the point where the tight serving at present ends. Now take hold of the upper-most, or left hand, loop and continue your serving with that. You will find that the other loops will disappear miraculously. When you find that there is only one loop remaining and that this does *not* encircle the string, pull on the end which you have held under your left finger, draw the loop in tight, and cut off the end close to the serving. Thus you have accomplished a 'whip-finish'. Wax the whole serving, and your string is complete.

All this is cumbersome to describe; it is, in fact, so very much simpler than it sounds. Write a detailed description of how to do up your shoelace, or better still of how to put on your collar and tie, and you will see what I mean.

And now, while the mood is on you, make a spare string. You will want it. And make one more, a very strong one of, say ninety strands, to fit a bow of 5 ft. 10 in. from nock to nock. You cannot make a bow without a string to test it with as you go. That is why I put the making of the bowstring first.

One word of caution. Do not seek to save yourself the trouble of making a proper bowstring and think that a piece of good, strong hempen whipcord will do as well. It will not. It will break, and so most likely will your bow with it.

ASCHAM'S NOTES
Of strings

'An ill stringe breaketh many a good bowe, nor no other thinge half so manye.'

'Now what a stringe ought to be made on, whether of good hempe, as they do nowe a dayes, or of flaxe, or of silke, I leave that to the judgement of stringers, of whom we must buy them.'

'Great stringes and little stringes be for divers purposes: the great stringe is more surer for the bowe, more stable to pricke withall, but slower for the cast. The litle stringe is clean contrarye, not so sure, therefore to be taken heede of, lest with long taryinge on, it break your bowe, more fit to shoote

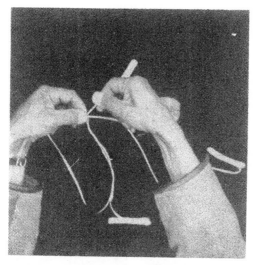

Twisting. The left hand grips all three skeins;
while the right forefinger and thumb twist
one skein hard, in the direction the thumb
is pointing

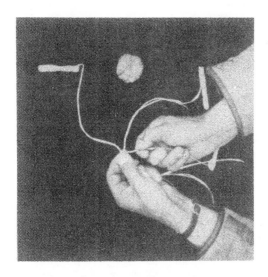

Twisting. The hard-twisted skein is brought
downwards, over the other two, and tucked
away under the left thumb

7. *String-making II*

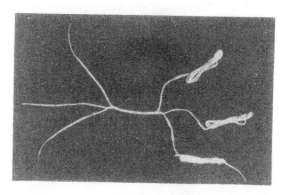

The little rope

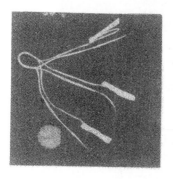

The little rope looped,
the skeins paired

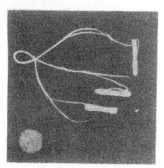

The skeins waxed together
and married

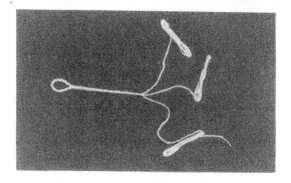

The completed loop

8. *String-making III*

farre, than apt to pricke neare, therefore when you know the nature of both bigge and litle, you must fit your bowe according to the occasion of your shootinge.'

'You must looke that your bowe be well nocked, for feare the sharpnesse of the horne shere asunder the stringe.'

'You must mark also to set your stringe streyght on, or els the one ende shall wrieth contrarye to the other, and so break your bowe.'

'When the stringe beginneth never so litle to weare, trust it not, but away with it, for it is an ill saved halfpeny, that costes a man a crowne.'

'Thus you see how many jeopardyes hangeth over the selye poore bow, by reason onlye of the stringe. As when the stringe is shorte, when it is longe, when eyther of the nockes be noughte, when it hath but one way, and when it taryeth over longe on.'

DIMENSIONS of SOME ACTUAL BOWS

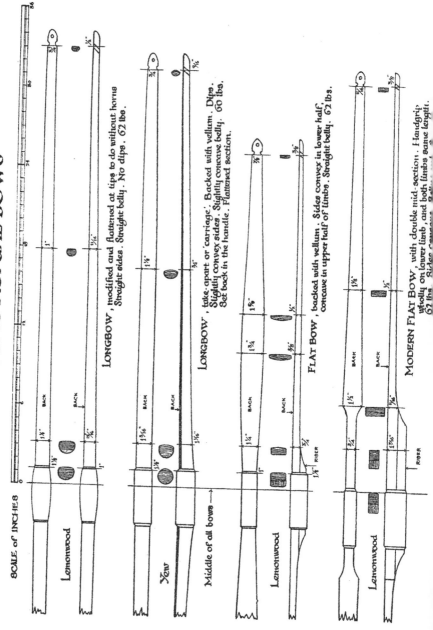

SCALE of INCHES

Lemonwood

LONGBOW, modified and flattened at tips to do without horns. Straight sides. Straight belly. No dips. 62 lbs.

Yew

LONGBOW, take-apart or 'carriage'. Backed with vellum. Dips. Slightly convex sides. Slightly concave belly. 60 lbs. Set back in the handle. Flattened section.

Middle of all bows →

Lemonwood

FLAT BOW, backed with vellum. Sides convex in lower half, concave in upper half of limbs. Straight belly. 62 lbs.

Lemonwood

MODERN FLAT BOW, with double mid-section. Handgrip wholly on lower limb, and both limbs same length. 62 lbs. Sides concave

THE BOW

'The Bowe is a weapon wonderfull readie in all seasons.'
SIR JOHN SMYTHE, *Certain Discourses.*

PRELIMINARY

There is no mystery in bowyer's work: nor is the making of a bow of the simple sort with which we are here concerned an intrinsically difficult thing. But patience is required and a temperament which will tolerate the seemingly endless trials until all is right and just as it should be. A bow is something more than a stick which will bend. Time also is necessary; how much I cannot say. Starting with a prepared stave you may want a few hours or a few days; given a standing yew tree you will want three or four years maybe.

So approach your bow making without undue impatience. Bear constantly in mind the fable of the Hare and the Tortoise; bowstaves are not grown in a day but can be ruined in a moment by one injudicious cut. Remember, also, that you are not a cabinet- or pattern-maker but a bowyer; you are not making anything to strict measurements; your bow will evolve gradually as your work proceeds, and that precisely is the fascination of the thing. A bow is a work of art; work only therefore when the spirit is upon you: 'Sone enough if well enoughe; wherewith every honest handy craftes man should measure, as it were with a rule, his work withall.'

This is no treatise on bows, and here I shall not, even if I knew enough, discourse of bows of wood, horn, bone, bamboo, and even steel; of bows simple, backed, laminated, reflexed, eared, set back in the handle, and takedown; of bows high-stacked and flat; of longbows and shortbows; of bows of the West and of bows of the East. No, there is material for a life's work almost. Let us confine ourselves to what is practical and necessary as an initiation to the bowyer's art, and to such types as can be made with materials easily obtainable; wood for material, and for types the traditional longbow of England, the shorter flat bow characteristic of the North American Indian,

PRACTICAL

and perhaps one or two variations of each. When you have mastered these you may begin to cherish the same ambition as myself, which is to make one of those wonderful reflexed composite horn-wood-sinew bows of the East; but that time is not yet.

DEFINITIONS

Bowyers use technical language like other professional people and craftsmen. Here are some terms you will want to remember.

The back is that side of the bow that is farthest from you as you shoot. It is flat or slightly rounded.

The belly is the side of the bow nearest to you as you shoot. In the longbow it takes the form of a Roman arch; in the flat bow the arch is drastically flattened or indeed there may be no arch at all, the belly being quite flat.

Stack—a bow is said to be 'high-stacked' when the arch of the belly is deep in proportion to the width of the bow. The higher the stack the more readily will the bow break.

The handgrip (or handle) is just that. It is *not* in the centre of the bow.

Riser—a modern term applied to a piece of wood fixed to the belly of a flat bow to increase the depth and to strengthen it at the handgrip.

The tips are the last four or six inches at each end of the bow.

Whip-ended is when the tips are weak relative to the rest of the limbs.

The limbs, upper and lower, are the halves of the bow above and below the handgrip respectively. Measuring from each end of the handgrip the lower limb is shorter than the upper by 1½ in.

Set back in the handle is when the whole of each limb has a slight forward inclination, i.e. towards the back, when the bow is unstrung.

The nocks are the grooves at each end of the bow which receive and retain the loops of the string.

The dips—when the belly of a bow dips sharply from the full depth at the handgrip to a lower level it is said to have 'dips'. A modern innovation due to one Buchanan and said to make for less jar in shooting. The old longbow had no dips; the line of the wood ran in an even taper from handgrip to tips.

The arrow-plate is a little piece of ivory, shell, or fibre inlet or stuck on to the side of the bow immediately above the handgrip on the left-hnad side as you shoot. It prevents the arrow from damaging the surface of the bow in its passage across it. For hunting, a buckskin arrow-plate has the advantage of being noiseless.

Backing is anything glued on to the back of the bow either to preserve it from accidental damage or to reinforce its ability to stand tension when the bow is drawn. Bowyers will never cease to argue about the utility of this.

To tiller a bow is to observe the shape and character of the limbs when the bow is drawn, fully or in part, and to correct irregularities where they show themselves.

The weight of a bow is that number of pounds which, if attached to the centre of the string, would draw the bow to the full draw of the archer who owns it.

To brace a bow is to set the string in position ready for shooting.

Fistmele is the distance between the handgrip on the belly side and the string when the bow is braced. If you place your clenched fist on the handgrip and stretch up your thumb the tip of the latter should just touch the string. Hence the name. A bow which is highly strung, i.e. where the distance is more than ordinary fistmele, will shoot more cleanly, if with slightly less power, than one which is not.

Cast—is the way a bow causes the arrow to fly. A bow which has a good cast will send the arrow in a flatter trajectory than one which has not. An important characteristic since a bow with good cast helps to reduce an archer's main difficulty, viz. the estimation of distance and hence of aim.

OF BOW WOOD

The bow is essentially a spring. The material of which it is made must therefore have the necessary characteristics. It must endure being bent repeatedly and to an extreme degree, and must then return, faithfully and with great rapidity, to its original shape when the strain on it is released.

Notwithstanding the diversity of materials of which bows can be made, in regard to wood (to which we shall confine ourselves here) bowyers are agreed that only three varieties can properly be called first class. These are Osage Orange (*Maclura Aurantiaca*), Yew (*Taxus Baccata*, or *Canadensis*), and Lemonwood (*Calycophyllum Candidissimum*). There is, indeed, a suspicion that box was used sometimes in medieval times; but I have not been able to verify this. You may, if you like, experiment with hickory, wychelm, or ash, the 'mean woodes' of the old English bowyers; but I shall not. They will make bows of a sort, but not good ones.

Osage Orange you are not likely to get in this country; it is a very tough North American wood of which I have no experience. Those who know it say that it is just a little bit better than yew. Try it, by all means, if you can get a stave, but remember it is abominably difficult to work.

PRACTICAL

Yew is the classic material for the English longbow. Irregular and difficult to work, it makes a bow lovely both to shoot and to look at.

Lemonwood, which the timber trade calls '*Degame*', grows in Cuba. It is a hard, heavy, yellowish-buff wood without any apparent grain. It is difficult to saw, but delightfully easy to work with edged tools. Together with lancewood (somewhat similar, but more brittle and not recommended), it was used by the makers of carriage shafts and is still used by the makers of fishing-rods. It makes first class bows; it is easy to work; and, all things considered, is the most suitable material for your first essay in bow-making. Its only drawback, if indeed it is one at all, is that it 'follows the string' a little; that is, it takes on a slight permanent bend. But since this bend, once taken, does not increase, there is no harm in it. So be advised, and begin with lemonwood.

I cannot tell you any more about it than this, as I have always bought prepared staves, except that I have noticed a tendency to the development of fine, hair-like cracks parallel to the bow's length. These I bind (like a cricket bat) whenever they appear. I have broken several yew bows in the making and in use, but, so far, no lemonwood bow has come to grief in my hands.

Do not waste time trying to make a bow out of a whole sapling or thin branch of any wood. Serviceable bows can not be made that way.

Of yew in particular

The yew is a queer tree. A dark, forbidding thing, which in England grows freely on the high chalk of the south. A yew tree is unmistakable; never really big however old it may be; and some are almost incredibly old. Dark needle foliage, short irregular trunk, many branches, and smooth, scaly, reddish bark. In exposed places the whole tree is often twisted and gnarled to a degree. Trees may be male or female, the latter being easily distinguishable, at the proper season, by the bright cerise 'berries' which it bears, which are not berries at all, but just a fleshy growth surrounding the single seed. Some bowyers say these female trees will not yield good bows; some say they are as good as the male. The foliage is highly poisonous to cattle, and it has even been said that working in yew wood has upset the craftsman in some mysterious way.

The English yew is called *Taxus Baccata*, the American *Taxus Brevifolia* or *Canadensis*; the latter is the better, since it grows high up in exposed mountainous country. The English sort will make bows all right, not of the best quality but good and serviceable. It is rather too open in the grain compared with foreign varieties, a fact which was well recognized centuries ago. In the

80

'Hatfield Papers' (1574) four districts are mentioned as sources of good bow-staves: Salzburg, in Austria; Switzerland, above Basel; 'Revel, Dansk, Polonia, and all countries East of the Sound'; and Italy, staves from whence were pronounced very fine. In short, the best yew (and also probably the most irregular and difficult to work), is that grown slowly, high up in a dry country. This will be hard, heavy and dense, and has the finest cast of anything in the world. The Americans can get all they want from the mountains of the west; we must put up with what we can get in England, and really it is quite serviceable even if it does follow the string about as much as lemonwood. I have two bows, as nearly identical in length and tiller as two bows can be; one is of lemonwood and the other of English yew. Both are of the same weight, which means that the yew one is bulkier. There is little to choose between them, but to be really honest I prefer the lemonwood. I cannot tell you exactly why, so little is the difference between them.

Yew is a peculiar growth; and whoever first thought of using it for bows was a genius. On the outside there is a thin, scaly bark, which can be easily removed. Under this is a layer of 'cambium', never more than an eighth of an inch or so thick, which is also to be removed. Next comes the sapwood, white, tough, leathery stuff, varying considerably in thickness even in the same tree. Lastly we reach the heartwood, which is, when thoroughly seasoned, brittle and springy, and may vary in colour from pale buff to deep red.

The secret of the yew bow lies in the combination of the heart- and sapwoods; the former drives the arrow with its spring and sharp recovery; the latter acts as a natural backing and prevents the heartwood from breaking. It follows that, to make a bow, you require a stave which comprises some of each, and this can, obviously, only be split from the outside of the tree. The heartwood will then form the belly of your bow, the sapwood the back; the former will endure compression as the bow is drawn, the latter can withstand the corresponding tension. It is an ideal combination.

The difficulty is to find a tree which contains a clear piece long and straight enough to make a stave for a longbow. Yew is a twisted, knotty growth, and has, besides, innumerable 'pins', which are very small knots from which twigs grow. Furthermore, the surface usually has all sorts of bumps and hollows in it, and the sapwood may be of the most irregular character. It is most difficult to select, from outside inspection alone, a piece which will be satisfactory. There will be many failures in your selection, however skilled you may become. It is, naturally, much easier to find two shorter pieces which can be joined; if at all possible, these should be cut from the same billet, side by side.

Which leads us on to the time at which yew should be cut; and here, as in almost everything else, bowyers differ. Some say the winter is best, for the sap is then 'down'; others say sap doesn't matter. My own experience leads me to prefer the winter, and here is an extract from an old letter in support:

'Also you shall understand here is plentie of yew for bowstaues. I caused three horse loades to be brought us for to know the trueth: but they were cut out of season this moneth of April, the sap being in them. Three moneths I neuer left speaking to the Country men to bring some. Your Agent will send some home for example.'

('Mr. Arthur Edwards, 26th April 1566, in Shamaki, in Media, to the Right Worshipful Sir Thomas Lodge Kt and Alderman.')

Hakluyt's Voyages, 1599 (Edn. of 1809)

There was a time, before the war, when you could import fine bowstaves from the United States, and maybe that time will come again before we are too old for archery. But until then you will have to content yourself with English yew; and the first step towards that is to locate a wood where there are suitable trees, on high ground for preference, and on the chalk. That done, your first trouble will be to persuade the owner that you are in your right mind, and your second that your object is worthy of the sacrifice of one of his trees. Yews have a certain sanctity in England; and whereas I have not usually found private owners very helpful, I have had much courtesy and assistance from the officers of the Forestry Commission. This finding of the tree, and obtaining permission to cut it, difficult though it may prove, are by far the easiest parts of the whole proceeding. The rest will be, if my own experience is any guide, pain and grief mixed with some small particles of triumph. Do not be discouraged with this. A yew bow, made as it were from the very beginning, is worth all your pains, and is something to have accomplished.

The tree you want will be not much more than six or nine inches in diameter, straight and smooth, and without little side branches or knots. The billet that you will want to get out of it will be six feet, more or less, long and about three inches wide on the sap side. And a merry hunt you will have before you find what you want!

When you have found a tree of the right diameter, with a stem clear of all major imperfections, and straight for six feet or more, put away all idea of haste. Regard it slowly and reverently as the gift of God that it is. Mark in your mind's eye the parts of it that you think will yield you bowstaves; and then saw it as close to the ground as possible, since the lower part is tough and valuable.

If one side of the tree is blemished, as is so often the case, and if it is convenient to have the tree fall in that direction, you can save a lot of hard work by cutting a deep notch on that side with the axe, but be very careful that the notch does not cut into the good side at all.

When felled, cut off the top. Green yew is very heavy, and, if alone, it is most unlikely that you will be able to move the log at all, other than to roll it over. Take your time, and make up your mind exactly where it ought to be split in order to get the most out of it.

To split, I use two old axes and a sledge-hammer. Starting right at the butt end of the log, hold an axe with the blade parallel to the log's length. Make very sure that the line from back to edge of the axe points truly towards the centre of the log; and then hammer the axe in until a crack just starts. Into the thin end of this crack insert the second axe six or eight inches away from the other, and hammer that in a little. The first axe will now be loose, and is inserted again farther along.

The great thing is to get a split true to the centre of the log, to lead the split fairly down the log's length, and not to hammer one axe in too much until it has been followed by the insertion of the second.

With your log now in halves, you can see the peculiar structure of sap- and heartwood. Split the halves into segments three or four inches wide on the bark side; and put all away to season, preferably on the rafters of some outhouse.

My first experience may show you some of the pitfalls, but do not imagine that it is always so exasperating. I had obtained permission from the authorities in charge of a certain part of Salisbury Plain to get what I wanted from one of their copses. I examined score upon score of trees. After days of search I had located four trees which seemed suitable, and they were duly cut as close to the ground as possible. There followed four years of seasoning in a covered shed. Yes; four years. Perhaps three would have done as well, but not less. There is a method of seasoning yew more quickly than this, by immersion in running water, but I cannot tell you anything about it. Good seasoning is absolutely essential; without it your bow will be flabby and have no cast.

Now this was my first experience with yew, as I have said. I knew it was not in the least like lemonwood, and that the run of the grain was all-important, so that it might go clear from one end of the bow to the other. I knew also that both heart- and sapwood were required. So, taking my first log, which was only some five inches in diameter and so rather small, I determined to split it with wedges, lest by sawing it I should cut too much across the grain. Greatly hoping, I began—and the log slit spirally. Wind-twisted; but impossible to tell in the standing tree. The second log did the same, but not so badly that I could not get from it some pieces long enough for half a bow; of which more later. Somewhat discouraged (and who would not be after waiting four years?), I determined to saw the third log, and took it to the mill. Not very satisfactory; the sapwood proved to be very thick and irregular, and goodness knows how much grain the saw had cut through. Still, the wood was sound and, having to leave the work for a space, I consigned my split and sawn billets to the rafters of my workshop until I should return; but not before had made myself an odd little flat bow from one of the short pieces of the second log. Two years later I did return, and forthwith made a good bow from two more of these short bits.

But I still had to tackle my principal treasure, seven feet of apparently flaw less yew, some nine inches in diameter. To split, or to saw? I split, and again achieved a spiral, a full quarter-turn in seven feet. And there was more yet! have already said that the sapwood is white and the heartwood reddish; and there is a sharp, clean line of demarcation between them. But here between them lay a thin, dark-purple, almost black line, as it might have been drawn by an indelible pencil. Sap-rot; and the sapwood itself was brash and not rubbery as it should be. However, hoping against hope, I roughed out a bow albeit somewhat twisted in the back, worked it up gradually, and shot two arrows with the full draw. At the third draw the bow broke into four pieces So ended this adventure.

The disappointment was mitigated by the fact that I had learned a great deal; and one does not, I assure you, always have these disasters. Yew is much too nice to be discarded because of any initial failures.

I have no experience of imported yew; but with English yew of my own cutting and seasoning I find that, while all of it follows the string to about the same extent as lemonwood, the heavier, harder, more densely-grown sort does so least; compensating for this (or so it seems to me) by being rather more brittle than the softer, light-coloured kind.

Try it, anyway. You cannot call yourself a bowyer till you have used yew

ASCHAM'S NOTES

'As for Brasell, Elme, Wych, and Asche, experience doth prove them to be but mean for bowes, and so to conclude, Ewe of all other thinges is that whereof perfite shootinge would have a bowe made.'

'Everye bow is made eyther of a boughe, of a plante, or of the boole of the tree. The boughe commonlye is very knottye, and full of pinnes, weake, of small pithe, and sone will folowe the stringe. . . . The plante proveth many times well if it be of a good and cleane groweth, and, for the pith of it, is

A hedgerow Yew
No good for the bowyer

A woodland Yew

9. *Yew Trees I*

A very large old Yew, and staves from some of its branches

Old Yew, showing the characteristically fasciated trunk

quicke enoughe of cast, it will plye and bowe farre before it breake, as all other yonge thinges do. The boole of the tree is cleanest without knot or pin, having a fast and hard wodde, by reason of his full groweth, strong and mightye of caste, and best for a bowe, if the staves be even cloven, and be afterwards wrought, not overthwarte the woode, but as the graine and streighte growinge of the woode leadeth a man, or els, by all reason, it must sone breake, and that in many shivers. This must be considered in the roughe woode, and when the bowe staves be overwroughte and fashioned. For in dressinge and pykinge it up for a bowe, it is too late to loke for it.'

'The beste colour of a bowe that I finde, is when the back and the bellye in workinge be much what after one maner, for such oftentimes in wearinge do prove like virgin waxe or golde, having a fine long graine, even from one end of the bow to the other; the short graine, althoughe such prove well sometimes, are for the most part very brittle.'

LENGTH OF BOWS

Here is a subject on which only a bold man will dogmatize. The old rule for the longbow was that it should be at least equal to the height of the archer; and the longbow was used principally for warfare in open fields. We, on the other hand, are not going to war (although I did in fact make a dozen special arrows in the hope of stalking enemy parachutists in the stirring days of 1940), but to hunt. A bow of six feet or more will cumber you in the woods and will prevent you shooting comfortably, if at all, when kneeling or squatting, unconventional and even scandalous positions. Make a traditional bow if you like; it will shoot safely and sweetly but I do not think you will use it for long. What you want is a bow that is at once short and durable. Well, then, what governs the permissible length? Three things—the nature of wood itself, your own dimensions, and the form to which you shape the stave.

Wood cannot be bent without limit; there comes a point at which it will snap. Everybody knows that but nobody can tell you just when that point will be reached. Wood is not, in this respect, responsive to exact mathematical calculation. We must therefore go by experience and chance the occasions when our stave will surprise us by either its goodness or badness.

Secondly, your own dimensions. I cannot tell your height nor, more important, the length of your reach. You may be like the Long Man of Wilmington, or you may be one of the Seven Dwarfs. It matters not so long as we know. So measure your reach or 'draw'. Stand up, sideways so that the line through your two shoulders points towards your target. Stretch out your left arm towards this target holding a thick stick in your hand as if it were a bow. Your arm should be straight but do not lock your elbow joint. Hold your head up, turn it to the left, and look directly over your left shoulder at the target. Now get somebody to measure the distance between the back of your left forefinger and the point on the angle of your jaw vertically below your right eye. That is your 'draw'. Record it permanently somewhere. It is more usual to measure from the jaw to the back of the bow; I prefer to take the longer length to the back of the forefinger. When you have a bow and a barbed broadhead arrow you will see why. Your draw, if you are a 'Long Man', may be twenty-eight inches or more: if a 'Dwarf' twenty-six or twenty-seven inches.

Inches are important things, both in bows and in arrows; do not think of them as trifles.

The longer your draw the longer must be your bow.

Now the third factor, the way you fashion your stave, i.e. the shape you would see were you so hardy as to bring yourself to cut your bow across with a saw. When a bow is bent the back is stretched and the belly is compressed; and the thicker the bow from back to belly the more the crushing strain on the latter. One can to some extent assist the back (although bowyers disagree on this) by artificial means, but nothing can be done to help the belly. One dare not, therefore, make a bow too thick, or 'stack it too high' in archers' language. There is a limit beyond which it is not safe to go.

Conversely, a bow that is thin from back to belly can suffer proportionately greater bending without risk of breakage. You can bend a woodshaving right back on itself without fracture, but such has no spring or driving force; it is too thin. So we have two limits; an upper limit of thickness which will either prevent you from bending the bow at all because it is too strong for you or, if you can bend it, will impose such crushing strains on the belly that it will give way; and a lower limit of thinness beyond which the bow will lose its power of driving the arrow.

For equal weight the thick bow must, of course, be correspondingly narrow, the thin bow correspondingly broad across the back. The former is the traditional longbow of England; the latter is characteristic of many 'primitive' peoples.

So we have considered the three things which must perforce control the length of your bow. And in terms of actual feet and inches? There you have me. I will not invent and publish a table relating lengths of bows to lengths of draw; I will merely give you a guide. Dr. Pope, to whom all of us should pay the utmost respect, has said that his longbows (narrow and thick) varied from 5 ft. 6 in. to 5 ft. 8 in. in length. I, who claim no respect whatever from you, say that I have found 5 ft. 3½ in. to 5 ft. 7 in., from nock to nock, safe and comfortable, and my draw is 28¾ in.

In regard to flat bows (wide and short) Mr. Gordon in his *The New Archery*, recommends 5 ft. 3 in. to 5 ft. 6 in. for draws of 27 to 28 in. and over respectively. I have found 5 ft. 3 in. quite satisfactory. You can, of course, go shorter if you like to try. Ishi, the Yana Indian with whom Dr. Pope had such a delightful partnership, used bows of only 3 ft. 6 in., with a draw of 26 in. His bows were made of juniper, with a heavy backing of sinew. For a draw of 28 in. the corresponding length would be about 3 ft. 10 in. This is very short indeed. The little yew bow which I have mentioned previously is only 4 ft 1½in. long; it weighs 62 lb., but is hard to shoot as so much of the weight is in the last two or three inches of the draw. I would not put too much trust in it in the field; it is a freak, but nevertheless has shot a good many of my long arrows, and demonstrates what can be done occasionally with luck. I have also a very nice, easy-shooting bow of 4 ft. 3 in., in lemonwood, backed with stout vellum. It is a matter of conjecture how long this will last. I do not really think that any wooden bow much shorter than 5 ft. is to be relied upon for a man, of, say, 28 in. draw, if it is to be used continually.

So make your choice; and remember that you will be eternally struggling for the most satisfactory compromise between length, which means safety and sweet shooting, and shortness, which means ease of carriage, the ability to shoot from queer positions, and perhaps a somewhat flatter arrow-flight.

THE WEIGHT AND CAST OF BOWS

Your bow must be within your compass and under proper control. The temptation to have a bow too strong for you is one which it is very difficult to withstand. It is easy enough to work up to a strong one, but do not begin with it, or you will never learn to shoot properly. For an average grown man whose muscles of fingers, arm, and body are not yet accustomed to this unusual exercise a weight of 45 lb. is not too low. Anything heavier will be a struggle. Ishi's bow was of this weight, and he found it quite adequate to his needs. Work up gradually. I find bows of 60 to 62 lb. about right for me; 70 lb. I can manage, but not with any real comfort since I have not persevered. Exercise and constant use are indispensable; I could not draw any of my bows to the full after three or four years of absence. Dr. Pope used bows up to 85 lb.; but there are no grizzly bears in England, nor do we want to use ⅜ in. diameter arrows.

It does not follow at all that the heavier the bow the faster and lower will the arrow fly. A heavy bow can, and indeed after 70 lb. or so must, project a heavier shaft; but it may not have the cast of a bow two-thirds of its weight. For every stave there is a weight at which its cast will be a maximum. How to determine what this weight is I cannot tell you, nor do I believe anyone else can. All I can say with assurance is that the bows I make for myself, according to the methods given here, weigh about 60 lb. and have a point-blank range of seventy-odd yards with birch arrows and seventy-five to eighty yards with bamboos. By 'point-blank' range I mean that range at which the centre of the target will be hit when aim is taken in such a way that the arrowhead seems to rest on that centre. Do not let ourselves be unduly worried with theory. If your bow is sweet to shoot and strong enough for your purpose surely that is all that matters.

There are two ways of weighing a bow. If you have a spring-balance capable of reading up to 80 lb. or more, hang it up on a strong hook on the wall, or suspend it from a beam. Cut a lath about six inches longer than your arrows. Right at one end bore a hole big enough to slip over the hook of the balance; and, measuring from the edge of the hole nearest to the end of the lath, mark off the length of your draw. Hang this lath on the balance-hook so that it hangs down vertically. Brace your bow. Place the string over the balance-hook so that the latter comes exactly where the nock of the arrow would be. Holding the handgrip of the bow with both hands, one on each side of the lath with the forefinger steadying the latter, press down until the bow is at full draw as shown by your mark. Read, or get somebody else to, the indicator on the balance. The number of pounds registered is the weight of the bow.

If you have no balance, you must resort to cruder means involving the kitchen scales, and must determine the weight piecemeal. First lash a little piece of flat wood to the back of the handgrip of your bow, projecting an inch or more on the side where the arrow comes. Unstring the bow, so that one loop is right off; pass the bow under the handle of a good big bucket; re-string so that the string passes over the handle of the bucket; and then brace the bow. Somewhat of a conjuring trick, this, but not difficult. Fill up the bucket with sand, stones, bricks, or anything else you like (water won't be heavy enough) and put a box or trestle on each side of it. Now get up on the trestles, one foot on each, taking an arrow with you. Let this arrow rest, point downwards, on the little piece of wood lashed to the handgrip. Take hold of the string at the nocking-point and draw the bow (the arrow being steadied by, and sliding between your fingers), not to the arrow-neck, but, seeing that your arrowhead is rather more 'within the bow' than it normally would be, to a point somewhat short of this which you will already have determined and marked on the shaft. The bucket will either lift from the ground or not. In the former case, add more weight to it; in the latter, throw some out. Adjust like this until the bucket is just, and only just, lifted at the full draw. Then undo the whole contraption and weigh the bucket and its contents in penny-numbers according to what your scales will take at one go.

Why go to all this trouble when I could much more easily hook the string over a nail in the wall and hang weights on the bow's handgrip? Because if I did, I should keep the bow drawn for much too long at one time, and probably ruin it.

LEMONWOOD BOWS

The Longbow

Unless you care to buy a whole log from a timber importer, as you could before the war, and go to the trouble of having it sawn up and seasoned (which I believe is rather troublesome with this material) you will buy your lemonwood staves ready cut. The proper size for a longbow stave is 6 ft. by $1\frac{1}{8}$ in. square. You will find it heavy and hard and probably it will be covered with shellac to prevent the development of cracks. The grain will be hardly perceptible, if at all. Look it over; if it is straight and true it doesn't matter which side you make into the back of your future bow. But if it has a curve one way or the other, then let the concave side become the back. If the stave is twisted at all square it up with the plane before you do anything else; and in any case plane it up clean all over. Now, turning the future back uppermost, mark the centre of the stave; mark also a point $1\frac{1}{4}$ in. above this and another $2\frac{3}{4}$ in. below. Take these lines right round the stave. The space of 4 in. which you have so marked will form the handgrip, and you will note that this is not central with the stave's geographical middle.

Then drive a small tack into each end of the stave, stretch a thin thread or wire as tightly as you can between them and mark off a centre line right down the stave's length. This apparently simple process can be troublesome. Make sure that your line is really straight and that it bisects the handgrip part exactly; your bow will be a failure otherwise.

Now, from each end of the handgrip section draw straight lines to each end of the stave so that the width there will be reduced to $\frac{3}{4}$ in. Straight lines, I say. Your bow is now marked out, and your next task is to remove the surplus wood at the sides to form the taper. Now lemonwood is hard to saw but easy to cut with an edge. It planes beautifully. You can therefore plane off the surplus if you like. Personally, I should use my small axe, and when I had

PRACTICAL

finished I should light my pipe and watch you getting hotter and hotter as you worked away. Every man to his choice; and in any case I should use the plane to finish off with, exactly to the lines marked, and square with the back.

Now turn the stave on its side. At each end, measuring from the back, mark off a thickness of $\frac{1}{2}$ in. Do the same for the other side: and then draw straight lines from each end of the handgrip section to these marks. Here is some more surplus wood for you to remove.

Your stave now tapers from side to side and from back to belly, while the handgrip section remains $1\frac{1}{8}$ in. square as you received it.

So far you have been carrying out a rather dull mechanical operation. You will note that you have not touched the back other than to make lines on it. Nor will you; the back, except for a slight rounding of the edges later on, remains inviolate. Now you begin real bowyer's work.

Lay your stave back downwards on the bench. Then sharpen your plane. Your task now is to round the two upper edges of the stave, including the handgrip, as it lies before you until they coalesce and the belly assumes a smooth curve from side to side. Close to the handgrip section this curve should have the form of a rather fat 'D' of which the back forms the straight line. As you go farther up the limbs this 'D' should get progressively thinner until at the tips the bow's section becomes nearly flat. This is not the true longbow style; in this the 'D' section remains practically constant throughout. But I like the modification for two reasons; it leaves wide tips to take the nocks safely and it makes for greater safety in the draw.

Now just round slightly the sharp edges of the back. Be careful in all the foregoing not to leave ridges or hollows; the limbs of your bow must be smooth and true from end to end.

Cut temporary nocks in the tips of the limbs, the groove to come about $\frac{3}{4}$ in. in from the ends. Use your large rat-tail file for this and smooth off all sharp edges with steel wool. Note carefully the shape of the nock; at its deepest point, where it cuts the edges of the bow, it should be just, and no more, a full semicircle. Note also that the flat part of the back is not cut into at all. There is no need to finish the ends of the bow now unless you wish to keep the full 6 ft. length. In that case put the nocks a full inch from the ends.

Most of the bows that you have probably seen in shops will have had horn tips on them. These are very pretty, difficult to make and fit, and quite unnecessary. Do not bother yourself with them. Plain nocks, cut in the ends of your bowstave, provided it is left wide enough as I recommend, are a matter of ten minutes' work, and perfectly reliable and satisfactory.

Your bow now lies before you in embryo. Test it for strength. To do this hold it at the handgrip, belly up, with the left hand. Put one end against your left instep and hold the other in your right hand. Spring it a little, carefully, downwards. You can thus form an idea of what it is like.

Your task now is so to reduce it that you can get a string on to it. If you have followed the directions so far the taper of the belly from handgrip to tips will be a straight line. This has to be reduced to a long, smooth curve. If this curve is made very gradual you will be making a longbow as it used to be made; if, on the contrary, the curve dips sharply from the handgrip and then flattens out again into the limb you will be making 'dips'. The latter is preferable. So go to work with your spokeshave or your shoemaker's rasp, whichever you prefer. Remember continually that it is easy to take wood off but impossible to replace it; and that a very little taken off has a great effect on the ultimate bow. Very frequently stop and test your bow again.

When you feel that you could manage to bend it sufficiently to brace it with a string, fit your strong string to it. Adjust the bowyer's knot in the lower nock (the lower limb is that which has $2\frac{3}{4}$ in. of the handgrip on it) so that the loop at the other end of the string is about 3 in. from the upper nock. Now hold your bow in your left hand, at the handgrip, back up this time; lower end against the left instep, right hand resting on the back with thumb and finger ready to push the loop of the string up towards the nock. Now pull upwards with the left hand and press downwards with the right hand. Let the latter slide up the bow until the loop can be pushed into the nock. This will be a hard struggle. If you can't manage it at all reduce the bow a little more. Don't ever let the fingers of the right hand get between the string and the belly of the bow; if they should you may get hurt.

Now, having strung your bow after a fashion take it and draw the string very cautiously and only a little. Do this several times. Reduce the bow still more, taking the utmost care to reduce evenly all along the lines. When you can brace your bow to the extent that the string stands about 3 in. away from the handgrip at the belly side (the necessary shortening of the string being done by adjustment of the bowyer's knot) you have come to the point where really fine and careful work is required.

These are the things to aim at:

There should be no bend in the handgrip; nor any apparent bend for two or three inches above and below it.

Each limb must bend evenly and equally; the curve, when full-drawn, must be without lumps, hollows, or unevennesses of any kind.

The lower limb should be slightly stronger than the upper.

There should be no tendency for the bow to twist in the hands while being drawn. If there is, the odds are that your bow was not marked out straight.

Your bow, when full-drawn, should be perfectly straight when viewed from the back, the string should bisect the whole length of it, and it should bend in a clean, uniform arc with a flattened centre part at the handgrip.

Work slowly and carefully with your rasp. I find it a great help to work with the bow actually braced. Repeatedly draw your bow, a little way only and observe progress. I do this in front of a large mirror, which I prefer to the use of a tiller. If you haven't got a mirror then make a tiller. This is merely a piece of wood, say 2 by 3 in. and 3 ft. long, with a block at one end to hold the handgrip, and notches or nails up its length to take the string. If you use this do not leave the drawn bow on it for a moment longer than is absolutely necessary. That is one reason why I prefer the mirror; one cannot hold the bow drawn for more than a second or so.

So continue, slowly and returning over and over again to your mirror or your tiller. Draw the bow a little farther each time. Weak spots will show as an angle in the bent limb; reduce the bow on each side of them until they disappear. You will notice at some time about now that your lemonwood is beginning to take a slight permanent set, to 'follow the string'. Never mind; you can't prevent it, it doesn't matter, and it will only go so far and no farther.

It is when I have been working on my bow for some time and am getting it well into shape and have almost reached full draw that I am gripped with an Emotional Crisis. Probably the making of your first bow has been exciting all along; this wears off with the making of others, but the crisis to which I refer does not. It is the decision to draw the bow to the full. Shall I do it now, risk the consequences, and get it over? Or shall I yet wait a little, think it over, and prolong the agony?

'A bow full-drawn is seven-eighths broken,' said Thomas Waring, the eighteenth-century bowyer—sometimes a new bow full-drawn is eight eighths broken, but mercifully not often. So approach the full draw in prayerful mood, and, whatever you do, do not guess it. Fix an arrow, or a stick the length of an arrow, on the string, brace yourself for an effort, put your weight into it, and draw slowly, steadily and with faith. There! It's over! Now never, never draw your bow one fraction of an inch beyond this. You have tempted Providence sufficiently and he has been kind to you.

At full draw the curve of the bow should be as we have already said, a

A perfect Yew   The same   The yield of staves
                       split

Endgrain of Yew, showing   Riving out the surplus
the white sapwood,   heartwood from a stave
and red heartwood.
Rather coarse grain

11. *Yew Staves*

Yew Longbow, 5ft. 5.5 in.

Lemonwood Flatbow, with
double mid-section, 5ft. 1.5 in.

Lemonwood Flatbow, 4ft. 3in.   Yew Flatbow. 4ft. 1.5 in.

12. *Bow Lengths*
All measurements from nock to nock. The draw is 28.75 in.

clean, even sweep with a flattened middle. If it is not, make such corrections
as may be necessary; and then, if you find the bow too strong for you (as it
should be at this stage) weaken or 'sink' each limb evenly and proportionately all along. But be careful how you do this. A new bow will become
lighter with use as the wood settles and becomes limbered up; be careful
therefore not to sink it too much at first. If you do make this mistake, the
only remedy is to shorten it by cutting fresh nocks, and then you will have
to go through all the agony of the full draw trial again. This you will have to
do in any case with your present bow unless you want to keep it at the 6 ft.
length. So finish up with your bow in the rough just a little heavier than you
like. Never mind about weighing it yet on actual scales.

Drill a $\frac{3}{16}$ in. diameter hole in the extreme tip of the upper limb above the
nocks. Scrape the bow now all over with the steel scraper or the sharp edge
of your pocket-knife until all ridges and file marks have gone. Then go all
over it, except the handgrip, with the finest grade of steel-wool that you can
get; this will produce a most lovely surface. Never use sandpaper.

Now for the arrow-plate. 'Vulcanized Fibre' is tough and practically ever-
lasting. Cut a piece, $\frac{1}{32}$ in. thick, about 1$\frac{1}{4}$ in. long by $\frac{3}{8}$ in. wide. Round one
end into a semicircle. On one surface bevel all edges until they are sharp like
a knife. Lay the arrow-plate aside until you have finished the handgrip. This
fibre is, however, rather noisy; an arrow sometimes hits it hard in passing and
makes a most undesirable crack. For a silent shot, a piece of very thick, soft
buckskin is preferable, even if it is not so durable.

So long as the handgrip is comfortable and not too thick it does not matter
what you do with it. Make it to suit yourself and pad it out with slips of wood
or leather on the back of the bow if you feel you need it. Personally I don't.
Just cut a piece of good leather with a roughish surface, like buckskin, allow-
ing for a reasonable overlap on the back of the bow, wet it thoroughly, and
glue it on with casein glue, or having first covered the wood with glue, you
can wind on whipcord instead, which makes for a good rough surface.

Take then, your arrow-plate and, if it is of fibre, soak it thoroughly in
water until it is quite soft; this will take an hour or so. Cut your leather, bevel
with a safety-razor blade the edges which will overlap, and soak it. Mix your
casein glue rather thick. Cut two lengths of $\frac{1}{4}$ in. or $\frac{1}{8}$ in. tape. Have handy a
short roll of 2 in. wide surgical gauze bandage, and a foot of string. The
arrow-plate goes on the left hand side of the upper limb where the arrow will
pass; its base should come just below the upper edge of the handgrip leather.
Glue it on in position and bind it temporarily with a piece of string. Cover the
handgrip with glue and also the inner surface of your leather from which you

have squeezed out all surplus water. Put the leather on and see that the overlap comes central with the middle of the back of the bow. Take the temporary binding off the arrow-plate, and bind everything tightly with your bandage, from top to bottom and back again, two layers. Casein glue sets very slowly; so after half an hour or so unwind your bandage and make any little adjustments that may be necessary. See that all the edges of the arrow-plate are right down on the wood surface. Glue one surface of your tapes and bind round the upper and lower edges of the leather so that these become neatly bevelled off down to the surface of the bow all round. Then replace your bandage, and leave the whole thing overnight.

Your bow is finished, except for something to keep out the damp.

For this I use boiled linseed oil. Smear this on thinly with your finger and rub it well in. Lightly wipe off any excess and hang your bow up for a day or two. Repeat once or twice. When the oil is quite dry polish with a soft rag and you will obtain a most beautiful satin finish which will not chip off (because it is in and not on the wood) and will keep out moisture indefinitely. Some people use shellac; I can't think why. This produces a hard, shiny, brittle surface coating. It has nothing whatever to recommend it.

Decoration? Certainly; but not too much. A little colour on the back at each side of the handgrip sets the bow off nicely. The bow is to be your partner in the woods. You have eyes, so why should not the bow also? So I put eyes on mine. Nonsense? Possibly. But are you prepared to be categoric about it? Is there not just a chance that it may help your shafts to fly true? Are not two pairs of eyes better than one?

The Flat Bow

This has no historical or ethnical relation to the longbow; the two are half the world apart. And yet, if you have stacked your longbow as I recommend, you have already begun to approach the flat variety. The flat bow is shorter, wider and thinner than the longbow; dimensionally it is different, in principle identical. Its main advantage is that it is handier.

We have already discussed the question of length. So take a lemonwood stave some four to six inches longer than your bow is to be, 1½ in. wide (or 2 in. if you want to experiment with a very short bow), and ¾ in. thick, and plane it up clean on all sides. Choose which is to be the back, mark the middle of it, run a centre line down it from end to end, and mark off a 4 in. handgrip section in the same position relative to the middle as for the longbow. This handgrip should be ⅞ in. wide; mark it out. Mark also four lines across the back and right round the stave, 1 in. and 1½ in. above and below the ends of the handgrip; let us call these lines, starting from the uppermost on the upper limbs, A, B, C, and D respectively. Prolong each end of the lines, marking out the handgrip straight up and down as far as lines B and C; and prolong them further from B and C in a fair curve so that the latter meets, almost tangentially, the ends of lines A and C where these cut the edges of the stave. This will give you a handgrip section of the usual 4 in. plus a straight extension of 1 in. each end and an additional extension of ½ in. in which the handgrip swells out to the full width of the bow. Now from the points where each end of lines A and D cut the edges of the stave draw straight lines to the ends of the stave so that a width of ¾ in. is left there.

Remove the wood to form this taper; and remove also that part outside the marked handgrip-plus-extension section. Be particularly careful to cut and finish the sides of the handgrip square with the back.

Your bow is now roughed out in one dimension, but obviously the hand-grip is not thick enough. You must fit a 'riser' i.e. attach a piece of wood on the belly side to ensure the rigidity of the handgrip and to give you something to take hold of when you shoot. For this riser you can use any piece of sound hardwood; hard mahogany (not the soft, trashy baywood often called mahogany) looks well. Cut this very carefully, and accurately square on all sides and ends, ¾ in. thick, 7 in. long, and as wide as the bow is at lines A and D. This has now to be fastened permanently to the belly side of the handgrip; the ends coinciding with lines A and D. Make quite sure that the surfaces of stave and riser to be joined fit accurately (which is exceedingly difficult), and then do the trick with fairly thick casein glue and clamps or a vice. Leave it to set for forty-eight hours. Now either you trust glue or you don't. I don't, particularly with hard, dense wood. We are asked to believe that the hand-grip of a bow is static and does not bend; nor does it visibly, but actually it must do so infinitesimally. Furthermore, we put on the riser to prevent the thin ¾ in. stave from bending as it most certainly would without it; and what attaches the riser to the stave is a glue film. Evidently therefore this film is under strain when the bow is drawn, since without it the riser would come off and the handgrip would bend. Therefore I do an unspeakable thing—from the belly side of the riser and into the stave, but without reaching through to the back, I drill for and insert three screws, all within the 4 in. section of the handgrip proper: and I sink the heads ¼ in. below the surface and plug the holes with wood! So disgraceful is this procedure that I have not dared to include screws and a screwdriver among the lists of tools and materials. But however shocking it may be, at least I know that of the elements, Earth, Air, Fire and Water, to which my bow will be exposed only the third has the power to detach my riser. If you decide to follow me in this, put your screws in properly; drilling three sizes of hole, one for the threaded part, one for the smooth part above the thread, and one to take the head. And use steel screws, not brass. If you don't do it, don't blame me if one day the riser flies off in your face and your bow breaks. Alternatively, of course, and if you don't mind the extra expense and labour, you can start with a stave of such a thickness as will make an attached riser unnecessary.

Having done all this you are now ready to begin on the belly of the bow. First of all, file or rasp the edges of the riser until they are flush with the sides of the bow and handgrip all along. Then, starting about $\frac{1}{4}$ in. above and below the 4 in. handgrip cut away the wood of the riser in a sharp downward curve which will cut into the lemonwood just short of lines A and D; flatten out sharply so that the thickness of the lemonwood at, say $\frac{1}{4}$ to $\frac{1}{2}$ in. beyond lines A and D is $\frac{1}{2}$ in. This $\frac{1}{2}$ in. thickness will now be very gradually diminished until, at the tips of the limbs you have a little over $\frac{5}{16}$ in.

Your bow will now bend; cut the nocks and fit a string but not of course to fistmele. Have a look at your bow in the mirror or on the tiller. Do the adjusting as for the longbow, but even more carefully since the flat section develops weak spots easily. Reduce the depth of the handgrip from belly to back until it is about $1\frac{3}{8}$ in. deep, and round the edges on the belly side until it is comfortable for the hand. Round the edges of the back, and round the edges of the belly rather more. Tiller and finish as before.

This bow will probably follow the string more than your longbow. It will shoot neither better nor worse, but it has the advantage of being shorter.

If you don't like its looks (and indeed I think the sudden swelling out from the straight handgrip to the full width is ugly) there is no need to confine yourself to that shape. Ishi's bow was widest at a point halfway up the limbs; so you can make the limbs in the form of a very attenuated leaf or spearhead if you like. But remember, if you experiment in this way, that width and thickness together make up the strength of the limb; and that if you reduce or increase one you must correspondingly increase or reduce the other, in proportion of course to that part of the tapering limb on which you are working.

There is a scientific variety of this bow described by Mr. Gordon. This varies from the description given above in two particulars only; firstly, the upper end of the 4 in. handgrip section coincides with the middle of the stave instead of being placed $1\frac{1}{4}$ in. higher, and has immediately above it a similar 4 in. section; and secondly the taper of the sides of the limbs is not straight but has a very slight curve of which the convex side is towards the centre line of the back. If the limbs are properly tillered they will then bend in arcs of a circle. The handgrip, being wholly below the middle of the bow, allows the arrow to be discharged from the middle line, and the whole bow is symmetrical. This is said to give greater efficiency. I have no doubt it does, but I am not a good enough archer to have been able to notice it. The doubled handgrip section of course lengthens the bow; or, conversely, shortens the limbs for a given overall length; both are drawbacks for our purpose.

THE YEW BOW

Do not, I pray you, attempt a bow in yew until you have mastered and become thoroughly familiar with the general principles of bows in lemonwood; and do not, for the reasons already given, use English yew unless no other is at hand; lemonwood will make you a much better bow. Yew and lemonwood differ as much as do chalk and cheese. You have seen 'The Mikado'? And you remember the poor wretch whom Gilbert condemns to play (I quote from memory only):

On a table untrue,
With a twisted cue,
And elliptical billiard balls?

Unless you are extremely lucky, that is more or less the fate which awaits you when you are confronted with your first yew stave.

The principle and lay-out of yew bows are exactly the same as for lemonwood; but there the similarity ceases. In lemonwood, grain is no great matter; the stave can be planed up true and square; and you can cut it freely and as you like as you proceed. In yew, grain is the primary consideration; and it is prominent, irregular and frequently twisted. Emphatically you can not cut yew as you desire; you must mould your bow round the eccentricities of your stave. And it is not easy. Probably, as we have discussed earlier, you will have to get your stave by splitting from a log of your own cutting; and you will remember that it is the outside part of the log that we want. The stave will consist of an outer layer of thin, scaly bark, an inner layer of more or less thick white sapwood, and an inmost layer of reddish heartwood. You will be extremely lucky if you can find a suitable stave six feet long. Yew is full of twists, dips, lumps, knots and tiny little knots called 'pins', all of which have to be taken account of. You have, of course, no choice as to which shall be back or belly; the sapwood is the back, and the general idea is that this shall run from end to end of the bow in a nice even layer about $\frac{3}{16}$ in. thick; a pretty thought! So contemplate your stave with some care. You will have cut it (if

G 97

you can) 6 ft. long and about 3 in. square. Remove the scaly bark with the edge of your axe. The axe, by the way, is the tool *par excellence* for dealing with yew; it follows the grain automatically and without any thought or care on your part. It will also follow a flaw in your stave and so save you the trouble of working unbeknownst on a faulty piece of wood.

If you think your stave will make a bow at all (and many won't) clean up the square ends with rasp and file until you can see the end-grain quite clearly. Note that the sapwood runs in an arch from side to side of the stave; the curve of this arch has to be preserved all down the back of your future bow. Then axe off the bulk of the surplus sapwood and finish roughly with the rasp until you have a mean thickness of about ¼ in. everywhere. In doing this follow carefully all the twists, dips and lumps of the back; and where any knots or pins show themselves on the back leave extra wood around them so that they stand up a little from their immediate surroundings. You can tell very well by the feel of the axe whether the sapwood is tough and rubbery, or brittle and short; it is no good persevering at all with the latter kind. Observe the back again and decide in your mind's eye what sort of a bow you can make of it. The vertical dips and lumps will not present much difficulty, although they must be preserved. It is the sideways twist which makes things so awkward if it exists. You have to decide whether, starting from the plane of the part where the handgrip will come, the deviation from that plane in the middle or ends of the limbs will be too much, or whether the narrowing of the bow as the ends are approached will reduce the twist of the back (perhaps with a little cheating in regard to the thickness of the sapwood layer) to an amount which can be tolerated. Or, a little juggling with the plane of the handgrip may ease matters materially and bring the rest of the stave into a manageable relation. It is all a matter of judgment in which written instructions cannot help much.

It is said that one layer of this sapwood should be carefully followed throughout. If you do that there will, of course, show no 'feather' or pattern of grain on the surface of the back; and it will besides be an immense drudgery. I cannot for the life of me follow why it should be necessary so long as there is a minimum thickness of $\frac{3}{16}$ in. of unbroken and uncut grain everywhere. I do not say there is no virtue in this one-layer technique, but I feel pretty confident that it is of small moment.

Suppose, now, that you have made the best job you can of the back and are ready to begin on the belly. Use your axe again here, but take care of knots. These are very hard, and if cut through with force the blow may tear out great pieces of wood and go much deeper than you want; the grain is always curly near knots. Much better use your rasp here; and leave all knots a little 'proud' of the surrounding surface. When you get near your final shape it is better, unless the knots are really sound and undecayed, to drill them out completely and replace with a hardwood or yew plug carefully shaped and set in glue. These plugs must be a tight fit and have to be driven in. The belly will naturally follow the ups and downs of the back since the grain of both is more or less parallel. Be more than ordinarily careful in tillering your bow, and care not what it looks like at rest so long as it strikes a fair curve when drawn.

Remember also that English yew will follow the string and will weaken a good deal after a little use. Be very cautious and careful how you come to full draw; indeed, confession of weakness or not, I do not like to do this at all until I have backed the bow with vellum. In this I follow Dr. Pope, who said he had many bows break in his hand until at last he took the advice of Ishi the Yana and backed them; after that, he said, no bow legitimately used had broken. Backing is the reinforcing of the bow's back with something else which will help it to stand the strain when the bow is drawn. Yew has a natural backing in its own sapwood, but even this is prone to produce raised splinters under strain. The ideal backing material is vellum, which is calf-skin cleaned and prepared for bookbinding, drumheads, and similar uses. Vellum cuttings, from the edges of skins, can be bought quite cheaply as semi-waste. Get them about 2 in. wide and as long and thick as you can. You will find the best of it almost as thick as a postcard, with one rough white and one smooth yellowish side. The rough white side is the one which goes in contact with the bow's back. The strips should run from the tip of each limb to the handgrip where, if possible, they should overlap. They should cover the whole width of the back but should not extend on to the sides of the bow. Cut them a little wider than you finally require: the vellum has a tendency to become narrower during manipulation and any excess which gets glued on to the sides can easily be cut and filed away afterwards. Soak thoroughly in cold water until they are soft and flabby in every part. Then cover the whole of the back of your bow with a thickish mix of casein glue, letting this come also well down on to the sides. Fix the bow in a vice by the handgrip so that the whole of one limb is accessible; you will want both hands for what follows. Take one of your vellum strips and wipe the excess water off it. Do not stretch it or you may end up with a thing like a thick bootlace. Lay the rough white side, which will now be the concave side, on to the glued surface of the bow, and smooth it out with your forefinger, squeezing out excess glue and setting the strip in place. Take now a 2 in. wide gauze surgical bandage and wind this tightly over strip and bow from tip to handgrip and back again. So easy; and yet in the combination of wet vellum and slippery glue there lurks a particularly malignant little devil! As you wind on your bandage the strip will develop a passionate desire to slip round the bow under the bandage, and the tighter you wind the more pronounced this slip becomes. Struggle against this as best you can; this is where both hands are wanted. I find the best way is to adjust the strip fairly accurately, wind on, and leave everything for half an hour. Then I take the bandage off and find the strip much more amenable and the glue having come to anchor as it were. The strip can now be pushed properly and finally into place; and with care in re-winding the bandage all will be well. Do the other limb, and leave everything overnight. In the morning take off the bandages and let stand for an hour or two to get quite dry. Then cut or file off the vellum which has stuck along the sides of the limbs, so that the back only is covered.

Now you can go to your full draw; and finish off the bow as before. English yew or not, perhaps it is as well that you do this once; you will get the experience and you will be more likely to be successful if ever you do manage to come by a really good hard stave.

Joined Limbs

Hitherto I have assumed that you have been working with a full-length stave. Since such are hard to get it is likely that you will have to join two pieces. This in itself is a potent argument for using lemonwood which can always be got long enough. The joint is difficult to make and I have doubts, possibly quite unreasonably, as to its reliability in a heavy bow. My faith in glue is, as I have said before, not strong. If, therefore, you feel impelled to join two limbs, know that they join at the handgrip by means of a devilishly difficult thing to make called a 'double fishtail joint'.

Square up the butt ends of your two limbs accurately on all four sides, and ends; taking, of course, due account of the thickness of sapwood that it is necessary to preserve. Do this before ever you attempt any tapering of the separate limbs. Lay the two limbs back uppermost, before you on the bench. Mark out, with the most meticulous care, on each the outlines of the proposed joint viz. two V's, each 4 in. long, cut into the wood of one limb, and two similar V's cut so as to project from the end of the other. The base of each of the four V's will be half the width of the back, so that they meet accurately on the centre line of the bow. Put the limbs vertically in the vice with the back facing you and cut out the V's with a tenon saw without a back (such can be bought, or you can have the back removed). This is really

Side   Back   Belly

13. *The Nock*

An early stage. The limbs still in the square

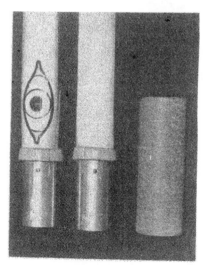

The finished joint
View of the back

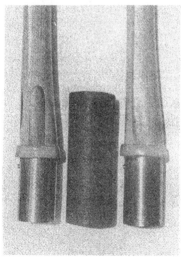

The finished joint
Side view

14. *The Carriage Bow*

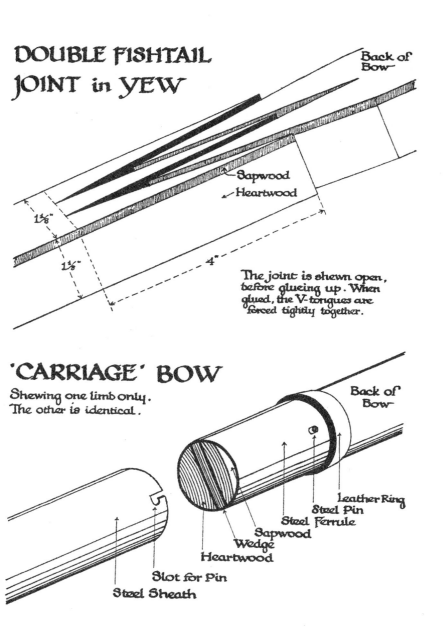

DOUBLE FISHTAIL JOINT in YEW

Back of Bow

Sapwood

Heartwood

1⅛"

1⅛"

4"

The joint is shewn open, before glueing up. When glued, the V-tongues are forced tightly together.

'CARRIAGE' BOW

Shewing one limb only. The other is identical.

Back of Bow

Leather Ring

Steel Pin

Steel Ferrule

Sapwood

Wedge

Heartwood

Slot for Pin

Steel Sheath

difficult to do well. The cuts must be square from back to front and exactly on the marked lines. The theory is that the pairs of V's fit into each other; if they don't then resort to fine and careful filing until they fit really well everywhere. When they do fit, perhaps after much patient toil, put a good coating of casein glue on all joining surfaces, bring them together tight, and screw up hard in the vice for forty-eight hours. Then proceed to lay out your bow as if you were working an ordinary full-length stave. The importance of accurate layout will be apparent now; since if it were not well done the centre line of your bow may run all awry on one or both of the limbs.

The jointing of the limbs in this way allows you, if you like, to make a bow 'set back in the handle', and so to offset to some extent the effect of the following of the string. Also this set-back makes a pretty bow; but it should not be overdone or your bow will not stand the full draw. To make it it is merely necessary to clamp up your joint so that the limbs make a very, very obtuse angle with each other. It will be sufficient if, when you lay the joined stave on its side and stretch a thread between the ends of the limbs, the thread stands off from the back of the handgrip section (where the joint is) by, say 1½ or 2 in. in a 6 ft. length. Remember, also, that this set-back will require you to have a slightly greater thickness of limb from back to belly at the handgrip section in order to allow for the wood which will have to be cut away to bring the handgrip level again on back and belly.

A lashing of thin whipcord, set in casein glue, to cover the whole of the fishtail joint is a good thing and an extra insurance against anything starting there.

THE CARRIAGE BOW

I do not know why a bow which is made so as to come apart in the middle should be so named. The other name is 'demountable', a horrid word. Why not jointed? But whatever it may be called, it is a fact that it is quite practicable, and at times most convenient, to have a bow which can come apart at the handgrip and be packed in a small compass. It is practicable, that is to say, for bows up to about 60 lb. in weight, but not, I think, above that: and it is intended to be applied to the longbow type. The principle is that the butt end of each of the two limbs fits into a metal ferrule; and these in turn slide into, and are there locked into, a larger sheath which holds them both; exactly like a large double joint on a fishing-rod. The ferrules and sheaths, all three, must be of seamless steel tubing. Such as I have used have been of American make, of metal $\frac{1}{32}$ in. thick. The ferrules are $2\frac{5}{16}$ in. long, and $1\frac{7}{32}$ in. outside diameter. The sheath is, correspondingly, 4 in. and $1\frac{9}{32}$ in. It would be better in all ways if the thickness of the sheath were $\frac{3}{64}$ in., with a corresponding reduction of the inside diameter so as not to enlarge the handgrip. The $\frac{1}{32}$ in. stuff is liable to distortion after the bow, if it is at all heavy, has been in use for some time. This would have the additional advantage that a normal bowstave of $1\frac{1}{4}$ in. square could be used, which is not the case with the above sizes. Mr. Gordon recommends an assembly in which the outside diameter of the sheath is $1\frac{3}{16}$ in.; this would be less bulky in the hand, but I have not tried it.

The two ferrules must be an accurate sliding fit into the outer sheath: on no account must there be any side play. It is best, for the same reasons as were given in describing the making of a bow from two pieces of wood, to fit the ferrules to the limbs before doing any tapering of the latter. Otherwise, you may find that some slight inaccuracy will spoil the whole.

Prepare, then, the backs of your two limbs and run a centre line down each. Mark off all round the limbs a line $2\frac{1}{4}$ in. from the butt (handle) ends, and square the ends. Take each limb in turn, and, with the tip resting on the floor, stand on the butt end one of the ferrules, so that the outer surface of the back coincides with the inner surface of the ferrule as you look down through it. Then strike the ferrule a hard blow with a wooden mallet: on no account use a hammer, and take care that your blow falls evenly on the whole circumference of the steel. This will mark you out a neat circle on the end grain of the limbs; and accurately to this circle and for the space of $2\frac{1}{4}$ in. must you now cut your wood.

Put your limb in the vice, horizontally, back up, and rasp off the corner facing you until the far edge of your cut nearly touches the centre line. Turn it round and do the other side. Similarly for the two corners of the belly. Arrange for some 'set-back' if you wish: you will have to work this out: it will mean cutting into the surface of the back at the forward end of the ferrule, and this, if you are using yew, is a serious matter which might, if the sapwood were not thick enough, take you right through the thickness of it and so to certain disaster. But, set-back or not, be most careful to keep the direction of the part you are reducing to a circular section in proper alignment, whichever way you regard it. Mark lines on the sides as well as the back if you are at all doubtful of the power of your eye to keep you straight.

Now reduce the eight corners that you have, and abandon the rasp for the file as you approach the final stages. Be very careful that you do not take too much off the extreme end.

When the ferrule will just begin to show signs of going on, tap it slightly with the mallet, remove again, and file to the marks which will be left on the wood surface. So continue until you can push it on with the hand (but with difficulty) about two-thirds of the way. Now square up accurately the shoulder at the forward end of your work, and file up carefully the remainder of the wood over which the ferrule has not yet gone. Then cut off the end of the limb so that the ferrule, when fully home, shall project $\frac{1}{16}$ in. beyond it.

It is necessary to wedge the end of the limb into the ferrule. So put the limb vertically in the vice and cut a V-shaped slot, parallel with the lines of the end grain, about 1 in. deep and $\frac{3}{16}$ in. wide at the top. Make a wedge of soft wood which, when driven home, will slightly expand your V-cut.

You are now ready to put the ferrule on. Mix some casein glue (I am not sure whether this really does any good or not, but I put it on as an extra insurance) and cover the cut end of your limb with it. Stand the limb vertically with its tip on the floor, put on the ferrule, and drive it home hard with the mallet. Then put glue in the V-cut, and on the wedge, and drive the latter home firmly but not so violently that you will risk distorting the ferrule. Then grind or file off the projecting rim of the ferrule and the protruding end of the wedge until all is fair and square.

The other limb is, of course, treated exactly the same. Now insert both limbs into the sheath, so that they meet accurately at the centre. In this position they have to be locked before anything else can be done; and the best way of doing this is to arrange that a small pin projects from each ferrule which can be engaged with a suitably shaped slot in the sheath. For this you require some small pieces of $\frac{1}{8}$ in. diameter mild steel rod and an $\frac{1}{8}$ in. diameter drill. Remove one limb from the sheath without disturbing the position of the other. Clamp the limb which still has the sheath on it vertically in the vice. On the centre line of the back of the sheath, and with centre $\frac{1}{4}$ in. from its end, drill a hole through it and the ferrule, and into the wood beyond for a distance of $\frac{3}{8}$ in. Take the sheath off, and into the hole in the limb drive a length of $\frac{1}{8}$ in. steel rod so that it projects about $\frac{1}{8}$ in. Now take the sheath and with a rat-tail file enlarge the hole sideways for a space of $\frac{1}{8}$ in., taking great care not to disturb the size or shape of the original hole. From the end of this enlargement, file upwards (or cut downwards towards it with the hacksaw if you prefer) a channel $\frac{1}{8}$ in. wide out through the edge of the sheath. You have now an L-shaped slot into which the steel pin in the limb will enter and lock by a slight turn. Enter it so, and file the pin off flush with the outer surface of the sheath, or even a shade below it.

Now insert the other limb in the sheath and so turn it until you are quite satisfied that the backs of the two limbs are in the correct relation to one another. With lemonwood this is easy: with yew some considerable cogitation is frequently required. When you are satisfied beyond all doubt, clamp the whole bow most carefully in the vice and proceed with the second limb as you did for the first.

Your two limbs being now locked in a permanent relation to each other (but of course, 'demountable' whenever you feel like it) you can strike a new centre line down the whole back and proceed to the fashioning of the bow in the ordinary way.

For the finish of the handgrip, cover the sheath with leather, and put a bevelled band of thick leather round the base of each limb to come flush with the ends of the sheath.

I like this type of bow. The only real disadvantage is that the handgrip is a fixed size and shape, and may be found rather too fat for comfort at first. It also makes the bow rather heavy. Both disadvantages are, I think, amply compensated for by the fact that the bow can be packed up small at a moment's notice.

Keep the ferrules and the inside of the sheath very slightly oiled.

ASCHAM'S NOTES

Marks of a Good Bow

'If you come into a shoppe, and fine a bowe that is small, longe, heavye, and stronge, lyinge streighte, not windinge, not marred with knotte gaule, wind shake, wem, freat or pinch, bye that bowe of my warrante.'

'A bowe is not well made, which hath not woode plentye in the hande.'

'And likewyse as that colte, which, at the first takinge up, needeth little breakinge and handlinge, but is fitte and gentle enough for the saddle, seldome or never proveth well: even so that bowe, which at the first byinge, without any more proof and trimminge, is fitte and easye to shoote in, shall neither be profitable to laste longe, nor yet pleasant to shoote well. And therefore as a young horse full of courage, with handlinge and breakinge, is brought unto a sure pace and goinge, so shall a newe bowe, fresh and quick of caste, by sinking and cutting, be brought to a stedfast shootinge. And an easy and gentle bowe, when it is newe, is not much unlike a soft spirited boye, when he is young. But yet, as of an unrulye boye, with righte handlinge, proveth oftenest of all a well ordered man: so of an unfit and staffish bowe, with good trimminge, must needes follow always a stedfast shootinge bowe.'

To Improve a Bow

'Take your bowe into the fielde, shoote in him, sincke him with deade heavye shaftes, looke where he cometh moste, provide for that place betimes, least it pinche, and so freate: when you have thus shotte in him, and perceyved good shootinge woode in him you must have him againe to a good, cunninge, and trusty workman, which shall cut him shorter, and pike him and dress him fitter, make him come round compasse every where, and whipping at the endes, but with discretion, leaste he whippe in sunder, or els freete, soner than he is ware of: he must also laye him streighte, if he be caste, or otherwise need requyre, or if he be flat made, gather him rounde, and so shall he both shoote the faster, for farre shootinge, and also be surer for near prickinge.'

ARROWS

'He purveyed hym an hondred bowes,
The strenges were welle dyght,
An hondred shefe of arrowes good,
The hedes burnyshed full bryght.
And every arrowe an elle long,
With pecocke well y dyght,
Inocked all with whyte sylver,
It was a semly syght.'
From *A Lytell Geste of Robyn Hode* (c. 1500).

Arrow-making is a tedious, tiresome, difficult, almost mass-production job. Much rather would I make a whole bow than six broad-head arrows. And yet they look so simple! You will remember that in the case of Archers Nos. 1 and 2, I cruelly constrained them to make their arrows first; knowing full well that if they had the skill and patience for this the rest, bow and string, would seem easy by comparison. I advise you to do the same.

In the old days a 'flight' of arrows was three; but that is rather few to make at once. I like to make arrows in sixes: that is about as much as I can put up with at any one time. If any professional fletcher should chance to read this he will smile, he who turns out arrows by the gross; but I think there will be sympathy and understanding in him too, since he knows how skill and dexterity grow with use, and how few shafts, comparatively, the amateur is likely to make.

The making of target arrows is a very exact business: yet for hunting-arrows we need not be quite so meticulous. After all, in hunting we never know exactly the range at which we shoot. Any miscalculation of the distance will far outweigh some slight variation in the arrows' behaviour one from another; and by the laws of chance this variation is just as likely to correct our miscalculation as not. Moreover, no good sportsman will shoot at long range; and the shorter the range the less will be the effect of variation in individual arrows. So, while it is nice to have all our arrows precisely uniform in all respects, it is less important than one might think at first. At a fixed and known distance of course, as in target shooting, it is fatal not to have them all as nearly identical as you can make them. Clearly it is an advantage, for any purpose, that your arrows shall not vary unduly among themselves; but if you strive for perfection your labour will be immeasurably increased without sufficient corresponding advantage. The permissible variations you must discover for yourself by actual shooting.

Arrows consist of four parts: the shaft itself, or stele; the head; the shaftment where the three feathers are; and the nock into which the bowstring fits.

THE STELE OR SHAFT

This is not only the body of the arrow, but its mind as well. Upon its qualities (and sometimes, apparently, its temperament also) depends the whole behaviour of the arrow in flight. Two seemingly identical shafts, of the same dimensions and substance, may behave quite differently. These vagaries cannot be predicted. The only test is that of shooting.

Whatever the shaft may be made of it must have three properties; be of a suitable weight; be sufficiently rigid to withstand the sudden push of the string; be sufficiently springy to behave in accordance with the 'Archer's Paradox'.

When an arrow is on the bow, the string drawn, and aim taken, the nock lies in the plane of the centre of the bow's belly while the head is to the left of this plane by half the width of the bow. At the loose the nock receives an impulse directly toward the centre line of the bow, while the head is held rigidly, by the side of the bow, to the left of that line. The net result, one might think, would be that the arrow would be discharged away to the left. The Paradox is that, normally, that does not happen. What does happen is that the push of the string is so violent and sudden that the nock begins to move before the head does so: and that can only happen by a bending of the shaft. The position of the arrow is such that this bend has its convex side to the left. The result of the bend is that as the arrow moves away past the bow, the head is directed slightly to the right, thus correcting its initial deflection to the left. The shaft then snaps straight again, and the arrow proceeds (at least we hope it does) on a straight path to the target. Sometimes this straightening of the shaft occurs while it is actually in passage across the bow; you will then hear it smack hard against the arrow-plate, and your shot will probably not be good. Evidently, then, our shaft must be both rigid and springy to the exact degree required by these complicated movements. These properties are usually called 'spine'; and

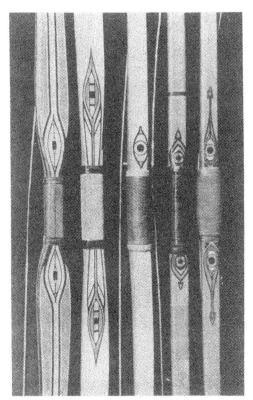

Bow Decoration

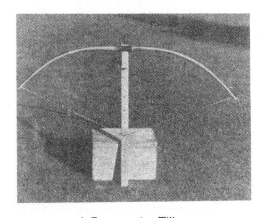

A Bow on the Tiller

15. *Decoration; and the Tiller*

Arundinaria japonica, the Japanese Bamboo

Betula alba, the White Birch

16. Arrow Wood

some archers devise little mechanisms for measuring spine before they make up their shafts. Do so, if you like—so many pounds' weight to deflect a shaft, held at both ends, so many inches—but I think you can do much better by selecting sound material, making up your shaft, and then shooting it. This is the 'official' explanation of the Paradox. I have often thought, however, that the passage of the two 'hen' feathers across the bow must at least assist, if they do not originate, the correction of the arrow's direction.

As in the case of bows, let us come straight to the point and say that, for hunting-arrows, for durability, and for accessibility, only two materials are worth our attention. These are white birch and Japanese bamboo. Both, if of good quality, possess the necessary properties. Birch you can get at the ironmonger's. Ask for $\frac{5}{16}$ in. 'dowel sticks'. These are made for cabinet makers, are thirty inches long, and come in bundles. Select only those which are straight (or nearly so), have grain running the full length, and have a good steely feeling. Reject all crooked, twisted, broken-grained, and flabby sticks. The good ones make admirable shafts, if perhaps a little on the heavy side. Failing these ready-made sticks, you can of course have some birch sawn up at a mill; but then you will, after further seasoning, have the additional labour of rounding and reducing to size.

Bamboo is a very ancient material for arrows, not used in medieval England for obvious reasons, but used throughout Asia from time immemorial. The right kind for our purpose is the Japanese, *Arundinaria Japonica*, clumps of which are common in gardens throughout the country. It is a remarkably accommodating growth and a plant of it will provide a surprisingly high proportion of shoots of the right dimensions. If possible, select those which are dead, dry and hard; but green ones, so long as they are not of the current year's growth, will do as well if carefully seasoned. Some are practically of uniform diameter throughout their length; but more commonly they taper slightly. Cut them, at the nock end of the future shaft, 1 in. above a joint, and at the head end 3 or 4 in. longer than you will eventually want. Use a knife for this; secateurs are apt to split the stem. Select them so that the diameter is approximately $\frac{5}{16}$ in. at a point one-third of the way up the shaft from what will eventually be the head end; the part forward of this can be reduced to the same diameter if the wall is sufficiently thick. As in the case of birch, keep only those which are stiff and steely; and those which have a good thickness of wall with a central passage of not much over $\frac{5}{32}$ in. in diameter. Tie them in bundles and set away to dry and season thoroughly.

Whichever material you use, the first operation to be performed, after the preliminary selection and rejection of the unfit, is to straighten the shafts.

PRACTICAL

This you do by heat. Twist the shaft in your fingers over any convenient small flame, heating only the place which you desire to correct, and avoiding any scorching of the wood or fibre. When hot, bend straight with the fingers and judge your result by eye. Bamboo is particularly easy to straighten: heat makes it instantly pliable and it regains its rigidity at once on cooling. When you have straightened a batch of shafts, cut them to the correct length, which, you will remember, is individual to you, and was determined before ever you set about making your bow. This must allow for the part that enters the socket of the arrowhead. In cutting bamboo, let the end of the nock come ⅜ in. above a joint; the latter will then most conveniently form the base of the nock and no plug or filling will be required. Then smooth up the whole shaft with a file (for bamboo, where the projecting rims of the joints must be removed) and sandpaper, and cut the nock. The birch shafts will be parallel-sided throughout: the bamboo will increase in diameter towards the head. If you like to equalize the weights of your set of birch shafts, well and good; and do it by taking off wood at the nock end. You cannot do much correction with bamboo. But there is one thing which you must do with bamboo and that is to plug the head end with wood to strengthen the walls and to give a firm seating for the base of the arrow blade. Any soft wood will do for the plug, which should be about an inch long. See that it fits moderately tightly and fix it with any adhesive you like to use.

THE NOCK

This is ⅜ in. deep, and of such a width that the whole arrow will just hang on your particular bowstring without falling off. The base of the nock may, with advantage, be just a shade wider than the jaws. If your nock be too wide you will have difficulty in keeping your arrow on the string as you go through the woods; if too narrow, your string will likely split it at the loose. To make the nock in birch set the shaft upright in the vice, file the end perfectly smooth so that you can see the grain, and make a preliminary cut with a saw at right-angles to this grain. This point is important, as we shall see later. Enlarge your cut to the proper width with the flat warding file; round off the sharp corners at the bottom so that the string will not be in danger of being cut by them. Round also the sharp corners at the top of the nock: and sandpaper the whole quite smooth.

For bamboo, set your shaft in the vice so that the axil (the little depressed place just above the joint, where a side shoot either has been or might have been) faces you, and make your nock with the file only. It will be found quite easy, much easier than with birch. Then finish as above.

SETTING-ON THE HEAD

The shaft must be reduced in diameter so that it will enter the socket of the head right up to the metal filling of a practice head and just slightly farther than the base of the blade in a broad-head. To enable the latter to come about, a shallow groove is filed, in the same plane as the nock, about $\frac{1}{16}$ in. deep. This seats the shaft nicely and prevents the head from turning. To allow surplus adhesive to be extruded, thus avoiding an air lock which would prevent the head going fully on, it is a good plan to file a longitudinal 'flat' on the entering part of the shaft.

As an adhesive I use plain black cobbler's wax, a messy but most effective substance. Have a little of this melted in a large metal spoon, warm the end of the shaft slightly, dip it into the wax and roll it round a little, insert it into the head socket (also warm), push, and the thing is done. See that the socket is fully home up to the shoulder which you have formed on the shaft by reducing the diameter, and that the blade of broadheads is truly in the plane of the nock. Any wax which gets extruded in this process can easily be chipped off after cooling in cold water. Heads so fixed will never come off unless you want them to; and then they can, by warming, be removed in the twinkling of an eye.

It doesn't matter at all whether you put heads on before or after fletching. I like to do it before, so that, after fletching, I can go straight on to the restful and gay work of painting—port after storm, as it were!

MARKING OUT THE SHAFTMENT

First of all, if you are using bamboo, roughen slightly the last seven inches of your shaft with a file; bamboo does not take glue well, and this helps a great deal. Then lay your batch of shafts together flat on the ground or work-table with their nocks all in line. The pencil marks which you are now going to put on them will be determined, as to position, in part by the length of feather vane which you propose to use. For reasons given later on, it is better to stick to one length, and that is, 5 in. of vane plus $\frac{1}{4}$ in. of bare quill at each end to take the binding. So, take a T-square, and, using the nearest shaft as a base, draw lines across the whole batch of shafts as follows, all measured from the nock end: $1\frac{1}{8}$ in., $1\frac{3}{8}$ in., $6\frac{3}{8}$ in., $6\frac{5}{8}$ in. Take these lines right round each shaft, and you are ready for the most difficult job of all, the preparation and setting on of the feathers.

FEATHERS

There is no substitute for these wonderfully intricate and beautiful mechanisms. Had there been, one can be quite sure that their use would have been abandoned long ago in favour of something less exasperating and time-consuming. When you have time, go and seek out a large-scale model (there is, or used to be, one on view at the Science Museum in Oxford), and wonder at the marvellous ingenuity which goes to their construction; it will be some recompense for your trials. It is possible to use arrows without feathers, but only for very short distances. Beyond these, the shaft requires guidance. We cannot use just any feather; we require something at once stiff, durable, flexible, irrepressible; and it must be easily got. Ancient ballad-writers frequently refer to peacock's feathers. You have already had an extract from Chaucer, and here is one from the Wardrobe Account for the fourth year of Edward II:

'*Pro duodecim flecchiis cum pennis de pavonae emptis pro rege, de 12 den.*'
    i.e. 'To twelve arrows with peacock's feathers, bought for the King, 12 pence.'

These are not the tail-feathers, but the red-brown pinions, which are very strong and thick, but harsh and brittle. Apart from the expense, this is sufficient reason for not bothering further about them.

Tradition talks, or sings, of the 'gray goose', and indeed Ascham writes a delightful eulogy of the virtues and the benefits conferred on us by that homely and disdainful bird. Goose feathers are good, but nowadays it is more common, I do not know why, to use turkey. Both are readily obtainable, so make your choice. When I first became interested in the matter, in the days when there was no black market and we lived a free, unregimented life, I ordered from an advertisement in an agricultural paper a turkey for Christmas; and added a request that the breeder would also send me some feathers. All went well; the bird duly arrived and with it a huge paper parcel. From the snow storm that sprang out of this, like the Djinn out of the Bottle, I extracted score upon score of the most beautiful white pinion feathers: and the stock so acquired has lasted me ever since. That was before it had occurred to me that there exist feather merchants from whom we can buy what we require. You will notice that I was lucky enough to acquire white feathers; and that colour I have held to ever since. It is such a great help in finding arrows after the shot. Also they look nice; but the common grey-barred-black turkey is more usual, and perhaps you will prefer to have, in any case, a distinctive colour for the 'cock' feather, of which more later.

You will notice also that I said 'pinion feathers'. These are the big, strong, narrow feathers on the outside of the wings; no others are any good. Only one side of these pinion feathers carries a web broad enough to use. The feathers on each wing curve a different way, and are termed 'right' and 'left'. It does not matter which you use, provided that all three vanes on any one arrow are 'rights' or 'lefts' and are cut from as nearly as possible the same parts of the individual feathers. Select, therefore, sufficient pinion feathers to fledge your batch of arrows; they should be clean, unbroken, strong and thick in the web. To get the correct length to carry a broadhead, it is unlikely that you will be able to get more than one vane out of each feather.

PREPARATION OF THE VANES

Since we only require the web of the feather, and not all the thick quill also, the one has to be separated from the other; and this can be done in two ways. A 'stripped' vane is one which is just torn off the quill; it is a spineless, flabby thing to work with and, although it is quite satisfactory in use and in durability, I do not like it.

To strip a feather, hold it vertical with its upper (convex) surface towards you, and separate the web at the extreme tip, so that your right thumb and finger grasps only (for a 'right' feather) the right-hand side of the web. Then, holding the top of the quill with your left hand, pull firmly and continuously downwards with your right. If you are lucky, the whole web will come away with only a thin sheet of quill attached to it. This requires some practice before it can be done with confidence. I will confess at once that I have never reached that condition! But do not be put off with this; commercial arrows are fletched almost exclusively with vanes prepared in this way. When you have thus torn the web off, trim the quill until only a little projects on each side of the web. There is no more to do.

The way I like better is to cut or pare the vanes from the quill. This method takes up a very great deal more time and requires the exercise of some considerable skill. But it produces a robust and easily-handled vane and I like it on that account. So did Ascham, who regarded stripped vanes as a manifestation of laziness. Provide yourself therefore, with some discarded safety-razor blades; those which have a sharp edge on one side only are the best. Take a feather, upper or convex side toward you, and point uppermost, in your left hand, and slit the quill from top to bottom with the razor blade. In doing this you should cut as near to the web as you dare. Make the cut very slowly and carefully: if you don't, you will run either into the middle of the thick quill or into the web and spoil the feather. Keep your left hand below the blade and push the feather up on to the edge, little by little. When you have got the web off thus you may still have to do a little paring to attain an even width of quill all down the feather. Then put the web face downwards on a board or table, near the edge so that your right hand can be slightly below the web, and pare off the thick ridge of quill on the back. What you want to aim at is a web with an even base of about $\frac{1}{16}$ in. width to stand firm upon the shaftment, and as thin as you can reasonably cut it. Even up the quill as well as you can with the razor blade. Select a length of $5\frac{3}{4}$ in. from the most uniform part of the web and cut it out; then trim the web away at each end so as to leave $\frac{3}{8}$ in. of bare quill there. Now put it into a long paper clip—one of those things with two flat steel spring jaws made to hold a bunch of papers—and rub the quill on a sheet of sandpaper until its under surface is smooth and even. Cut off the upper end of the web square, and it is ready for gluing.

DISPOSITION OF THE VANES

Each arrow carries three vanes. These are set so that the webs, not necessarily the quill bases, stand out from the shaft at equal distances round the circumference, with their surfaces at 120° to each other. Since vanes are not uniform either in their natural curvature or in the angle at which the web stands to the quill base we may find, and usually do, that to get the above result the bases will not be equally spaced. That is no matter; it is the web which counts.

But, over and above this first requisite of correct spacing, there is the requirement that the vanes shall be put on in a fixed and definite relation to the bow when the arrow is on the string. The vanes brush past the side of the bow at the loose. If their position was variable, arrow for arrow, the effect of this brushing would also vary at every shot; and no two arrows would fly alike. The position of the vanes relative to the bow must therefore be fixed This position is such that when an arrow on the string is viewed from the nock end one vane projects to the left at right angles to the string while the other two point inwards, or to the right, at equal angles. These two will then bear equally and evenly on the bow at the loose. The vane which projects to the left is called the 'cock feather', and is frequently of a different colour from the others to facilitate quick nocking or setting on the bow. This spacing and proper relation to the string and bow is not all. We can put on our vanes in either of two ways; so that the arrow rotates in flying, or so that it does not. Ascham thought, I do not know why, that as soon as an arrow stops rotating it stops flying. His observation cannot have been good. Arthur W. Lambert, Jr., the American target archer, prefers arrows that do not rotate. Again I can give no reason. From which you can easily deduce that both kinds give good

ARROW VANES

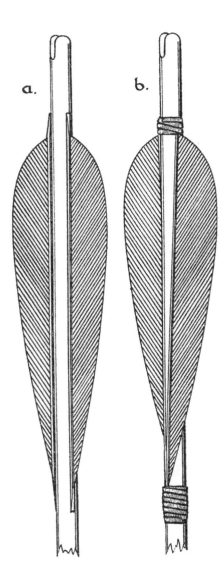

a.

b.

a. Vanes on straight.
Arrow will not spin.
Viewed from nock end
looks like this:

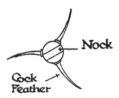

Nock

Cock
Feather

b. Vanes at an angle,
exaggerated.
Arrow will spin.
View from nock end is:

Enlarged Sections of
c. Stripped Vane
d. Cut Vane

c.

d.

results; as indeed is the fact. An arrow that spins as it goes certainly seems to fly more truly and is more graceful to watch; and I have, therefore, a preference, part aesthetic and part mechanical, for that sort. But my own limited experience tells me that the non-spinning and occasionally tail-wagging kind in fact flies just as truly, even if it does at times induce just a suspicion of anxiety as to the outcome. It is simple so to adjust the vanes that you have either kind. For the non-spinners see that the vanes are for their whole length set on parallel to the axis of the shaft. For the spinners, set the vanes on so that their length makes a slight angle with the shaft's axis; all three vanes, of course, being inclined in the same direction.

For a wobbling, gadding, and useless arrow make the mistake of mixing one 'right' vane with two 'left' ones, and vice versa, or incline one vane of a spinner in a direction opposite to that of the other two. Such arrows are dangerous.

So much for the relation of the vanes to the circumference of the shaft. In the longitudinal direction they must be put as near the nock as will allow sufficient room for the tips of the fingers of the drawing hand. The web should not, therefore, be placed nearer the extreme tip of the nock than $1\frac{3}{8}$ in.; and we have already marked our shafts accordingly.

And one other point, which has to do with your safety and not with the performance of the arrow. It is applicable to wooden shafts but not to bamboo. Take a birch shaft (or, better still for demonstration, a pine or cedar one) and sandpaper it quite smooth. You have cut the nock across, and not parallel with, the lines of the end-grain. Look now at the length of the shaft. In the plane of the nock, i.e. on the upper and lower surfaces of the arrow when it is on the string, you will see the 'feather' of the grain (a confusing term, this, when we are talking so much of real feathers) pointing either forwards or backwards in a series of long, sharp-pointed loops. On the sides of the arrow, i.e. at right angles to the plane of the nock, you will see parallel lines of grain running the full length of the shaft. These are the edges of the layers which make up the substance of the wood. Now, if your arrow should break at the loose it is most unlikely to do so sideways, since the layers are strong in that direction. Your shaft will break upwards or downwards, and as it does so it will pass across your left hand. If you don't want your hand to be pierced by the broken shaft you will have taken care that the 'feather' on the underside of your shaft points backwards, that is, towards the nock. And this consideration removes from you any choice as to which side of the shaft you shall put your cock feather. It must be placed on that side which will permit the 'feather' on the underside of the shaft to point backwards.

SHAFT GRAIN, & THE NOCK

a.   b.

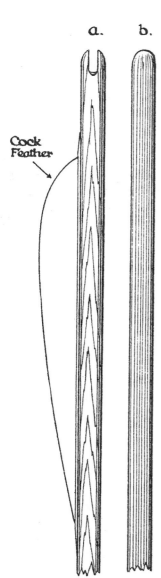

Cock
Feather

a. Underside of shaft. Grain must
   point towards nock, if any is
   visible.

b. The side of the shaft that runs
   against the bow.
   The grain is here shewn truly parallel to the length of the shaft, and
   no points, as in 'a', will appear.

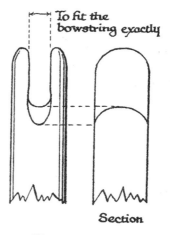

To fit the
bowstring exactly

Section

The nock is cut
across the end-grain

PRACTICAL

So now assemble your vanes in threes, 'rights' or 'lefts' as the case may be; mark the proper side of your shafts for the cock feather; and prepare for a trial of skill and patience.

GLUING VANES

The choice of an adhesive depends upon the use to which your arrows are to be put. Target arrows are fastened, by professional fletchers, with ordinary cabinet maker's glue, and a very good job it makes. It will not, however, tolerate damp, and can therefore be dismissed for hunting gear. We want a waterproof substance, and our choice lies between a celluloid cement and casein glue. I prefer the latter since it sets very much more slowly and is easier to manipulate on that account. Moreover, it makes an excellent joint. At the time of writing these notes I have just recovered an arrow which had been lying in the open, in damp grass, for over six weeks. Apart from the loss of a little paint in one or two places it is still a perfectly good arrow, and all the vanes are secure. The vanes were stuck with casein glue on to bamboo.

So mix your casein to a thick treacly consistency and let it stand for half an hour or so after mixing.

Professional fletchers deal with a whole batch of arrows at one time, waiting until their glue is tacky and then putting the feathers directly into place, where they stick. A slight adjustment here and there and the batch is done. It is difficult and tricky work, dependent upon the glue and the weather, and is not applicable to what we want to do. Casein glue takes eight or nine hours to set and will not, at first, hold the vanes without some help. It is quite sufficient for us to deal with one arrow at a time. When you have mixed your glue you can soften your feathers a little while you wait for the glue to 'season'.

I am never quite sure whether this softening process helps or not, since the feathers dry so quickly afterwards. But try it once, and then make up your own mind. Spread out your whole batch of vanes between the folds of a damp towel, and put a weight on top. So leave for about half an hour. Take these vanes out three at a time: they will be straighter and less refractory than dry ones for a short while.

Take up a shaft, fasten a piece of sewing cotton, or some of your bowstring thread, round it tightly just below the lowest pencil mark, and then spread a good dose of glue evenly all over the shaftment, particularly at the ends where the bare quill of the vanes will come. Your forefinger is by far the best tool for doing this; so have handy a little pot of water to cleanse it each time. It is quite fatal to attempt to put vanes on with sticky fingers; keep them clean all the time, and if ever you do touch glue rinse them at once.

Set your shaft aside for the glue to soak in a little. Sometimes a second coat seems advisable; use your judgment in this.

Take up each vane of your three in turn, and with a little stick spread a liberal dose of glue on the base of the quill. Don't let any get on to the web. Set them aside so that you can pick them up easily again and take up your shaft in the left hand, horizontally with shaftment pointing towards your right, so that your thumb will come just about where the lowest of your pencil marks is, and so that the place for the cock feather is toward you.

Now pick up the vane that is to be your cock feather, insert the lower end of the quill under the left thumb, so that the web starts at the second lowest of your four marks, and hold it there while you just grip it with a partial turn of the thread, winding away from you. Never mind if the vane flops about, as it will; so long as the end of the quill is firmly held it will be all right. Rotate the shaft one-third of a turn towards you and repeat the process with the second vane. To do this, keep your thumb on the first vane and hold the second with the tip of your left forefinger. As soon as the thread has gripped the second vane, you can release your thumb from the first and transfer it to the second. Rotate another third, fix the third vane, and then take two or three tight turns over all three. Be careful to see that all webs start at the correct mark. Don't bother about any other adjustments at this stage, but see that the quills point straight up and down the shaft. Now reverse the thread so that it winds towards you. To do this, extend your left forefinger a little, still holding the shaft as before, wind over its tip, then bring the thread back towards you above the shaft and take two or three tight turns over the last few coils that you have wound previously. This is difficult to describe satisfactorily, but any friend who ties salmon flies will show you the trick in an instant. When you have done this, turn the shaft so that the vanes are vertical. The problem now is to wind the thread through the webs so that the quills are bound firmly to the shaftment. The turns should be about ⅜ in. apart, and must be tight. Rotate the shaft to the left as you do this and be careful not to spoil the web by binding down any of its fibres; the thread must go right down to the upper surface of the quill between the fibres, which should be little if at all displaced. It is convenient to control the tension of the thread with the little finger; this will leave the right thumbnail free to adjust the position of the quills, as each turn over them is taken, to ensure that they run evenly and straight and are not pulled round out of place. When you come to the bare quills at the nock end take two or three turns over them, spiral up to the end of the nock, and there secure by two half-hitches.

Now survey the unpromising looking object in front of you! Or, perhaps it is not as bad as that, and you have done a neat and tidy job at the first attempt. Whichever it may be, turn the shaft and look at it from the nock end. Begin with the cock feather and adjust the position of the quill at the nock end until the web stands out truly at right angles to the nock. Then work down the whole vane until it is straight all along, either parallel with the shaft, or at a slight angle as required for an arrow which is to spin. Have more regard to the web than to the quill. The web must not kink or cockle, and this can be controlled by slight adjustments to the position of the quill. Take care that the vane is sitting fairly on its base, and not on its side; sometimes tight winding of the thread pulls a vane right over where the quill has been cut too narrow.

Deal similarly with the other two vanes, remembering that they must each run evenly on the bow, and must be symmetrically placed both in that respect and with regard to the cock feather.

Having made all these adjustments look over the whole thing from all angles, and, if satisfied, set it aside to dry and harden up overnight.

Admittedly this method is difficult and clumsy; but I know of no better which will permit casein glue to be used. This requires a little pressure to be brought to bear on the surfaces to be joined, and this the thread does. Casein will make such a joint on birchwood that the webs will suffer themselves to be torn away piecemeal and still leave the joint sound. With bamboo the results are, in my experience, not so thoroughly reliable in all cases. A reasonably slow-setting celluloid cement has sometimes, but not always, given good results on bamboo. It seems to depend very much on the individual bamboo and the degree to which its surface will, or will not, allow the adhesive to penetrate and take hold.

Of one thing I am sure: bind as tight as you can, and bind closely.

After twelve hours or so remove the thread and examine your vanes closely for any faults in the joint. Should you find any places where the glue has not taken hold (and you should not) insert a little more glue under the quill with the point of a knife, or a sliver of quill itself, and bind up again.

I am told that all this long, tiresome process can be avoided if one uses the glue (whatever that may be) which makers of model aircraft use to fasten together the pieces of balsa wood of which the plane is constructed. By this method, the vane is held in a long paper-clip, or between two strips of wood, and is pressed up against the shaftment on which a layer of glue has been smeared. By the time one has counted 100 slowly the vane will be sufficiently set to allow you to let go of it. Before actually doing this, both vane and shaftment should have been smeared with glue which is then allowed to dry;

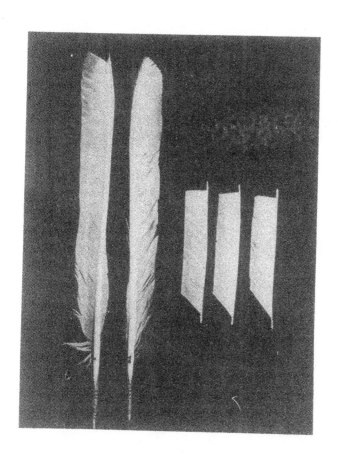

Left and Right feathers   Three Vanes cut from
                              a left feather

17. *Feathers*

Splitting the Quill

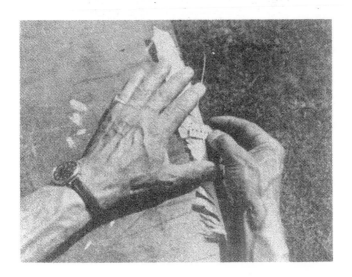

Paring off the ridge of Quill

18. *Vanes I*

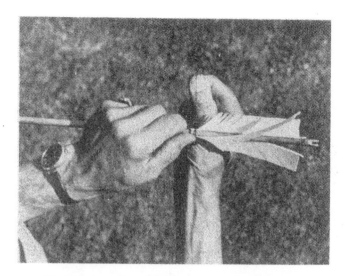

First Stage. Securing the ends of the Vanes.

Second stage. Running the thread up through the fibre
of the Vanes. Note that the second and third turns are
not properly down to the base of the fibre

19. *Vanes II*

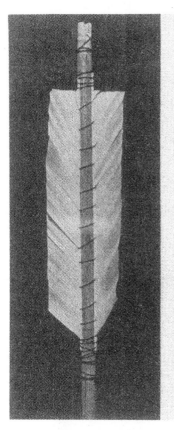 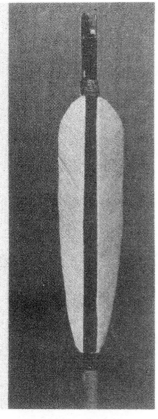

Vanes glued, and bound   Vanes trimmed and
temporarily with thread   ends bound with tape

20. *Vanes III*

a second coat is then applied to the shaftment immediately before the vane is to be fixed. I shall try this next time I turn fletcher.

If all vanes are tight on clean up the shaftment between them, with the edge of a file, to remove any little ridges or blobs of glue, and then trim the ends of the quills. Bevel them off first with a razor blade so that they merge neatly into the level of the shaft, and then, if this has not already automatically shortened them, cut them evenly to your pencil marks on the shaft. These ends must now be bound to secure them. Target arrows are not usually bound at all; but then they do not tear through bush and grass as will ours. For binding the most convenient material is the narrow ⅛ in. green silk tape which you can buy at those shops which cater for lawyers' stationery; or thread, carpet thread for choice, will do if you don't mind the business of making a whip-lash finish each time.

If you use tape, cut off as many 5 in. lengths as you want, two per arrow. Cover one side with any convenient adhesive (I usually use the old-established 'Seccotine') and lap it round neatly and tightly to cover the quill ends. See that the end is firmly stuck down. When dry give a good coating of celluloid varnish and the whole will be waterproofed and smooth.

TRIMMING THE VANES

The vanes keep the arrow point foremost and on a steady course. It is immaterial just how this is accomplished; whether by simple air drag as some say: or by a rudder effect as others assert. Let us not go further into an unprofitable discussion; but be thankful that it is so.

The bigger the feathers the greater the effect, and the more slowly will the arrow fly. So we are, as so often in this matter, up against a compromise. Fine, big, upstanding vanes will make your shaft fly as steadily as a rock, if it is in other respects sound; they will also make it fly deliberately and without zest. Small vanes may be barely sufficient to hold the shaft on its course; but your arrow will fly like the wind.

A speedy arrow is not only good in that it reaches the mark more quickly but your point-blank range is much increased by it; both advantages to the hunter. We are, however, limited in the smallness to which we can trim our vanes by the size and shape of the arrowhead we use. A big broadhead requires a correspondingly big vane. Cut the vanes too small and your arrow will either dive head first into the ground or swoop most violently and dangerously to unexpected points of the compass. On the other hand, a plain bullet jacket point, carrying no blade at all, can be held true by quite tiny vanes, as in flight arrows used for shooting to extreme distances.

PRACTICAL

The shape of the vanes matters little, whether triangular, arc-shaped, or parabolic. But since the vane has the greater effect the farther it is from the arrowhead it is clearly an advantage that its greatest breadth shall at least be in its rear half, if not actually at its rearmost point. Also you will find that some shapes are much easier to cut than others. So I advise you to adopt a simple one. The easiest to cut is the plain triangle, with its greatest width at the nock and no width at all at the forward end. This, however, is not pretty, and I modify it to the shape of a very elongated and rather flat-sided peg-top.

The height of the vanes is, as already said, conditioned by the arrowhead; but there is no sense in having them a fraction higher than you must. Quite apart from the speed of flight, the narrower the vane the more easily your 'twelve lives' will fit into the quiver or storage box, and the less will they damage each other. So we conclude that a long, low feather is the most practical. Dr. Pope used immense broadheads 3 in. long and 1¼ in. wide. To carry them he found it necessary to use a vane 5 in. long, ¼ in. high at the forward end and ⅞ in. at the rear. With a ⅜ in. shaft that means that the diameter of his whole arrow was over 2 in. A quiverful of these monsters must have been an awkward thing. Mark you, I do not criticize; he had made exhaustive experiments; and for his particular game, frequently dangerous, and for the heavy bows he used, I have no doubt such gear was advisable. We in this country, where deer will be our largest mark, can use a smaller head. For those I describe later it is satisfactory to have vanes 5 in. long, level with the shaft at the forward end, ½ in. high at a point about ⅝ in. from the rear end, and from that point rounded into the shaft at the rear binding. If you want to use smaller vanes for smaller heads, then you will find 4 in. long by ⅜ in. high suitable for the little broadhead, and 2 in. by ⅜ in. for the plain bullet jacket; but this introduces a variation into one's arrows of which, for constancy of shooting, I am somewhat doubtful.

Various means have been advocated for the actual business of cutting the web—razor blades, knives, sharp steel templates, and so on. On all counts I prefer a long, sharp pair of scissors, with which a neat and tidy job can be done in very short time. To cut feathers you must always attack them against the direction of the fibres, i.e. from the top of the feather downwards. It is difficult enough to make a regular cut even in this way; but it is quite hopeless in the reverse direction, even if you can get a hold at all. Practise on some spare feathers; you will then find how easily the scissors and the feathers will conspire together to produce a ragged cut, and to run in closer to the quill than you desire. At the nock end of the vanes you will indeed have to cut the reverse way; but there you will be cutting almost square across the fibres and no trouble will arise.

An easier way, perhaps (but I have not tried it myself), is to hold the web between two shaped metal templates, and to burn off the projecting part of the feather with a taper, I can well believe that this is a very quick and accurate way of doing a rather difficult thing.

Do not cut your feathers as low as you intend them finally to be. After some shooting they will probably settle a little. Then bring them to their proper size.

TRIAL OF THE SHAFT

Before you go on to painting try your shafts by actual shooting. Shoot each several times, noting the character and direction of the flight.

Reject, resolutely and without compunction, those which do not perform steadily and straight.

Target archers number their shafts and record whether each shoots to the right or left, and how much. So they can group them and make the necessary allowances in a match. You cannot do that when suddenly confronted with your game. You must know that the arrow on your string, or the next one you take at random from your quiver, will go straight and true if only you hold and loose properly.

PAINTING

This is a jolly business, a welcome and light-hearted relief from all the painstaking work that has gone before. A hunting-arrow should be a brilliant thing, not just for gaiety but so that you will have more chance of finding it again. I paint mine, below the shaftment, a bright vermilion, and to this colour I owe many a shaft which otherwise would have been lost in the grass. The shaftment can be any colour you like. It is a convenience, if you make your arrows in sixes, to keep a separate colour here for each batch.

Behind the feather I paint the nock end a different colour according to the head; black for big broadheads, red for small broadheads, and white for the plain point. So you can select what you want from your quiver. Also, to distinguish the cock feather (if your vanes should be all alike) I put a spot of white paint both above and below the shaftment in line with that important vane. One can then nock the arrow quickly and correctly.

I do not worry about a personal mark on my arrows, as do target shooters.

PRACTICAL

Your arrows will bear your own imprint and style clearly enough: there is no need to distinguish them further.

For paint use something which will dry hard and glossy. One of the modern synthetic finishes will do well. Start painting at the nock end. Stick your arrows, when done, into a flower-pot full of dry earth or sand. So you can easily deal at once with a dozen or more.

Do not shoot your arrows until the paint is thoroughly hard; otherwise you will scrape off long streaks against the bow.

VARIATIONS

Our hunting-arrows are plain cylindrical shafts of strong, durable material. Because of the weight of their heads they balance, as they should, somewhat forward of their middles. There is, therefore, no need for us to have 'footed' shafts. Nor need we bother about 'chested', 'bob-tailed', or 'barrelled' arrows, in which the diameter is not constant. These refinements, of doubtful value even among target archers, are quite unnecessary for us. Similarly, we need no fancy work in our nocks, insets of hard wood and the like; the tough birch, or the hard diaphragm of the bamboo are very serviceable and need no reinforcement.

Let us keep to plain, straightforward gear.

ARROW WEIGHTS

The modern custom is to weigh arrows in grams or grains. The older fashion is to use silver coins.

English silver can be counted by weight; thus two separate shillings and a sixpence weigh exactly the same as a half-crown piece; and so for all values. This holds even for our modern 'silver' coinage, that shoddy stuff, with which the King's effigy is disgraced.

You will find that your big broadhead arrows will weigh about 'seven shillings', if they have birch shafts; with bamboo the weight will be reduced to 'five and sixpence'. An ordinary target arrow, in pine or other light wood, will weigh 'four and sixpence' or thereabouts.

It is convenient to keep a set of new coins as weights, including the silver threepenny bit if you can get one.

ASCHAM'S NOTES

Of arrows. 'A shaft hath three principall parts, the stele, the fethers, and the head.'

ARROWS

Of arrow wood. 'Steles be made of divers woodes: as,

Brasell	Servicetree
Turkie Woode	Hulder
Fusticke	Blackthorne
Sugercheste	Beche
Hardbeame	Elder
Byrche	Aspe
Asche	Salowe
Oake	

... Brasell, Turkie Woode, Fusticke, Sugar Cheste, and such like, make dead, heavye, lumpishe, hobbling shaftes. Again Hulder, Black thorne, Servestree, Beache, Elder, Aspe, and Salowe, eyther for theyr weakness or lightnesse, make holow, starting, scudding, gaddinge shaftes. But Birche, Hardbeame, some Oake, and some Ashe, being both stronge enoughe to stande in a bowe, and also light enoughe to fly farre, are best for a meane, which is to be sought out in every thinge.'

'Yet, as concerning sheaffe arrowes for war (as I suppose) it were better to make them of good Ashe, and not of Aspe, as they be now a dayes. For of all other woodes that ever I proved, Ashe being bigge is swiftest, and againe hevye to geve a great stripe withall, which Aspe shall not do. What heaviness doth in a stripe every man by experience can tell, therefore Ashe being both swifter and heavyer, is more fit for sheafe arrowes than Aspe, and thus much for the best wood for shaftes.'

Of Cornus (dogwood). '... this wodde is as harde as horne, and verye fitte for shaftes.'

Of bamboo. 'Yet of all thinges that ever I marked of ould authors, eyther Greeke or Latine, for shaftes to be made of, there is nothinge so common as reedes. Herodotus, in describinge the mightye hoast of Xerxes, doth tell that three greate countryes used shaftes made of a rede, the Ethiopians, the Lycians, (whose shaftes lacked fethers, whereat I marveile most of all) and the men of Inde. ... In Crete and Italy they used to have theyr shaftes of reede also.'

Of steles. 'A stele must be well seasoned for castinge, and it must be made as the grain lyeth, and as it groweth, or els it will never flye cleane. ...'

'And how bigge, how small, how heavye, how light, how long, how short, a shaft should be particularly for every man, seeing we must talk of the general nature of shootinge, can not be toulde. ... As it is better to have a shaft a little too short than over longe, somewhat to light, than over lumpishe, a little to smal, than a great deal to big, which thinge is not only truly sayde in shootinge, but in all other thinges that ever man goeth about, as in eatinge, tankinge, and all other thinges like . . .'

'The under hand must have a smal brest to go clene away out of the bowe, the fore hand must have a bigge breste to bear the great might of the bowe.

The nock. 'The nocke of the shaft is diversely made, for some be great and full, some handsome and litle; some wyde, some narrowe, some deepe, some shalowe, some rounde, some longe, some with one nocke, some with double nocke, whereof every one hath his propertye. The great and full nocke may be well felt, and many wayes they save a shaft from breakinge. The handsome and little nocke will go cleane awaye from the hand, the wyde nocke is noughte, both for breakinge of the shafte, and also for sodaine slippinge out of the stringe, when the narrowe nocke doth avoyde both those harmes. The deep and longe nocke is good in warre for sure keeping in of the stringe. The shalowe and rounde nocke is best for our purpose in pricking for clene deliverance of a shoote.'

Footed arrows. 'Peecing of a shaft with Brasell and Hollie, or other heavye woodes, is to make the ende compasse heavye with the feathers in flyinge, for the stedfaster shootinge. For if the ende were plump heavye with lead, and the wood next it light, the head ende would ever be downwards, and never flye streight.'

Of feathers and fletching. 'Now to loke on the feathers of all manner of byrdes, you shall see some so lowe, weake and shorte, some so course, store and harde, and the ribbe so brickle, thin and narrow, that it can neither be drawen, pared, nor yet well set on, that except it be a swanne for a deade shaft (as I know some good archers have used) or a ducke for a flight, which lastes but one shoote, there is no feather but onlye of a goose that hath all commodities in it . . . thus for our purpose, the goose is the best feather, for the best shooter. . . . Yet well fare the gentle goose, which bringeth to a man, even to his doore, so many exceeding commodities. For the goose is mans comfort in warre and peace, sleepinge and wakinge. What praise soever is geven to shootinge, the goose may challenge the best part in it. How well dothe she make a man fare at his table? How easily dothe she make a man lye in his bedde? How fit even as her feathers be only for shootinge, so be her quills fit only for wrytinge. . . . The old goose feather is stiffe and stronge, good for a wynde, and fittest for a dead shaft: the young goose feather is weak and fyne, best for a swift shafte, and it must be couled at the first sheeringe, some-what hye, for with shootinge it will sattle and faule very much. . . . Betwixt the winges is litle difference, but that you must have divers shaftes of one flight, feathered with divers winges, for divers wyndes: for if the wynd and the feather go both one way, the shaft will be caryed to much. The pinion feathers, as it hath the first place in the winge, so it hath the first place in good featheringe. . . . The coloure of the feather is least to be regarded . . . yet surely it standeth with good reason to have the cocke feather blacke or greye, as it were to geve a man warning to nocke right. . . . Wherein you must looke that your feathers be not drawen for hastinesse, but pared even and streight with diligence. . . . This thing, if a man take not hede on, he may chaunce have cause to say so of his fletcher, as in dressinge of meate is commonlye sayde of cookes: and that is, that God sendeth us good feathers, but the devill noughtye fletchers. . . . The length and shortnesse of the feather serveth for divers shaftes, as a large feather for a longe, heavye, or bigg shafte, the short feather for the contrarye. Again, the shorte may stand farther, the longe nerer the nocke. Your feather must stand almost straight on, but yet after that sort, that it may turn rounde in flyinge. . . .

'Both the feather in makinge your shaft, and you in nockinge your shaft, must take heede that two feathers equally runne on the bowe. For if one feather runne alone on the bowe, it shall quickly be worne, and shall not be able to match with the other feathers; and again, at the lowse, if the shaft be light, it will start, if it be heavye, it will hoble. . . .

'To shere a shaft highe or lowe, must be as the shafte is, heavye or light, great or litle, long or short, the swyne backed fashion maketh the shaft leader, for it gathereth more ayre than the saddle backed, and therefore the saddle backe is surer for daunger of weather, and fitter for smothe flyinge. Again, to shere a shaft rounde, as they were wont sometimes to do, or after the tryangle fashion, which is much used now a dayes, both be good. . . .'

ARROWHEADS

RIVETTED BROADHEAD

TANGED BROADHEAD

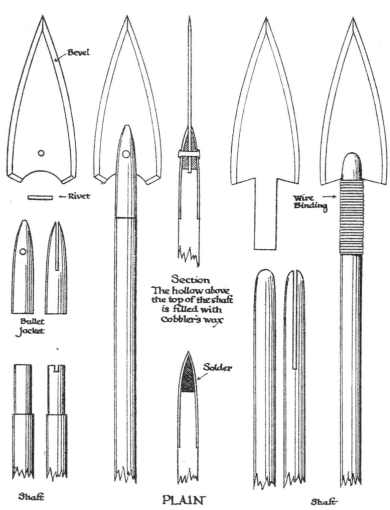

Bevel

← Rivet

Bullet Jacket

Shaft

Wire Binding

Section
The hollow above
the top of the shaft
is filled with
cobbler's wax

Solder

PLAIN
PRACTICE HEAD
in Section

Shaft

ARROWHEADS

ere (risking your wry and deprecatory look) is the point of the whole matter. All that we have considered hitherto is but the vehicle. When, by a combination of good shooting and good fortune, you land your arrow in the mark let it be one that carries a head fit for its task.

All sorts of materials have been used—bone, horn, sinew, wood, stone, glass, metal, and even the spikes from a sting-ray's tail. Our choice need not be so catholic, for we have sheet metal at our disposal, and, properly chosen and treated, it is the best, save in one respect.

What do we require from our arrowhead? Very simply that it shall cut deep and wide. Cutting without penetration gives merely a surface wound. Penetration without cutting gives a deep and grievous wound indeed, but not a merciful one since there is little bleeding. Such a point was the old-English 'bodkin', an armour-piercing affair of square or diamond section, a terrible thing feared wherever the English archers went.

We can insure a wide cut by choosing a suitable width for our blades; we can ensure depth of penetration by a suitable shape, by the keenness of the point and edges, by the strength of our bow and the weight of our shaft.

The power of an arrow never ceases to astonish me. Here is a light thing, flying most leisurely as we count speed nowadays, which yet will deliver such a blow as would skewer two men together were they so foolish as to stand one behind the other and offer themselves for a mark; which can penetrate chain-mail and plate armour; which can be shot through a door without any arrowhead at all; and which will slay almost everything that walks or crawls upon the earth. Compared scientifically with a rifle bullet the arrow is nothing. Compared by its results it is in some respects superior. Let us consider a few figures. A modern cartridge for a game rifle may carry a bullet which weighs 180 grains and discharge it at an initial velocity of 2,700 feet per second. Such a bullet, after it has gone 100 yards, will have a remaining energy of some 2,500 foot/lb.; or, in plain language, it will deliver upon

PRACTICAL

the mark a blow equivalent to that which would be given by rather more than a ton weight dropped from a height of one foot.

An arrow, on the other hand, will weigh approximately twice as much as the above bullet, but will only have a velocity of some 150 feet per second, and an energy of 25 foot/lb. These are Dr. Pope's figures.

Since it is the energy which counts, one might conclude that the bullet would be one hundred times as effective as the arrow. It is not so. Then what do we conclude? Simply, I think, that we are not comparing like with like. Now if we were to compare the effect of an arrow, of the broadhead sort, with that of a sword-thrust we should be on firmer ground. Both penetrate deeply, both cut widely. The bullet is outside the picture; it is a different thing.

As to actual killing power, anything, be it bullet, arrow, or sword, which reaches a 'vital' part will be effective. But Pope, who was a physiologist as well as an archer, maintained that the arrow was more humane than the bullet in that death would ensue rapidly from a body-hit in a non-vital area; a characteristic which all sportsmen must value highly.

The arrow kills by the depth and extent to which it severs the organs of the body; not by the shock of the blow it delivers. We must therefore so construct it as to be capable of this to the highest degree.

MATERIALS

Good steel for big broadheads; spring steel properly tempered. But mild steel if you can get no better; although this will not take or keep a really good point and edge, and will bend and buckle badly if it whacks into anything hard.

For small broadheads, rabbit arrows, we do not need spring steel; mild steel will do quite well.

The spring steel should be $\frac{1}{32}$ in. thick, in strip 1 in. wide. The mild steel for the strong, small broadheads is $\frac{1}{16}$ in. thick, in strip $1\frac{3}{4}$ in. or 1 in. wide according to which kind you propose to make, i.e. with or without a tang.

Some day I want to try flint or glass arrowheads. These cut much better than steel on account of their naturally fluted edges. Pope showed that one of these would penetrate thirty inches of animal tissue against the twenty-two inches of the steel broadhead. They are, of course, very brittle; and to make require long practice in an all-but-forgotten art. Two excellent reasons why I can tell you no more about them. But Ishi, the Yana Indian, made them quickly and easily and used them for all his hunting. For ordinary practice arrows the steel, copper-covered jackets of rifle bullets serve very well. These

ARROWHEADS

are, of course, the empty jackets without the lead filling. For a $\frac{5}{16}$ in. shaft the proper size is the ·311 in. calibre, more commonly known, perhaps, as the German 7·9 mm. service bullet. Failing these, brass or steel tube of the proper diameter, the end filled with a round-headed screw soldered in. Or, if you don't mind the expense, use the regulation steel target pile.

If you like a practice head which shall be of the same weight as your broadheads (a good plan) you have only to use brass or steel tube of the correct length and fill it with solder to the proper extent. This, with a constant size of feather, will ensure that you will not be put off, after practice, when you come to use the broadhead in the field.

SHAPE AND SIZE

Generally speaking, the broadhead is triangular and barbed. I do not like the plain triangle, simply because, as in the case of arrow vanes, it is not a graceful shape; and I do not see the use of barbs, except to indicate to the archer, by pricking his finger, that he has drawn his bow to the full. Your arrowheads will look better, and be just as efficient, if you modify the plain, unaesthetic triangle so that it becomes a long, very nearly straight-sided ogive; this retains the narrow 'entry' of the triangle but pleases the eye much better.

The sharp triangular barb I modify into a rounded form, giving it a sharp cutting edge. This you can feel when drawing just as well as the sharp point.

Do what you will in these two matters; and, having decided, file out a blank shape which will serve as your template. Mine is $2\frac{1}{2}$ in. long, from point to lowest part of 'barb', and just a shade under 1 in. in width at the widest point which comes just above the 'barbs'.

The barbs, or their modification, are easily formed by filing the base of your triangle. Use a $\frac{1}{2}$ in. half-round file, and remove nearly a semicircle from the base. Then drill a $\frac{1}{16}$ in. diameter hole $\frac{5}{16}$ in. above the deepest point of the semicircle to take the rivet.

An alternative method of securing the head is to make it with a tang which will fit into a slot in the shaft. If you like this method, then cut your template with a tang at least 1 in. long and $\frac{5}{16}$ in. wide. This involves a lot of hard work and has, in my view, no compensating advantages whatever.

The little broadheads are precisely the same in design as their big brothers. I make them 1 in. long and $\frac{5}{8}$ in. to $\frac{3}{4}$ in. wide.

Both kinds have bevelled cutting edges. Let this bevel be wide and flat, about $\frac{1}{8}$ in. A narrow bevel will neither take nor keep a proper edge.

PRACTICAL

CONSTRUCTION

Heads, like shafts, are best made in batches of six. To make a *big broadhead* take your strip steel, lay your template upon it and scribe round it with a sharp point of some sort. If then you fix it in the vice, you will find, if you are using spring steel which has not been hardened, that you can, with a hammer and very little trouble indeed, crack off the rough shape of your future head more or less to the lines you have marked. If you find the steel over-brittle, anneal it first by heating to a bright red and letting it cool slowly in the air. Alternatively, you can saw out the head with a hacksaw; but I think you will soon abandon this method, although you must use it if you are going to have heads with a tang. Having thus got your rough shape, it can be ground or filed accurately to the marks. With handwork only I am not sure which is the quicker method. If you grind holding the blade in your fingers, have a little pot of water handy and keep the head (and the grindstone) constantly wet; otherwise you will suddenly, and with no warning at all, find your fingers severely burnt.

Now file your barbs, or cut your semicircle; and then file or grind the bevel to a keen, rough edge.

Now drill your rivet hole. Next the head must be tempered. We want it in such a condition that it will be neither soft, and so easily distorted, nor brittle, and so easily chipped or broken. It must be like a spring, tough and resilient. Light a gas ring, heat the head over it until it is a bright cherry-red, and drop it immediately into cold water. It will now be glass-hard. Polish up the surface until it is smooth and shiny. Now turn the gas ring low, and heat the head over a small flame, carefully and as uniformly as possible. You will see a series of beautiful colours form on its surface. First pale straw, then yellow, then blue, dark blue, and pale blue in succession. You want to stop the heating at the dark blue stage. When this is reached, throw the head into cold water again; and the job is done. An engineer would be horrified at this crude procedure; but its results are quite good enough for us. Don't polish the head again: the dark blue prevents it flashing in the sun too much, and also seems to me to be a good preventive against rust. This process is, of course, only applicable to your spring steel; it does not work, nor is it necessary, for your small broadheads made of mild steel.

The head must now be fixed in its socket. Take a bullet-jacket, set it upright in the vice, and file a small flat on its point. On this flat cut a small groove with the edge of a file. If you try to use the hacksaw without this preparation you will find it very difficult to start at all. Then saw downwards, straight, for ¾ in. The saw cut made by an ordinary hand hacksaw will fit the thickness of

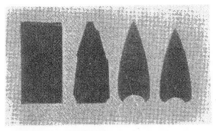

The steel blank; corners broken off;
roughly shaped; drilled, bevelled, and
tempered

A riveted Broadhead

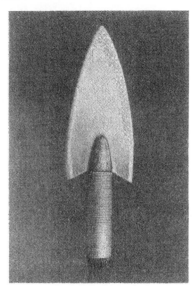

A tanged broadhead

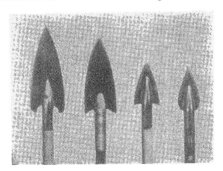

Broadheads, big and little

21. *Arrowheads*

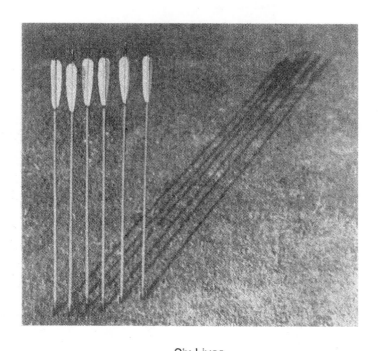

Six Lives

22. *A newly-completed batch of Broadheads*

your head. Be careful to get both sides of the cut the same depth, exactly; otherwise your head will not sit straight.

You must now drill a $\frac{1}{16}$ in. hole in the tip of your socket so that it and the hole in the head will come level when the latter is firmly seated in the saw cut. Take off all rough edges from the cuts and hole in the socket. Seat your head and rivet it in place with a piece cut from an ordinary soft iron wire nail of the proper size. Let the heads of your rivet be small and smooth them off all round with the file.

This one rivet is quite enough. Even if you have not been quite accurate in your work and find that the head is capable of some movement relative to the socket this will be eliminated completely by the wax with which you fill the point of the socket and secure the shaft.

Should you not be able to get any bullet-jackets you can make do, but not so nicely or so strongly, with steel or brass tube. With this you must hammer down the open end until the sides of the bevel thus formed are just $\frac{1}{32}$ in. apart. Mr. Gordon recommends that this be done over a suitably shaped piece of steel which slips inside the tube; a good idea. Then file off the top 'wings' of the bevel, which will leave you with a slot into which the head will fit. Then proceed as before. Such a socket will not have the strength of the bullet-jacket, the great advantage of which is that its point, into which the blade is seated, has a circular section, and thus has very great resistance to any sideways blow.

To fix a head with a tang, cut a slot in the shaft, in the plane of the nock of course, long enough to allow the extreme end of the shaft to come up on to the head for a distance of $\frac{3}{4}$ in. This end must be bevelled on both sides, so that the wood slopes down evenly and smoothly to the surface of the blade. Let this bevel be rather bluff; if it is too thin the wood will crack off at the first hard blow. No rivet is used, and you cannot use such heads with bamboo shafts. Drill a very fine hole, to take your binding wire, $\frac{1}{16}$ in. below the deepest point of the cut in your shaft. Start binding with fine brass or steel wire at the base of the head and continue till you come to the hole. Pass the end of the wire through, and break off by bending it backwards and forwards. A light tap with the hammer will secure it. It is an advantage if now you run a thin film of solder all over the binding. To be honest, I have never succeeded in doing this satisfactorily. Soldering is a weak point with me: one additional reason for not liking the tanged head, which in itself is heavier and much more fragile than the plain riveted variety.

Now that your heads are done, fix them on with cobbler's wax as already described, give them a light rub with steel wool, and oil them.

Keep them sharp with a file. This gives a better cutting-edge than a stone.

PRACTICAL

The little broadhead is made and fixed similarly, except that barbs, even embryo ones, are not necessary. These heads are roughly pear-shaped, with flat bases. Being of $\frac{1}{16}$ in. thickness a rather stouter hacksaw is required to make the cut in the bullet-jacket. They can be soldered to the bullet-jacket, instead of riveted, if you are clever at that art.

The plain practice heads should have soft solder melted into them until they reach whatever weight you want. When using the bullet-jacket I weigh them till the whole turns the scale at 5 grammes, or just over one-sixth of an ounce. The solder strengthens the point, helps the balance of the arrow, and gives a good firm seat for the end of the shaft. A head of this weight is, of course, not comparable to a broadhead, and arrows fitted into them will fly farther for the same elevation or point of aim.

ASCHAM'S NOTES

Of arrowheads. 'Our English heades be better in warre than eyther forked heades or brode arrowe heades. For first, the ende being lighter, they flee a great deale the faster, and, by the same reason, geveth a far sorer stripe. Yea, and I suppose, if the same little barbes which they have were clean put awaye, they should be farre better. For this every man doth graunt, that a shaft, as long as it flyeth, turnes, and when it leaveth turninge, it leaveth going any further. And every thing that enters by a turninge and boring fashion, the more flatter it is, the worse it enters, as a knife, though it be sharpe, yet, because of the edges, will not bore so well as a bodkin, for everye rounde thinge enters best; and therefore nature, saythe Aristotle, made the raine droppes round, for quicke percynge the ayre. Thus, eyther shaftes turne not in flyinge, or else our flat arrow heades stop the shaft in entering. . . . Thus heades which make a litle hole and deep, be better in warre, than those which make a great hole and sticke fast in. . . . I would wyshe that the heade makers of Englande should make theyr sheafe arrow heades more harder pointed than they be.'

'. . . You may desyre him to set your heade full on, and close on. Full on is when the woode is bet harde up to the ende or stoppinge of the heade; close on, is when there is left woode on everye syde the shafte, enoughe to fill the head withall, or when it is neyther to litle nor yet to great. If there be anye fault in any of these pointes, the heade, when it lighteth on an harde stone, or grounde, will be in jeopardye, eyther of breakynge, or els otherwise hurtinge.'

SUNDRY GEAR

ertain things are part of the traditional equipment of the archer. They are the bracer or armguard; the shooting-glove or, alternatively, the tab; and the quiver. Whether you will want all or any of them you can decide for yourself. The quiver certainly, unless you propose to carry your arrows in your hair as some wild peoples are reputed to do. The glove or tab most certainly at first, but not so surely later on. The bracer, perhaps; this is dependent upon your own anatomy and the height to which you string your bow.

THE BRACER

When you loose the string it will, or may, catch you a hard whack on the inside of your left forearm. It all depends on the shape of the arm and how you hold the bow. A highly-strung bow will hit you less severely than one which is low strung; it may, indeed, not touch you at all. If you shoot in an ordinary jacket the sleeve will take the blow—and deflect the shot.

So people lash or buckle a piece of stout leather on the part of the forearm just above the wrist, the lashing coming on the outside so that the bowstring shall have a smooth surface to strike on. Practically it is as good to tie up the wrist of your jacket with a piece of string or tape. I have never wanted a bracer at all. The 'stripe' of the string is not so severe that I cannot endure it on the bare arm for a dozen or so practice shots; and for the occasional shot in the woods, it is quite superfluous. But if you are going to practise in real earnest at a target then indeed you may want something. Make it to your own design; a detailed description is not necessary.

THE QUIVER

This holds your arrows. It should be about twenty-two inches long; five inches wide at the top and four inches at the bottom; flat-sided, soft, and collapsible. If you like a hard, rigid, tubular affair then of course your diameters will not be so great as the above figures; but don't take such a thing with you into the woods. The best thing to do, seeing that quivers are such individual things, is to take a sheaf of twelve broadheads and measure what will hold them comfortably; then make what takes your fancy. For hunting, a quiver must have certain indispensable characteristics. It must be noiseless; and this rules out hard leather, wood, and canvas, which all either cause the arrows to rattle as you move, or make an intolerable noise as you push through undergrowths. It must be roomy enough, so that arrows can be easily withdrawn, and so that the heads do not rub together too much and destroy their cutting-edges. It must have no projections whatever on the inside on which the arrow-head can catch as you withdraw the shaft. And, finally, it must keep out the wet. The best material I know for this is heavy, oil-tanned moosehide or horse-hide. Failing this, good, stout buckskin, or some similar thick, soft leather. Re-inforce the bottom with a double thickness. As an accessory, in case it rains while you are out, procure an oiled-silk or plastic sponge bag, with a draw-string. Slip this over the feathers of your arrows; it is true they are secured with waterproof glue, but wet does them no good and anyway makes the feathers all soft and liable to be crushed out of shape.

THE SHOOTING-GLOVE

This, or its much more satisfactory substitute the 'tab', is quite indispensable while you are learning to shoot, or when, having learnt, you intend to shoot more than a very few shafts.

The string is drawn with the tips of the fingers; and, as you draw, the tip of the forefinger, its inside surface, will get severely pinched in the angle between the string and the shaft. This can be avoided, but not altogether, by making the forefinger do more of the work of drawing than it is naturally inclined to do. Moreover, the surfaces of all three finger-tips cannot withstand for long the rub of the string unless they are protected.

The shooting-glove, or the tab, will not avoid the former ill, but will effectively ensure against the latter.

Do not bother about a glove, or even a modified one; they are hot, and always either too large or too small. Use the simple, ancient tab. This is a piece of supple leather, about $\frac{1}{16}$ in. thick, cut with two holes to slip over the fore- and third fingers, and projecting so as to cover all three of the working fingertips. A slot is cut between the fore- and second finger so that the shaft may come through. It is easy to make, always fits if made right in the first place, never falls off, and is completely effective. It also has the great advantage that, if turned back, it frees the hand at once for any other work.

After a little, when your fingers have hardened up, you may be able to dispense with this protection. But one cautionary word. Should the inside of your forefinger get sore, as described above, particularly in the neighbourhood of the nail, stop shooting at once, and do not go on until it is properly healed. Otherwise it will be, as Ascham says, 'long and long to ere you shoote againe', and you will have a painful sore for many days. Once, even, I had the whole thickness of the skin in this place removed at one shot. It was a painful lesson which there is no need for you to learn.

Besides these things you will want a bow-case, a pair of field-glasses, a small axe (the one you used for bow-making) in a leather sheath, a skinning knife, and a *rucksack*. Let the latter be reasonably large, and let it be of as soft a material as you can find so as to make less noise against the bushes and trees. It will hold all your spare gear and maybe your game as well. Being on your back and out of the way it is preferable to any kind of game-bag or haversack. It is quite enough to have the quiver dangling at one's side; one wants no more.

The bow-case is just a long bag of waterproof canvas. If it rains, out it comes and in goes your bow.

The field-glasses are better than any telescope, even though they do not magnify so much. Their field of vision and the light they let through amply compensate for a smaller image.

The axe you will want if you kill anything larger than a hare or rabbit. It is to cut through the ribs at the breastbone, and to sever the joint of the pelvis. Also you can, if you are in a truly wild place, and if you are wise you will, blaze the trees so that you can find your way back to your game should it be necessary to leave it overnight. But, as you value your freedom and your pocket, do not do this in these islands! Poor foresters as we are, the trees are sacred. A blazed trial will emphatically not make you popular with the owner of the land.

Keep your axe razor-sharp, with a smooth edge; and have a leather sheath made for the head.

The skinning knife need be only a small affair, with a blade some four inches long. Keep it really sharp with a file or very rough stone, and carry the latter with you as well as the knife. The edge has to cut skin and meat, and should therefore be rough. Our ancestors used a sharp-edged flake of flint for this, the most efficient cutting tool for the purpose that they could possibly have had. Its efficacy depends upon its wavy and serrated edge. A filed knife-edge is the nearest substitute. Don't carry an enormous hunting-knife. You will have no use for it.

PRACTICAL

ASCHAM'S NOTES

Of the bracer. 'Little is to be sayd of the bracer. A bracer serveth for two causes, one to save his arme from the strype of the stringe, and his doublet from wearing; and the other is, that the stringe glidinge sharplye and quicklye of the bracer, maye make the sharper shoote. For if the stringe should lighte upon the bare sleve, the strengthe of the shoote should stoppe and dye there. But it is beste, in my judgmente, to geve the bowe so much bent, that the stringe neede never touche a mans arme, and so shoulde a man need no bracer, as I knowe many good archers which occupye none.'

Of the shooting-glove. 'A shootinge glove is chieflye to save a mans fingers from hurtinge, that he may be able to bear the sharpe stringe to the uttermoste of his strengthe. And when a man shooteth, the might of his shoote lyeth on the foremost finger, and on the ringman, for the middle finger, which is the longest, like a lubber, starteth back, and beareth no weight of the stringe in a manner at all.'

'If yet you feele your finger pinched, leave shootinge, both because then you shall shoote nought, and againe by little and little, hurtinge your finger, ye shall make it longe and longe to or you shoote againe.'

MAINTENANCE AND REPAIRS

Archers' gear, like any other, will not look after itself. There is not much that has to be done, but that little is important. Damp and old age are the two things to beware of. Although you have, if you are wise, used casein glue throughout, yet this stuff is not waterproof in the sense that it actually repels water. A feather stuck on with it will not come off if it gets wet; but the glue will soften somewhat and no good will be done to the joint. The same applies with even more force to the vellum backing of your bow, if you have one. Damp, moreover, does not do wood any good; nor do extremes of temperature. So keep your gear in a dry, equable place; out of the wet, of course, but equally away from hot pipes and radiators and things of that kind. Store them in the same sort of conditions as you would your guns and fishing-rods.

Old age brings cracks, splinters, loose bindings, worn strings, and the like; which all lead to trouble if not carefully forestalled. In itself old age is no enemy; somewhere I have read that a good bow is capable of some 100,000 shots, so that you could, on this reckoning, shoot a dozen shafts every day of the year for nearly twenty-three years. But continual or intermittent use, it matters not which, coupled with neglect will not do. A stitch in time saves nine, or, as Ascham says, a grudged halfpenny will cost you a crown.

THE BOW

Apart from keeping the bow in reasonable conditions, there is nothing to do other than give it an occasional rub over with a very little boiled linseed oil, or a polish with beeswax if you prefer that. If it is a 'carriage' bow then a trace of oil (gun oil, not linseed) on the ferrules will make for easy dismounting and keep rust at bay.

Lemonwood may develop long, fine cracks, which do no harm if they are taken in hand in time. And both this wood and yew (unless backed) may produce splinters rising from the back. The palliative for these ills is to bind the bow in these parts as tightly as you know how. Use your bowstring thread for this, and soak it in boiled linseed oil when it is done.

Yew may also 'chrysal'. This is a minute crumbling of the wood on the belly side. There is nothing serviceable that you can do about this; when a bow is badly chrysaled it is unsafe and no longer fit to use. The trouble is most likely to begin in and around knots and pins.

If for any reason your bow should break it is finished and dead. You cannot repair it, except if it be a 'carriage' bow; in which case it is quite easy to drill the broken limb out of the ferrule and fit a new one. Ascham tells us of the several ways in which a bow can be broken. Over-drawing and a faulty string are the chief.

Never let anyone else use your bow. It is individual to you and is accustomed to your draw. Keep a spare for your friends to test their strength upon!

Hang your bow up when not in use; and not in a case which may attract the damp. A little leather thong passed through the hole in the tip of the upper limb is convenient for this.

When you go out to shoot, draw your bow little by little until it comes to full draw. This applies particularly to 'carriage' bows in which the joint may have developed just a suspicion of play. Be particularly careful about this with a bow that has been long disused.

THE STRING

Here is a frequent cause of disaster. A bowstring is not everlasting. Consider how sharply it is bent, and what strain is applied to that place where the arrow-nock fits. Consider what happens at the nocks at the tips of the bow. Consider the snap which it suffers time after time, as it returns to its position after the loose. It is marvellous that so thin a cord should endure as long as it does. If your bow-nocks are not really smooth they will sooner or later cut the string. But, more commonly, failure occurs under the whipping in the string's middle. One is disinclined to remove this whipping; all the more reason to do so to see whether all is well beneath. A string will sometimes give warning that it is about to break; queer irregularities will show under the whipping and it will seem as if the string is not pulled straight. Do not shoot then; you risk your bow.

Keep your string well waxed, and rub it smooth after waxing. Keep it straight, and do not hang your bow up by it. If, instead of a loop at one end and a bowyer's knot at the other, you have two loops, you can turn the string end-for-end after a while and so change the nocking-place. This will prolong the life of the string; but the bottom loop must be made in the right place

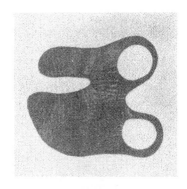

The Tab

The Tab in position

The Quiver

23. *Sundry Gear*

Bracing the Bow

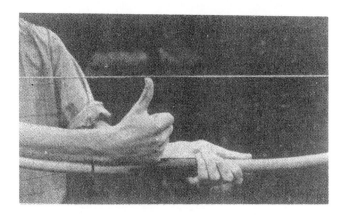

Fistmele

24. *Bracing the Bow*

since, if it is not, you will have to adjust it by twisting or untwisting the string unduly to bring your bow to fistmele.

ARROWS

If much used, arrows require constant attention. Feathers, paint, bindings, and head must all be kept in order. An arrow may warp and require straightening. It may lose its 'spine', and then it is fit only for the scrapheap. It may break, and often does, should it hit anything hard. Repair is then well worth while if the damage is in the forward half of the shaft. A break in the middle can sometimes be repaired satisfactorily, but the strain there at the loose is sudden and severe and any joint must be thoroughly sound.

Repairs in birch and bamboo require different methods. A broken bamboo shaft (I have never experienced one, except right at the head) cannot be mended at all. But if the arrowhead is just snapped off then it is a simple matter to replace it. File off the end of the shaft square. Take a piece of a birch shaft and reduce the diameter of one end so that it will fit snugly into the hollow of the bamboo for a length of an inch or so. The shoulder on the birch and the end of the bamboo must meet and fit tidily all round. Then set in this plug with glue; and when set, cut off the birch to the proper length and fit the new head to it.

To repair a broken birch shaft you must retain the feathered end and join a new piece to it. This join must be at least two inches long; two inches of actual glue-surface, that is. I find a plain 'scarf' joint quite satisfactory. This is easily made so that both pieces come into proper alignment by the use of a very simple contrivance. Get a little block of hardwood, three inches long by two inches square. Down the long axis of this drill a hole just a shade wider than the diameter of your shaft. On the upper surface of the block make two marks, each half an inch from the end; on this surface also trace the path and width of the hole. Draw a diagonal line joining the points where your two marks cut the lines of this trace, and prolong the line to the ends of the block. Now with a fine tenon saw cut vertically downwards, and stop when you have cut to about $\frac{1}{8}$ in. below the path of the hole.

If now you put a shaft through the hole, and saw again, guided by the cut you have already made, you will divide the shaft neatly and accurately and will produce a two-inch surface for your glue. And every shaft you put in will be cut to exactly the same length and angle; and so will fit neatly and truly together in line.

Having done this, smear the surfaces with thick casein glue, bring together, and bind up with string, taking care that in doing so the two parts retain their proper position and do not slip downhill (as it were) and spoil the joint. Leave for forty-eight hours. Such joints are thoroughly serviceable; but I usually put a band of yellow paint round the place to show that the shaft has been in hospital.

An accident to the nock makes also a fit subject for salvage. A thick string will sometimes split off one side of the nock at the loose. It will be your own carelessness if this happens, and you will endanger your bow. Still, if it does occur the nock is easily repairable by sticking on a new piece of birch, filing out the full nock again (wide enough this time!), securing the forward end by a fresh binding for the feathers and the rearward end by a narrow binding of thread.

Keep your feathers under constant survey; sometimes a part of the quill base gets torn loose. If so, a little celluloid cement insinuated underneath it will make all firm again. And see that the ends of the bindings do not begin to lift; the forward one gets rough treatment as it passes across the bow, and the rear one is continually subject to friction from your fingers.

Arrowheads need no attention beyond keeping them sharp and free from rust.

FINDING LOST ARROWS

Before I became an archer I had always imagined that an arrow landed so that its feathers stuck bravely up in the air for all to see. I found that, at a range of 100 yards or more, this was quite true. But at any less range, and particularly at the ranges at which we may expect to shoot game, it is lamentably untrue; and I suppose I have spent quite as much time in searching for lost arrows as I have in making the whole of my archery equipment. The reason is that at these ranges an arrow does not describe a fine 'head and tail rise' like a porpoise or a salmon, but flies with its axis almost horizontal throughout the whole of its parabolic course. As a result, it lands nearly flat with the ground. This is all right if you are shooting at a regulation target, and if you hit it. But if you are shooting at a mark on the ground, as you should be, then your arrows will either skid if the earth be hard, or will bury more or less of their entire length in the grass. Believe it or not, it is possible in this way to lose an arrow on a close-cut lawn. Be most careful, then, to mark the fall of your shafts; and be prepared to look painstakingly for them. You will remember what Bassanio said:

> In my schoole dayes, when I lost one shaft
> I shot his fellow of the selfesame flight
> The selfesame way, with more advised watch
> To find the other forth, and by adventuring both
> I oft found both.

MAINTENANCE AND REPAIRS

Well—follow his advice if you like; I do not think he had to make his own arrows. Pope said he always hunted a lost arrow for an hour, which was the time he took to make one. I have scythed a quarter-acre of meadow to find one before now—and then had it retrieved for me, quite by accident, by a casual visitor, from a spot thirty yards away! Elusive things; and one does so hate to lose one of a set. The vermilion shaft and the white feathers are great helps. So, if you are at practice, is a hay rake; this will get down just below the surface where the truants lie.

Be careful, therefore, where you shoot. Avoid, unless you are actually hunting, rough grass and mossy woodlands. These swallow arrows without trace.

REPAIR KIT

On your expeditions carry with you spare arrowheads, cobbler's wax, beeswax, bowstring thread and a spare string or two, a few vanes ready prepared and kept between two pieces of cardboard, casein glue, celluloid cement, a warding file, a few short pieces of birch shaft, and a piece of leather for smoothing your bowstring.

ASCHAM'S NOTES

Care of the bow. 'When you have brought your bowe to such a pointe, as I spake of, then you must have a harden or wullen cloth waxed, wherewith everye daye you must rubbe and chafe your bowe, till it shyne and glitter withal. Which thinge shall cause it both to be cleane, well favoured, goodlye of coloure, and shall also bringe, as it were, a cruste over it, that is to say, shall make it everye where on the out syde, so slipperye and hard, that neyther anye weete or weather can enter to hurt it. . . .'

Of frost. 'Yet if a man must needs shoote at any such time, let him take his bowe and bring it to the fire, and there, by litle and litle, rubbe and chafe it with a waxed clothe, which shall bring it to that point, that he may shoote safely enough in it.'

Of damp. 'Take heede also of mistye and dankinshe days, which shall hurt a bowe more than anye rayne. For then you must eyther always rubbe it, or els leave shootinge.'

'A bowe case of lether is not the best, for that is oft time moyst, which hurteth the bowes very much.'

Of bows breaking. 'A shooter chaunceth to breake his bowe commonly four wayes, by the stringe, by the shaft, by drawinge to farre, and by freates. . . .'

'When the stringe fayles the bowe must needes breake, and especiallye in the middes, because both the endes having nothing to stoppe them: but whippes so farre backe, that the bellye must needes violently rise up, the which you shall well perceyve in bendinge of a bow backewarde. Therefore, a bowe that foloweth the stringe is least hurte with breakinge of stringes.'

'By the shafte a bowe is broken eyther when it is to short, and so you set it in your bowe, or when the nocke breaks for litlenesse, or when the stringe slips without the nocke for wydenesse, then you pull it to your eare and lettes it go, which must needes break the shaft at the least, and put stringe and bow and all in jeopardy, because the strength of the bowe hath nothinge in it to stoppe the violence of it. . . .'

'The bowe is drawne to farre two wayes. Eyther when you take a longer shaft than your own, or else when you shift your hand to lowe or to hye for shootinge farre. This waye pulleth the backe in sunder, and then the bowe fleeth in many peces.'

'. . . The fourthe thinge that breaketh a bowe is freates, which make a bowe redye and apte to breake by any of the three wayes afore sayde. Freates be in a shaft as well as in a bowe, and they be much like a canker, creepinge and encreasinge in those places in a bowe, which be weaker than other. . . . Freates begin many times in a pinne, for there the good woode is corrupted, that it must needes be weake, and because it is weake, therefore it freates. Good bowyers therefore do raise every pinne, and alowe it more woode for feare of freatinge. . . . Remedy for freates to any purpose I never harde tell of anye. . . .'

SHOOTING

'PHIL: *What is the cheyfe poynte in shootynge, that every man laboureth to come to?*
'TOX: *To hyt the marke.*'

TOXOPHILUS

Now far be it from me that I should attempt to teach anyone how to shoot with the bow. I have not succeeded in teaching myself with any great success; although from time to time I am astonished at the sight of my arrow in the mark. By the laws of chance this must, I suppose, happen occasionally; and if it did not no one would continue with his archery. For, have no doubt about it, to shoot well with the bow is very difficult. It is easy enough to discharge arrows in the general direction of what you want to hit; and when you walk up to look at them it is also easy to persuade yourself that some of them have landed pretty near. But, as Ascham tersely points out, the object of shooting is to hit the mark; and how many of your pretty good ones have actually done that? 'Near misses', to use the modern phrase, do not count; certainly they are near, equally they are misses. No miss, near or far, will bring any game to bag. So we must learn to hit, and the road thereto is long and very, very narrow. Good field archery is a very skilled business; and that is, or should be, the spur which will drive you on to continue when all seems hopeless. For at times nothing goes right; and then will come a day (yes it will) when you will surprise yourself, when your arrows one after the other will fly straight and true, and when it all seems the easiest thing in the world. And you will then know that the power is at least in you to shoot well; and you will persevere.

String, then, your bow; set up a mark of some kind at its point-blank range, and see that your arrows are clean and straight. Ascham divided the art of shooting into five parts: standing, nocking, drawing, holding, and loosing. His directions as to what one should *not* do are much fuller than for the reverse; but what he says is sound and I cannot add much to his advice.

TARGETS

The regulation archery target is a thick disc of straw, at least four feet in diameter, propped up about two feet above the ground on a tripod; and has a cloth stretched over it painted in bright-coloured rings. It is expensive to buy, most laborious to make, and not necessary. I like to have a target on or near the ground, and of a dull colour; such more nearly resembles the game at which we shall be shooting.

If you want a circular taget, a very serviceable and easily-made one can be contrived out of corrugated cardboard, the stuff used for lapping round parcels. This can be bought in long rolls, and is about fifteen inches wide. If you roll this up very tightly, to any diameter you please, and then tie the circumference with string or wire, you will have a very durable and cheap target which holds arrows well. Do not roll it to and from your butt, which loosens it; carry it, and store it flat. At the butt, it needs no tripod but will stand up on the ground by itself.

It is also easy, and amusing, to construct a deer of straw. A few sticks or battens lashed together to form legs, backbone, and neck; some wisps of straw bound on to this skeleton with string; and you have a very life-like object, to which, if he is like mine, you will have to introduce your dog with due ceremony!

Easier yet; a handful of dry grass or hay just put on the ground. That represents your hare or rabbit.

Anthills and molehills are also good marks; but the former are usually much honeycombed, and do not hold arrows well. Whatever your mark may be, you will find it a great advantage to have behind it something to catch arrows which have skidded. Some long bundles of hay or straw serve quite well; or a low bank of earth or sand. Let this stop be of a good width to catch your bad shots. Without it, some of your arrows will be found to have skidded as much as fifty or sixty yards, and may be troublesome to find.

Let us remind ourselves first of all *how to string the bow.* Grasp it by the handle, back up, in the left hand. Put the tip of the lower limb into the angle between the instep of the left foot and the ground. Slide the palm of the right hand up the bow till the loop of the string is reached by the thumb and forefinger. Then, pulling up strongly with the left, and pushing down and out with the right hand, slip the loop into the nock. Make sure it gets properly into both sides of the nock; and do *not* get your fingers under the string.

STANDING

All sorts of instructions are given for this; but Ascham's idea is, I am sure, the most sensible. He wants you to be comfortable, and to stand as suits you best. The accepted rule nowadays is to stand with your shoulders in line with the flight of your arrow, or very nearly so, and to place your feet somewhat apart, and firmly. This is excellent for target shooting; but what about when you are in the woods and do not want to stand up like a telegraph pole? You must be able to shoot kneeling, or squatting; even perhaps from the back of a pony as so many nations used to do both in Asia and America. So find out how you can most comfortably shoot from unorthodox as well as orthodox positions; and having found out, stick to it. The great thing in archery is constancy, to eliminate as many variables as you can. How easy it is to give advice!

Whatever positions you do finally decide on they must be stable ones. When your bow is drawn you are under very considerable exertion. There is nothing left for any balancing feats.

NOCKING

Bearing in mind that the arrow lies on the left side of the bow, there are two other points only in this; to nock so that the cock feather is outwards, pointing away from the string; and to nock in the right place on the string, neither too high nor too low. This will require no thought, and hence waste of time when your game is in sight, if you have already made the two little lumps in the serving on the string as described earlier.

DRAWING

The bowstring is drawn by the tips of the first three fingers of the right hand. Mark you, the tips. The fingers should not be hooked round the string; but with a heavy hunting bow perhaps some slight approach to a hook may be tolerated both for security and ease. The less hook the better the loose. The nock of the arrow passes between the fore- and second fingers, so that there is one finger above and two below it. This is known as the Mediterranean Release, and is the most practical of all the possible methods. Make the forefinger do its full share of work. It is apt to shirk, and the more it does so the more will its inside get most painfully compressed against the arrow.

In drawing keep the right elbow up, so that at full draw, and indeed all along, the forearm is in line with the shaft. Any other position doubles your work, and cramps your freedom. Keep the right thumb doubled up out of the way, so that it will not touch your face or jaw.

Nowadays we draw neither to the breast nor to the ear. But either to the middle of the chin, or to a point on the jaw directly beneath the right eye.

PRACTICAL

You will find the latter 'anchor-point', as it is called, much more natural and easy than the former. Choose which you like and stick to it. Every shaft, whether your mark be at your feet or two hundred yards away, will be drawn full to this point.

You will already have made your arrows to suit this length of draw, and the barbs, or whatever you elect to finish off your broadheads with, will just touch the back of your left forefinger when the bow is full drawn.

And now, having given you the true and orthodox doctrine, let me, with all haste, ease my conscience. To hit anything much nearer than fifteen or twenty yards by this method is desperately difficult; and in a thick wood one often gets shots at rabbits and hares which appear suddenly almost at one's feet. Then I cast orthodoxy to the winds and draw direct to my eye. This cuts out all mental calculations, and the arrow is directed straight at the mark. I cannot quite manage the full draw in this position, but at so short a range that makes no practical difference.

With this confession let us go on to the actual act of drawing.

Here we have again to contend with diverse views; whether one should grip the handle tightly or loosely; whether we should extend the left arm fully and then draw with the strength of our right arm, or 'lay the body in the bow' as they did when archery was in its prime. To me it all seems to depend upon the weight of the bow. A light bow requires no particular effort; a heavy one may tax your strength to the uttermost if you are to draw it at all. Personally I hold the handle without any deliberate grip, and at the full draw my fingers only encircle it lightly and can be stretched out at full length with the bow's thrust taken in the crotch of the thumb and forefinger. I start with the arrow pointing downwards, as nocked, and the left arm extended straight, but not so straight that the elbow-joint is locked. Then, as I draw back the string, the left arm is steadily raised, until at the full draw it is in position with the bow vertical. But halfway through this simple, and indeed natural, performance, when the left arm is almost up and the right hand partly back, there comes an opportunity to use, apparently, one's body weight: and this, I think, must be the explanation of what is meant by 'laying the body in the bow'.

If at this stage of the draw, when the bow is beginning to show its strength against you, you square your shoulders, cock out your chest and advance it as if to get inside the bow between it and the string, you will accomplish the rest of the draw without trouble. I have never satisfied myself whether this motion is real or apparent; but without any doubt at all it is effective. It feels as if one were forcing one's hands apart by the weight of one's body. At all events I can think of no other explanation of the old expression. That it was something real is shewn by the following quotation from Bishop Latimer, of which more is given elsewhere:

'He [his father] taught me howe to drawe, howe to laye my bodye in my Bowe, and not to drawe wyth strength of armes, as other nacions do, but wyth strength of bodye.'

The fourteenth-century *Book of Roi Modus*, of which more later, has an even more graphic description of what is meant:

'. . . pource que larc est fort il fault estandre les bras et baissier le corps et soy plongier en son arc.'

To 'plunge into one's bow'; that describes admirably the feeling, if not the actual very slight motion.

The whole draw must be a steady, continuous motion from the beginning to the end. The left arm, the bow, and the right hand all move together, and arrive in their final positions simultaneously. The grip of the bow must be in such a position that the arrow comes against the arrow-plate, and not on part of the handle; and the bow must be vertical. A slow, deliberate draw makes for accuracy; a quick draw, followed by an almost instantaneous release, makes a strong shot, but probably not an accurate one. At the beginning of the draw you will have fixed your gaze on the mark, both eyes being open. Keep it there, and on no account let it wander. Never glance at or along your shaft, and then back to the mark again; nor look at your arrowhead. If you do, your concentration will go all to pieces and you cannot make a good shot. When you come to full draw you will find that your arrowhead will swim into your field of view (but do not focus on it) quite distinctly enough for you to aim it. Ascham is very insistent on this point. It it a thing that wants a little practice, since it rather goes against one's instinct. But it is not difficult to learn, and once learnt becomes a habit.

HOLDING

This is the moment between the attainment of full draw and the loose; the instant when you co-ordinate your mark and your arrowhead, making any necessary allowances for range and wind. The shorter you can make this moment the better your shot. The longer you hold the more tired both you and the bow become.

Range is the principal thing which is settled by this holding. Before ever you draw at all you will have estimated the range and will have thought where, in relation to the mark, your arrowhead must come. At point-blank range the head will seem to rest on the middle of the mark. Beyond that range it will have to come above it, and your bow-hand will partly or wholly obscure it. This is an 'underhand' shot. Below that range your head will be aimed below the mark; and this is a 'forehand' shot. How much in each case is a matter for you to determine according to the characteristics of your bow and shafts. The variations are much larger than you would expect, particularly at long ranges. Nor is it at all easy to hit something which lies almost at your feet—unless, that is, you break the rules as I have already told you how.

Allowance for a side wind is a chancy business. An arrow is not affected by wind to the extent one might expect, at the short ranges we shall use in hunting. Ascham liked his arrows to spin in a direction contrary to that of the wind: 'If the wynd and the feather go both one way, the shaft will be caryed to much.' Considered in the cold light of science I rather think that the contrary would be more correct; but in any case this is a refinement which may have its uses in target work but clearly is not applicable to our purpose where we shoot in any direction and with whatever arrow happens to be drawn from the quiver. Let us be content with the fact that we can for practical purposes neglect wind, unless it be very strong indeed, up to a range of eighty yards or so.

To sum up: the instant of holding is when you settle all these matters in your mind and adjust your arrowhead accordingly. The more quickly you do it the better.

LOOSING

This is the act of letting the string go; apparently very simple, in reality most difficult to do well.

The fingertips just slide off the string. There must be no backwards pluck, or your arrow will fly into the next county; there must be no weakness, or forward creep, or your arrow will fall short.

With a strong bow the loose is easier to do well than with a weak one: the string is so very ready to tear itself away.

At the loose, there are two things which must *not* happen. The right hand must not move from the anchor-point on the jaw; and the left hand and arm must not move at all. Both should stay in position until the arrow has done its flight. I find the greater difficulty with the bow arm; it requires a conscious effort to remember that, once the bow is drawn and aimed, the left arm has done its job and from that moment takes no part in the proceedings other than as an inert support for the bow. It takes no part in the loose; and it cannot affect the flight of the shaft by being waved about after the arrow has gone. More shots, I think, are spoiled by movement of the bow arm than by any-

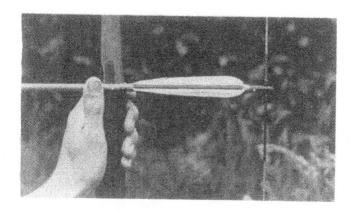

How the Arrow lies

The Mediterranean Release

25. *Position of the Arrow*

Standing and Nocking   Drawing

Holding   Loosing

26. *The Five Points of Shooting*

thing else at all. Keep it still; it is the right hand only which is the active agent at this moment. And let this latter stay against the jaw; do not move it backwards or outwards.

The loose, then, should be imperceptible. Your whole position, both before and after the arrow has gone, should be unaltered until the mark is hit.

When you have perfected your loose you will have done something which no other archer has yet accomplished.

These, then, are the five points. I will not, being a poor archer, presume to go further. Read and mark what Ascham says about them, particularly his insistence on 'cumlinesse'. Do not tie yourself into knots; avoid extravagant and unnecessary postures or motions; shoot plainly and easily, with a bow that is properly under control. And practise at all ranges, known and unknown, and at all kinds of marks, from all kinds of positions. Richard Carew (*Survey of Cornwall*, 1602), in speaking of the skill of Cornish archers, said that they practised at both target and field-shooting; but that the former was 'the first corrupter of archery' through too much precision, and was in earlier times little practised. Only—let your draw be constant, look fixedly at the mark throughout, and do not expect immediate or even quick results. It is a very highly skilled art which you have undertaken to learn. Remember what Philip Sidney said:

'Nothing is achieved before it be thoroughly attempted.'

ASCHAM'S NOTES
The two essentials

> PHI. How manye thynges are required to make a man evermore hyt the marke?
>
> TOX. Twoo.
>
> PHI. Whiche twoo?
>
> TOX. Shotynge streyght and kepynge of a lengthe.

The five points of shooting. 'Standinge, nockinge, drawinge, holdinge, lowsinge, whereby cometh fayre shootinge, which neyther belong to winde nor wether, nor yet to the marke, for in a raine and at no marke, a man may shoote a fayre shote.'

'To marke his standinge, to shoot compasse, to drawe evermore like, to louse everymore like, to consider the nature of the pricke, in hilles and dales, in strayght plaines and winding places, and also to espye his marke.'

'Standing, nocking, drawing, holding, lowsing, done as they should be done, make fayre shootinge. The first point is when a man should shoote, to take such footinge and standinge, as shall be both comely to the eye, and profitable to his use, setting his countenaunce and all the other partes of his bodye after such a behaviour, and port, that both all his strength may be employed to his own most advantage, and his shote made and handled to other mens pleasure and delyte. A man must not go hastely to it, for that is rashnesse, nor yet make to much to do about it, for that is curiosity: the one foote must not stand to far from the other, least he stoupe to much, which is unsemely, nor yet to nere together, least he stande to streyght uppe, for so a man shall neyther use his strength well nor yet stand stedfastlye. The mean betwixt both must be kept, a thinge more pleasaunt to behold when it is done, than easy to be taught how it should be done.'

'To nocke well is the easyest pointe of all and therein is no cunninge, but only diligent heede gevinge, to set his shafte neyther to hye nor to lowe, but even streight overthwharte his bowe. Unconstaunt nockinge maketh a man leese his lengthe. . . . Nocke the cocke fether upward always. . . .'

'Drawinge well is the best part of shootinge. . . . I never redde of other kind of shootinge than drawinge with a mans hand eyther to the breste or eare. . . . Leo the Emperour, would have his soldiours draw quicklye in warre, for that maketh a shaft flye apace. In shootinge at the prickes, hastye and quicke drawinge is neyther sure nor yet comely. Therefore to draw easely and uniformly, that is to say, not wagginge our hand, now upward, now downeward, but always after one fashion, until you come to the rigge or shouldringe of the heade, is best both for profite and seemlinesse.'

'Holding must not be longe, for it both putteth a bowe in jeopardye, and also marreth a mans shote; it must be so litle, that it may be perceyved better in a mans minde, when it is done, than seen with a mans eyes when it is in doinge.'

'Lowsing must be much like. So quicke and harde, that it be without all girdes, so soft and gentle, that the shafte flye not as it were sent out of a bowe case. . . . For clean lowsinge, you must take hede of hitinge any thinge about you.'

Of good style. 'Nothing is brought to the most profitable use, which is not handled after the most comelye fashion . . . the best shootinge is always the most comelye shootinge. . . .'

'But peradventure some men will say, that with use of shootinge a man shall learn to shoote; true it is, he shall learne, but what shall he learne? Mary to shoote noughtlie. For all use, in all thinges, if it be not stayed by cunning, will very easely bring a man to do that thing, whatsoever he goeth about, with much ilfavourednesse and deformitye.'

SHOOTING

'For you see that the stronge men do not draw always the strongest shote, which thinge proveth that drawinge stronge lyeth not so much in the strengthe of man, as in the use of shootinge.'

Of field practice. 'Use of shootinge maketh a man draw stronge, to shoote at most advantage, to keep his gere, which is no small thinge in warre: but yet methincke that the customable shootinge at home, speciallye at buttes and prickes, make nothinge at all for strong shootinge, which doth most good in warre. Therefore, I suppose, that if men should use to go into the fieldes, and learn to shoot mightye stronge shotes, and never care for anye mark at all, they should do much better.'

Of stringing high and low. 'But againe in stringinge your bowe, you must loke for much bende or litle bende, for they be cleane contrarye. The litle bende hath but one commoditye, which is shootinge faster, and farther shoote, and the cause thereof is, because the stringe has so farre a passage, or it part with the shaft. The great bende hath many commodities: for it make the easyer shootinge, the bow being half drawen afore. It needeth no bracer, for the string stoppeth before it come at the arme. It will not so sone hit a mans sleve or other geare, by the same reason. It hurteth not the shaft fether, as the low bend doth. It suffereth a man better to espie his marke. Therefore let your bowe have good bigge bende, a shaftment and two fingers at the least, for these which I have spoken of.'

Of care for your arrow. 'When you have taken good footing, then must you loke at your shaft, that no earth, nor weete, be left upon it, for so should it leese the lengthe. You must loke at the head also, least it should have any stripe at the last shote.'

Look at the mark. 'To loke at your shaft heade at the lowse is the greatest help to kepe a lengthe that can be, which thinge yet hindereth excellente shootinge, because a man cannot shoote straight perfectlye excepte he loke at his marke. . . . The chief cause why men cannot shoot streight, is because they loke at theyr shafte. . . . For having a mans eye always on his marke, is the only waye to shoote streight, yea and, I suppose, so redye and easye a waye, if it be learned in youth, and confirmed with use, that a man shall never miss therein. . . . The diversity of mens standing and drawing causeth divers men loke at theyr mark divers wayes: yet they all leade a mans hand to shoote straight, if nothing els stoppe. So that comlynesse is the only judge of best lokinge at the marke. . . . If a man would leave to loke at his shaft, and learne to loke at his marke, he may use this waye, which a good shooter told me ones that he did. Let him take his bowe on the night, and shoot at two lights, and there he shall be compelled to looke always at his marke, and never at his shafte: this thinge, ones or twice used, will cause him forsake loking at his shafte. Yet let him take hede of setting his shafte in the bowe.'

Of wind. 'The greatest enemye of shootinge is the winde, and the weather, whereby true keping a lengthe is chieflye hindered. . . . Therefore, in shooting, there is as much difference betwixt an archer that is a good wether man, and an other that knoweth and marketh nothinge, as is betwixt a blinde man, and he that can see. Thus, as concerninge the wether, a perfite archer must first learne to knowe the sure flighte of his shaftes, that he may be bould always to trust them. . . . The more uncertain and deceyvable the wynde is, the more heede must a wyse archer geve to know the wyles of it. . . . You must take heede also, if ever you shoote when one of the markes, or both, stands a litle short of a hye wall, for there you may be easely begyled.'

Of faults in shooting. 'All the discommodityes which ill custome hath graffed in archers, can neyther be quickly pulled oute, nor yet soone reckoned of me, there be so many. Some shooteth his head forwarde, as though he would byte the marke; another stareth with his eyes, as though they should flye out; another winketh with one eye and loketh with the other; some make a face with wrything theyr mouth and countenaunce, so, as though they were doinge you wotte what; another blereth out his tongue; another byteth his lippes; another holdeth his necke awrye. In drawing, some set such a compasse, as though they would turne about, and blesse all the field; other heave theyr hand now up now downe, that a man cannot decerne whereat they would shoote: another waggeth the upper end of his bow one way, the nether ende another way. Another will stand pointing his shaft at the marke a good while, and, by and by, he will geve him a whippe, and away or a man witte. Another maketh such a wrestlinge with his gere, as though he were able to shoote no more as longe as he lived. Another draweth softlye to the middes, and, by and by, it is gone you cannot know howe. Another draweth his shaft lowe at the breast, as though he would shoote at a roving marke, and, by and by, he lifteth his arme up pricke heyght. Another maketh a wrynchinge with his backe, as thoughe a man pinched him behinde. Another coureth downe, and layeth out his buttockes, as though he should shoote at crowes. Another setteth forward his left legge, and draweth back with head and shoulders, as thoughe he pulled at a rope, or else were afrayd of the marke. Another draweth his shaft well, until within two fingers of the heade, and then he stayeth a little, to loke at his marke, and, that done, pulleth it up to the head, and lowseth: which waye, although some excellent shooters do use, yet surelye it is a fault, and good mennes faultes are not to be folowed. Some drawe to farre, some to short, some to slowlye, some to quicklye, some hold over longe, some let go over sone. Some sette their shaft on the grounde, and fetcheth him upwarde; another pointeth up toward the skye, and so bringeth him downwardes. Ones I saw a man which used a bracer on his cheke, or else he had scratched all the skinne of the one syde of his face with his drawinge-hande. Another I saw, which, at everye shote, after the loose, lifted up his right legge so far that he was ever in jeopardye of faulinge. Some stampe forwarde, and some leape backward. All these faultes be eyther in the drawinge, or at the loose; with many other also, which you may easelye perceyve, and so go about to avoyde them.

'And afterward, when the shaft is gone, men have many faultes, which evill custome hath brought them to, and especiallye in cryinge after the shaft, and speaking wordes scarce honest for such an honest pastime. Such wordes be very tokens of an ill minde, and manfest signes of a man that is subject to inmeasurable affections. Good mennes eares do abhor them, and an honest man therefore will avoyde them. And besides those which must needes have theyr tongue thus walkinge, other men use other faultes, as some will take theyr bowe and wrythe and wrinch it, to pull in his shaft, when it flyeth wyde, as if he drave a cart. Some will give two or three strydes forwarde, dauncinge and hoppinge after his shaft, as longe as it flyeth, as though he were a madde man. Some, which feare to be to farre gone, runne backwarde, as it were to pull his shafte backe. Another runneth forwarde, when he feareth to be shorte, heaving after his armes, as though he would helpe his shafte to flye. Another wrythes, or runneth asyde, to pull in his shafte straight. One lifteth up his hele and so holdeth his foote still, as long as his shafte flyeth. Another casteth his arme backwarde after the louse. And another swynges his bowe about him, as it were a man with a shafte to make roume in a game place. . . .'

'Of these faultes I have very many myselfe, but I talke not of my shootinge, but of the general nature of shootinge. Now ymagen an archer that is clene without all these faultes, and I am sure every man would be delighted to see him shoote.'

Note that the soles of the feet, and the heels,
are flat on the ground

27. Unorthodox, but useful!

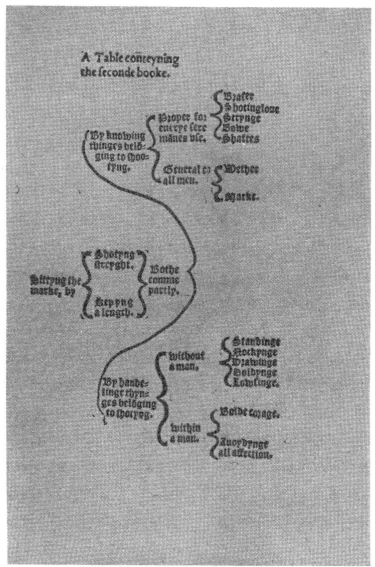

28. *Ascham's Diagram of all that goes to make Perfect Shooting*

Part Three

★

THE ART OF HUNTING WITH
THE BOW AND ARROW

HUNTING WITH THE BOW

'Now therefore take, I pray thee, thy weapons, thy quiver and thy bow, and go out to the field, and take me some venison.'

GENESIS, xxvii, 3.

GENERAL OBSERVATIONS

To anyone who lives in Great Britain the word 'hunting' has only one meaning. It means fox-hunting, with an occasional loosening-up to include the stag and the hare. Everywhere else, as far as I know, it means the chase of anything on this earth, other than fishes. It is in this sense that I use the word here—and you can include fishes too, if you like, since the shooting of them with the bow is nothing new.

The notes that follow are in no sense meant as instruction given by a skilled hunter to the new entry. On the contrary, they represent simply the cogitations of one who has, indeed, some experience of hunting game both large and small, but who is comparatively new to the use of the bow for the purpose. Regard them, if you will, as a disquisition on the elementary principles of getting up to your game, but with particular application to the peculiar and additional difficulties which beset the solitary archer. The notes may, and I hope will, be of some use to the complete novice; the seasoned hunter, the man of experience in these things, will see at once how little has been said, and how much more might have been included had he himself been the writer.

Just as Ascham has left us instructions, from the sixteenth century, on bows and their use for target-shooting, so there are two much older books on hunting with the bow. The first is *The Book of Roi Modus*; the second is the *Livre de Chasse* of Gaston de Foix; and both are of the fourteenth century. The former is much the more informative on our particular subject, and the printed edition of 1486 (which is the one I have used) is illustrated by the most delightfully naïve woodcuts. It seems, therefore, worth while, seeing that they took their hunting very seriously in those days, to include at the end of these notes certain extracts from these old manuals; they are at least entertaining if nothing else, and they are of the age when the bow was in its prime.

THE ART OF HUNTING WITH THE BOW AND ARROW

And now to our subject. First of all, let us try to visualize what we are about when we set forth after game with our bow and arrows.

The fox-, stag-, and hare-hunters, the shooters of pheasants and partridges, all pursue their object with energy, noise, a complete absence of concealment, and usually with a great company. They do actually pursue it; they go after it, literally, and it is the exhaustion of the beast they chase, or the forcing of it to go in a given direction, that enables them to do what they want.

We, as archers, must go to work quite differently; it is no use our 'chasing' in the ordinary sense. It is true that the ancient Assyrians in chariots, and the more modern North American Indian on horseback, used to chase lions and buffalo respectively; but that is not for us. No beasts of this formidable character live in these islands; even the last dragon has gone; so let us not dwell on the matter further.

We do not chase; the method that we must use is generally known, in America at any rate, as the 'Still-Hunt'. Still-hunting is woods hunting; and since an archer must come very close to his game, it is in woodland that he has most chance of success.

Stalking, by which I mean the careful approach to game in the open, is not ruled out by any means. Pope recounts the amazing feat of one of his friends who actually got up to within eighty yards of a Bighorn sheep in the Rockies, on a bare rock slope, and shot him dead. As I have no experience of this sort of thing (except for rabbits), I shall say no more, except that nothing would please me more than to have a chance of trying the method on red deer. To shoot the 'Great Hart' with an arrow, in the open, would represent the pinnacle of stalking skill; and some of my deer-stalking friends have told me that they do not think it impossible.

The thing that distinguishes still-hunting from all other forms is that you do not run after your game; at most you move very slowly and quietly; at best you let the game come to you. The underlying principle is very simple. All wild creatures are mortally afraid of Man; therefore, you must so act that they neither hear you, nor smell you, nor recognize you for what you are, even though you may actually be in plain view. Simple to describe, but abominably difficult to do.

A friend of mine said to me, not long ago, that it was an astonishing thing that a certain large wood held no grey squirrels, while there were plenty along the road leading up to it. Now, as a matter of fact that wood swarms with the little beasts. Why, then, the assertion of my friend, who is a keen shooter with the gun and sportsman generally? The answer, of course, is that the road-

From Gaston de Foix's *Livre de Chasse*

From Life. A German 20-pointer

29. *THe Great Hart*

eur· Item et quant au cerfz se tu laisse aller tes leureirs a lencontre il
est si royde de puissance et hault sur iambes et si fort de soy que a paine la
procheront Et pource doit on laisser aller au coste Au sanglier et a noy/
res bestes qui laisseroit aller a lencontre au sanglier par especial il sarre
stes et les atend et si come il vient ilz biennent·il les trespe pource las
se len aller apres le cul car aussi sont ce bestes que pores et truyes qui ne
vont mye toust Ainsi vous auons reduit et truise le reduit royal

Aprencis demande ce on fait ainsi tous buissons pour toutes
aultres bestes Modus dist nennil se ne sont pour les cerfz et
pour les loups Esquieulx chapitres vous sera dit et monstre
par raison aulcuns exemples qui sont bien a retenir Qui veult prendre
les loups a buissonner le tamps est la fin du moys de feureir et est le temps
ilz sont reparty de gestoire et de challeur pour quoy ilz sont familieux
Car tant come ilz sont en gestoire ilz menguent pou ou niant a pour les
assembler a vng buisson ou lon les veult prandre et deffrandre leur fault
donner a menger en ceste maniere Tu dois regarder es boys ou loups
hantet ou buissons fois des boys et cest pais auquel il aist eaue dedas
ainsi comme vng mare ou flacie ou il puissant boyre Puis prents vne

e ij

side squirrels have no fear of a car, which has never been known to molest them; while the woodland squirrels are terrified at the apparition of Man, who has.

The moral of which is that you will see very little by just walking through a wood.

Your approach has been seen, heard, or smelt by all the rightful inhabitants long before you come up to where they were then; and they have all taken 'avoiding action'. This does not necessarily mean that they have fled. On the contrary, your squirrel, to keep to our example, is still in his tree, at the back of a limb, motionless, watching you intently; and if you continue your walk you will never have known it. But stop and sit down nearby in some inconspicuous place. Wait, quite still, for twenty minutes or so, and your squirrel, forgetting his earlier fright, and seeing nothing but a motionless if rather unfamiliar lump on that log over there, will reappear; and after a moment or two's hesitation, will resume his daily affairs.

Let us consider this matter in analytical fashion. Every wild creature is ruled by four emotions, or senses, or whatever the correct word is. These are Fear, Hunger, Curiosity, and Sex.

Man, in hunting the creature, can turn these feelings to account; but, in doing so, he is countered by the beast's three powerful defences. These are the Ear, the Eye, and the Nose; perhaps also Form and Colour, although naturalists dispute hotly about the last. All game animals do not have these defences equally well developed. But it is not safe to rely on this, as an archer has to approach so close. Much better assume that everything is in first-class working order, as it most likely is.

By comparison, Man has let his equipment go all to pieces. His emotions are much the same, and he has others; but his defences are, in contrast, almost non-existent, at all events in communities which, oddly enough, call themselves 'civilized'.

When, therefore, Civilized Man enters a wood he is from that moment at a disadvantage. He can be heard, but cannot himself hear the listener; he can be smelt, but cannot smell out where the game lies; he can be seen, but cannot see the observer. Against these heavy handicaps he would be helpless were it not that he has a gift which his game has not. This is his power of conscious Thought. Knowing his deficiencies, Man *thinks* how to supplement his poor senses by care or stratagem. I do not for one moment deny to animals the power of thought, but Man's process is so far more highly developed as to make theirs insignificant by comparison. So we will think here for a little, and see what conclusions we reach.

THE ART OF HUNTING WITH THE BOW AND ARROW

Our problem divides itself into two parts; first, how to make use of the wild thing's emotions; and second, how to avoid or nullify its defences.

Fear we shall not make use of, unless one archer be driving game to another, which is not what we are considering. On the contrary, our whole aim in the still-hunt is to avoid alarm of any kind.

Hunger, also, is not a thing upon which we want to play. If you put down raisins to attract pheasants, or corn for deer, and then lie in wait, certainly your game will come. So will a weasel to a baited trap; but nobody would call that sport. No; the deliberate putting-down of bait we will rule out; but it is quite a proper thing, in my view, to lie up for a beast at the edge of his normal feeding-ground. That presupposes some skill, care, and observation on your part, and comes within the rules which we impose upon ourselves.

Curiosity is a well-marked trait in many creatures. No one who has ever pitched his tent in a field of cows needs be told this. So long as an object cannot be identified without doubt as a man, anything strange is likely to attract notice at once. If it moves oddly, but not alarmingly, it may even induce the watcher to come nearer for a better view. I have read, for instance, but never tried it myself, that deer can be attracted by fixing a bunch of grass to one's head, and bobbing up and down behind a bush which conceals one's body; and I know the shore-shooter can attract curlew within shot by waving a sheet of brown paper.

Two examples from Canada will illustrate the point.

Some years ago I was fishing in the St. Mary's River in Nova Scotia. It was a lovely morning in early summer, and I was in the river, fairly deep but close to the bank. I had risen nothing except trout, and feeling rather bored let my gaze wander downstream. About three hundred yards away I saw a couple of white-tailed deer. Between them and me was a completely open 'meadow', a long flat of lush grass. I kept my eye on them, and after a little they saw me. They decided that what they saw was nothing to worry about, but obviously they'd like to know what it was; and they fed on towards me, looking up every now and then. Each time they seemed reassured. Finally they came so close that I could, literally, have touched them with my rod. It was a wonderful and beautiful experience. They stood and gazed, and fed on past me quite unconcernedly; and I watched them out of the corner of my eye.

It was not till I moved that they took flight, and sailed off in glorious leaps.

Now why? The wind, of course, must have been from them to me. Man does not usually stand in a river. Man has two legs, and this apparently had none. That long thing sticking up at the side (my rod) looks something like the top of a sapling. It does not move. Funny we haven't noticed that tree-stump in the river there before!

The second occasion was on the other side of Canada, in the north-west of Alberta in the foothills of the Rockies. We were setting out for the mountains, seven mounted men and eight loaded packhorses. Just as we had started, and were a few hundred yards on the trail, out came a pair of mule-deer. They stood and looked at·us quite calmly, not the least nervous, and curious as to what all this cavalcade was doing.

Not until someone cried out did they leap vertically into the air, and off like the wind.

Now why, again? Horses, of course. And horses, even if they do have queer lumps on their backs, are harmless; they're always grazing round here somewhere. Not till Man made himself known by his voice did these lovely creatures take fright.

The common hare will give you an example of curiosity almost any time you meet one. If you put up a hare, and she goes off (why is a hare always 'she'?), whistle when she is a little way off. The odds are that she will stop, turn round, and look to see where that queer noise is coming from. That instant is your chance.

You cannot do this with a rabbit. But if you are good at making the squealing noise of a rabbit in distress others will come to find out what it is all about. So will those who hope to profit by it—the fox, the stoat, and the weasel.

Sex is an emotion which can only be played upon in the mating season. Every boy has read about calling for moose. The hunter makes a trumpet of birch-bark, and with it imitates the call of the cow. Another method is based upon the habit of the bull moose of thrashing about in the bushes with his antlers. So you do the same with a stick. He hears a rival, as he thinks, and will come to polish him off. Roedeer, which are very numerous and widely-distributed in England, can be called by bleating like a doe through a piece of wheat straw fashioned into a 'reed' such as many musical instruments have. I should think fallow deer would also respond to this, but cannot say so·for certain. If you should try this, remember, that the buck is as likely to approach you from behind as from the front, and will certainly circle to get your wind as he gets near. It is as well to remember, also, that any buck, even the roe, is liable to be dangerous during the rut. He is then bold, defiant, and looking for trouble. His mind is set on one thing, and one thing only; and rivals, or anything that looks in the least like one, are not to be tolerated. This, then, is the opportunity for exciting his curiosity.

The hare, when intent on matrimony, goes quite mad, and, if pursuing a doe, will take no notice of you at all. I once saw three bucks and one doe all together. They chased round and round in a small circle, about twenty yards away, till I felt quite giddy.

I neither like nor advocate this hunting in the mating season, and merely give you a fact or two about it. You will, of course, be restricted by, and obey, the Game Laws of whatever country you hunt in.

So much for the mind of the game. Now just a little about its equipment. The *Ear* in animals is an incredibly efficient instrument. Three things you must avoid. Talking, coughing, and sneezing, of course; noise in making your way through the brush; and cracking sticks underfoot.

Man is ideally equipped by nature for going silently, if only he goes naked. His skin makes no noise against the twigs and branches, his feet fall without sound and can feel everything underneath that might crack. The colour of a 'white' man is somewhat against him, but the sun can soon cure that. Never have I seen such a beautiful thing as the rich golden-copper colour of the men working on the beaches of Normandy in 1944. They had been exposed to the sun and wind for weeks, and their tan was such as any Red Indian might have envied. But white men have been taught that their bodies are an offence, even though God made them, and cover them up; and, anyway, our English climate does not encourage nakedness. So it becomes important that this covering shall be of suitable material.

Wear the skin of something else if you like; that is, leather or buckskin. that will be fine as long as the weather is good, but when you get wet you will look and feel as slippery and as clammy as an eel. It is not nice then; and one is so often wet.

Cotton, unless it be soft, like a shirt, is noisy against the brush. All rucksacks that I know of are of hard-woven cotton, and this is the one real disadvantage of carrying your kit in one.

On all counts wool is the best; good homespun for a jacket and flannel for trousers. The short type of 'battle dress' blouse is good, and does not catch in things. Trousers, although not very romantic, are much more practical than breeches of any sort, particularly in camp. They are not tight round the knee, nor so uncomfortable when wet.

As for your feet, rubber soles or rubber boots are moderately quiet but take away all feeling for what is underfoot. If you really want to get as nearly as possible to the feeling of bare feet, and go silently without breaking twigs, wear moccasins. The real article is of moosehide or thick buckskin; but if you can't get this, then I should say that ordinary soft chrome-tanned leather, which does not go hard after a wetting, would do just as well. With moccasins that have no hard sole attached, as some do, you can go in absolute silence, and feel your way almost by touch alone. The drawback is that your feet will always be wet if the ground is at all damp; but that makes no odds so long as you keep on the move and don't let yourself get cold.

In moving through brush, go slowly, and watch where you put your feet. Bend under branches, or push them out of the way quietly with a hand. In going through brambles, lift your foot up and tread on them. Avoid muddy places, which are liable to produce loud squelching noises; and dry leaves, which, especially if frozen, make it quite impossible to hunt quietly.

For quiet shooting, bind a thick piece of buckskin round the bow where the arrow passes, or fit a buckskin arrow-plate in place of the more usual bit of fibre or horn. It is also said to be a good thing to bind some fur round the bow, just below the nocks, to avoid the snap of the string against the wood as the bow straightens. With a reflexed bow this may be so, but I have not found it necessary with the ordinary type.

As you move, the arrows in your quiver will rustle loudly one against the other. Keep a hand on them to stop this.

If, in spite of all your care, you do make a sudden loud noise, stop, and stay stopped for several minutes. The things you have frightened may by then have recovered their equanimity.

And while you are thus going carefully and quietly, and slowly, hoping to avoid being heard, listen yourself. Sometimes it is easier to hear game than to see it.

As to the *Eye*, and being seen, there is little to be said that is not obvious. A man looking like a man is a sight that no truly wild animal will stay to investigate, unless it feels aggressive. But a man looking like a hummock or a tree stump, or just a piece of a man, is a different matter and may promote investigation. The most difficult thing in the world is to see before you are seen. Lt.-Col. Townsend Whelen, in his delightful book,[1] describes how he used to train himself by going out with his dog, trying to spot the things that the dog saw so often and so quickly. After a course of this he says that his observation improved enormously. Certainly I know myself what a tremendous help a dog can be in seeing things. His behaviour and direction will tell you where to look. But he must be a dog that knows his business, one that will keep as quiet as yourself, even in the most trying and exciting circumstances. Any other kind will spoil your hunt.

If you see game before it sees you, you have a rare advantage.

If you sit down, and stay still, in some likely and convenient place you are

[1] *Wilderness Hunting and Wildcraft*, S.A.T.P. Co., Marshallton, Delaware, 1927.

more likely to see before being seen than if you move about. But unless you are more or less in cover as well, you will give yourself away when you prepare to shoot.

If you are seen first, you will not know that it has happened, and you are not likely ever to see that particular animal at all. But if it should still be looking at you when you spot it, try not to let your eyes meet directly. An animal that thinks it has not been seen may stay to watch you further; but if it knows it is being looked at it will go at once. Try this on the next squirrel you meet. It is quite easy physically, but most tantalizing mentally, to pretend you are not looking at an animal, and all the time to watch him out of the corner of your eye. If, at the same time, you seize any opportunity to advance, do so diagonally, not directly, and you may get within range. It was by this method, and by advancing mainly when it was out of sight behind a ridge, that the bighorn ram was shot.

Avoid sudden movements; they catch the eye too readily.

As to disguise, we all know the value of camouflage. Let your clothes be of such a colour that they blend with the surroundings, but lighter rather than darker if there is any choice. Let the back of your bow, if it has a vellum backing, be broken up with colour, so that it does not show as a long, white, disturbing streak; and cover up the feathers of your arrows if they are conspicuous. I believe one could gain immense advantage by painting the face and hands, but I have never had the courage to do it. Certainly it pays, when waiting with a gun under a tree for pigeons, to shoot through a mask with eyeholes. Even the best-looking of us has a face which stands out in the woods like a full moon!

Train yourself, then, to see quickly, remembering that you will seldom see the whole of an animal at once, and that it is not likely to be in the picture-book attitude unless it has already seen you. And train yourself, also, to keep out of sight. Both are equally important—and difficult.

In the matter of *Nose*, Man is not a competitor at all. It is occasionally possible to smell game, if very close indeed; but in general one can say that Man's nose is quite useless to him. To an animal, on the other hand, loss of his powers of scent would be an irreparable and shattering calamity. His nose is his principle defence, far more so, I think, than his ears, and certainly, in close country at any rate, more than his eyes. The degree to which the power of scent is developed is amazing. One can imagine without great difficulty that a fox might leave such strong traces of his passage as to enable hounds to follow easily, although it is outside our own range of physical comprehension; but what shall we say of the ability of a retriever to follow a runner pheasant through a field of wet roots? Or of a bloodhound who will track and find a man over miles of country simply on the strength of a preliminary sniff at an old piece of his clothing? The power is beyond us to understand. When, therefore, you enter a wood, or indeed go hunting anywhere else, you advertise yourself loudly and inevitably to every creature down-wind of you for hundreds of yards. I say every creature, but whether birds have any power of scent I do not know. It follows that you must know the direction of the wind, the general direction that is, and hunt against it. If the wind is very light, you can discover its trend by throwing up a little dust, or some small bits of dry grass, or by watching your tobacco smoke. Wind is, however, a fitful thing, easily deflected by obstacles of any sort, and by variations in the contour of the ground. It then forms eddies, the behaviour of which cannot be predicted. Thus, unless you know your ground intimately, you may be caught out. In a really dense wood there will be little or no wind, however hard it may blow outside. There will, nevertheless, be a slow drift; and if you are moving, you may be able to keep pace with your own scent. Here, again, the smoke from your pipe will tell you whether you are doing this or not. I do not believe there is any harm in smoking while hunting. Tobacco has a strong smell, certainly, but it has not the terrifying smell of Man, and it cannot travel farther or faster than the latter, since scent is air-borne. I think the prejudice against smoking, where it exists, is due to a confusion of ideas. The danger of setting the woods alight is quite another matter, in which one cannot be too careful.

Scent has a tendency to rise. If, therefore, you can get above your game you may have some advantage.

One other point, which may be useful if you are attempting to follow up, say, a deer, particularly a wounded one. The procedure is the same whether you yourself are trying to track, as in snow, or whether you are using a dog to help you. Imagine you are going along a trail with the wind on your left. Your game, if wounded, is likely to want to lie down, and will turn off the trail to do so. He will turn to the down-wind side, i.e. to the right, go into the thicket a little way, then back parallel with the trail, and finally circle almost up to the trail again, where he will make his couch. Now, as you come along, you will pass close to him in his hiding-place, and he will have ample warning long before you have puzzled out his back-circle. So, instead of keeping religiously to the trail, reverse his procedure. Strike off to the right and into the rough a little, make a loop in the forward direction, and come up to the trail again. Keep on doing this, and you are likely to take him in the rear in spite of his ruse if you go quietly enough.

THE ART OF HUNTING WITH THE BOW AND ARROW

Apart from the emotions and the senses there is one other matter that has to be considered, unless one is content to hunt haphazardly.

Habit is as much ingrained in animals as it is in Man. Consider a city. Here the inhabitants go about their daily business in accordance with a plan—or at any rate think they do. They have their homes, their places of business, and their well-established routes between them. They have their eating and drinking places, and their parks and open places where they can sun and enjoy themselves. Their movements take place at regular hours, and Smith will always be found at his quick-lunch bar at one o'clock and hurrying to catch the 5.30 in the evening.

It is exactly the same with the wild things; not quite so rigid and humdrum perhaps, but nevertheless very similar. The wild creatures of a wood, or of a district, are not just scattered about at random. They work to a plan, too. The grey squirrel that you see running through the tree-tops is not just exercising himself. He is on his way to his winter nut-store, buried in a sunny bank at the edge of the wood. When he has got his ration, he will return to his home; and his route will be by exactly the same branches, twig for twig, as those he used on his outward journey. That rabbit is using his well-defined run through the undergrowth, and will come back along it sooner or later. Those pigeons that you see, flying home over there, will roost in that ivy-covered oak night after night, and will arrive at a fairly regular hour. The ducks that flight in from the salt marshes will always fly over that point of land there if there is nothing to put them off. Did you rouse a roebuck from that warm corner in the angle at the edge of the pine plantation? That is his regular sunning-place.

All these creatures have their habits, their roads and tracks, their feeding- and drinking-places, their playgrounds, and their homes. Making proper allowance for their kind, they lead regular, if not blameless, lives.

If you wish to hunt intelligently and successfully, you must make it your business to find out all these things; and you will find it fascinatingly interesting. Read up your natural history, and apply to your own ground the lessons learnt. Once you realize that all the creatures you meet are on business, and not, or seldom, just taking the air, you can really begin to plan your hunting. It is the absence of this 'local knowledge' which makes it so difficult when you go to a strange territory. Should you do this, remember the military maxim: 'Time spent in reconnaissance is seldom wasted.'

Apart from these questions of place, there is also time to consider. Game moves at more or less regular times, and favours the very early morning, the very late afternoon, and, of course, the night. You cannot shoot in the dark (but you can in bright moonlight), so that dawn and dusk are your proper times. If you are in position then, at the proper place which your observations have recommended to you, you will be hunting intelligently, and will have much more chance of success than will come from any casual invasion of a wood or other hunting-ground.

An archer must be a naturalist first, and a shooter second, if he is to fill his bag.

The actual act of *shooting* requires a little consideration, and some revision of ideas if a rifle has been the weapon used previously.

Range, of course, is very much reduced. In the open, your effective range for any game, is not likely to exceed eighty yards. In the wood it will be much less. Not that the arrow will not kill at greater distances; it will, up to the limit of its flight. But you cannot hit with certainty, and therefore will not shoot. It is not range so much as the restricted 'field of fire' which is the principal difficulty. With a rifle, at say eighty yards, you can shoot between two close branches or through a hole in the bushes thirty or forty yards away; or take aim at a head, or a shoulder, that just shows through a small gap. You know that the rise of your bullet above the line of sight will be inappreciable at this distance, less than an inch, probably. With an arrow, the corresponding rise is a matter of feet, six or twelve of them according to your tackle. The arrow requires more space, and plenty of it, in a vertical direction; much more, usually, than you would think. There is, therefore, no sense in hunting where the growth is too thick, or in hiding-up in a place overhung with branches.

Once I lost a roebuck through this. I had lain in wait in a plantation of young larches for the better part of a long, cold winter's day, with snow on the ground. In front of me was a corridor between the trees, straight and clear as I thought. Towards evening the buck suddenly appeared in this, tail towards me. Suspecting something, he jumped round and faced me. I was squatting partly hidden by a ditch, and he could not quite make me out, although the distance was only forty yards or so. As I rose, with infinite care and very slowly, drawing my bow as I did so, he advanced a pace or two and stamped. Then I loosed. My shaft flew—and glanced against one small, unnoticed twig, projecting across the path, sailing high over the buck's head. He vanished. I shall never forget. It was my first shot at a buck, and the memory of it is burnt into me.

Familiarize yourself, then, with the trajectory of your shafts at various ranges, and get the hang of things by shooting practice in an actual wood.

It is a great advantage to be able to shoot from a squatting position, both to diminish the effect of the high trajectory and to improve concealment.

THE ART OF HUNTING WITH THE BOW AND ARROW

There is nothing difficult in it, provided that your bow is short enough (as it can easily be), and that you are limber enough to be able to get right down on your heels. The soles of the feet must be flat on the ground, firmly. It is impossible to be effective if you are just perched precariously on the forepart of your feet. You can have no control over anything in that position. Kneeling is just as good; right knee on the ground, left knee up. The drawback is that a wet knee is an abomination.

Talking of squatting reminds me that I find it much more convenient to carry the quiver slung at the left hip. The usual place is on the other side; from which position, when you want to extract an arrow, it is necessary to wave the whole of the right arm in the air, away from the body, as you do it. And, moreover, the arrow comes up on the wrong side of the bow. Slung on the left, the arrow-nocks are comfortably to hand, particularly when squatting, and a shaft can be withdrawn easily and without any exposure of the arm. And the arrow comes up on the proper side, and can be nocked at once. Choose whichever suits you best; but try my way. I am sure it has advantages.

The bow you will carry in the left hand, pointing fore and aft, braced, back down and string up, with an arrow on the string ready for use. The arrow is kept in place by pressing it against the bow with the left forefinger. The left hand can also keep the arrows in the quiver quiet as you move, leaving the right free for moving branches, or anything else.

In your quiver there will be big broadheads for deer and large game of that sort, smaller ones for little creatures, and perhaps some blunt points for birds; a dozen or more in all. The different colours of the nocks will indicate which is which.

On your back is your rucksack with all your sundry gear in it—knife, hatchet, repair kit, and so forth. Have nothing dangling round the waist if you can help it.

As to what you can shoot, the answer is—anything; provided there are no elephants in your parish. Their hide is, so I understand, too tough for proper penetration. For ordinary thin-skinned game, the broadhead arrow is, within its range, fully as good a killer as the heaviest bullet ever made. But (and this is a substantial fly in the ointment) it is by no means as good a stopper. The arrow will kill, but it will not roll a beast over by main force, nor daze him with shock. Pope found this out with both bear and lion; and, without the timely assistance of a friend with a gun, might not have lived to tell his tale. He had, nevertheless, the courage to continue to shoot bears, including many grizzlies, and that gives us the measure of the man.

The traditional target of the English archer is the deer, and there are plenty of these wild in England to-day if you know where to go, and can get permission to hunt. At the end of this chapter there is a table which shows, very roughly, the present distribution of the various species of deer in England. The information from which this was compiled came from an article by Mr. Gerald Johnstone, published in the *Field* not long ago; and I am indebted to that newspaper for leave to make use of it here.

Regarding more humble sport, as a word of encouragement for you (and me), let it be recorded that Maurice Thompson, the American archer of the eighteen-seventies and eighties, used to shoot duck on the wing.

The above brief and elementary notes were written not long after I had begun to use the bow. They are the joint result of a considerable previous experience of the woods, armchair reasoning, and practical experiment. The practice of what they preach enabled me then successfully and often to come within range of deer, hares, and rabbits. Since that time many things have happened in the world, and matters other than archery have clamoured for attention. I cannot show you a picture of a brace of tigers shot with arrows, nor even of a buck. That is, however, no reason why you should not show me yours in due course. I shall, nevertheless, continue to hope that I may yet get in first.

'THE BOOK OF ROI MODUS'

This is a fourteenth-century work, to whose existence my attention was drawn by that entrancing book, *Bridleways through History*, by Lady Apsley.[1] This merely gives *Roi Modus* cursory mention; but there is a much fuller notice in Hansard's *The Book of Archery*, 1841, where the author has translated much of the part relating specifically to archery. This translation I have compared with the printed edition of 1486; and, although we differ in the rendering of certain minor matters (the old French is exceedingly obscure in places, and the printing is none too good), the general sense is not in doubt.

I cannot tell you who Roi Modus was (or was supposed to be), nor anything about his Queen Racio; that would entail a research outside the scope of these notes, although I should guess that they represent King Method and Queen Reason. But the author of the book was either Henri de Vergy, Seigneur de la Fère, or else one Henri Ferrières. Whichever it was, the manuscript was written at the beginning of the fourteenth century. It is a curious work, seemingly in two parts; the one dealing with hunting, the other with devotional matter. Archery is given a good place, although more from the

[1] Hutchinson & Co., Ltd., 1936.

point of view of hunting methods than of the handling of the bow. The numerous and delightful illustrations show clearly that the beasts of those days placed a high degree of trust in the intentions of the hunter; and that, even when hit, they displayed rather a well-bred surprise that such brusquerie should be possible than any sign of alarm or injury! It is also noteworthy that all the archers are left-handed. Or can it be that the wood-engraver found it easier to cut his blocks the right way round rather than go to the trouble of reversing the picture?

The title is: *Le liure du roy modus et de la Royne racio le quel fait mencion comant on doit deuiser de toutes manieres de chasses*; and it gives detailed instruction on the hunting and taking of all manner of beasts and fowl.

The chapter devoted to archery begins with a list of those things which a 'master of archery' should have or know. These are:

A silk string, which is stronger and more durable than that made of any other material; when well-made is more deadly in that it can cast a longer and heavier shaft, so giving a harder blow; and can be made any thickness to suit the archer.

A bow of a length, between nocks, of 22 'poñies'. This is evidently '*poignée*', a handful; and thus a delightfully vague measure. All we can deduce is that the bow was not less than 5 ft. 6 in. long. It would be a very small fist that was less than 3 in. broad.

An arrow of a length, from nocks to barbs, of 10 'poñies'; which, to my mind, settles the length of the unit as 3 in., since no arrow, if drawn to the head (as it was) can be much more than 30 in. long.

A light arrowhead, and low-cut feathers; but longer and higher-cut feathers for a heavy head. The barbs to be in the plane of the nock.

The distance between bow and string to be a full palm's width and two fingers.

The bow to be held in the left hand; the draw to be made with the right, using three fingers as in the Mediterranean release.

The arrow to be set properly on the bow, with the cock feather outwards; straight shooting is not possible otherwise.

He also mentions various other things, equally practical. An archer must never be without a file, and must keep his arrowheads really sharp. He should always carry a spare string; should dress in clothes of a colour to match the woods; and should have a well-trained dog.

He divides the methods of hunting broadly into two; hunting from a 'hide' ('*a fust*'), when the game is driven to the archer; and at view ('*a veue*'), which corresponds to the still-hunt. It is recommended that the bow for the former be a weak one; since, if it is not, the effort of drawing will attract the attention of the game. Moreover, the archer will be unable to hold his bow drawn, as is apparently correct form during the drive, and his aim will be unsteady. The strong bow is all right for the stalk, since the shot will be taken from a much greater distance and there is no need to draw until it is actually intended to shoot.

He recommends that you let your game pass you, if possible, before you loose. The arrow will do much more damage if it enters diagonally rather than straight through. There are three other reasons; the first, that the deer will probably give a bound as he sees the archer; the second, that the archer will probably jump as he sees the deer; and the third, that it makes it easier to allow for the speed of the deer. If the deer comes straight at you, then, of course, you will aim directly at the chest.

If a beast is only wounded, a good deal of information can be got from an examination of the blood trail. Dark-red and frothy blood is a good sign, and denotes a quick death. If it is clear, with some bubbles, but no froth, then you have hit a bone, and your beast will not die. If there are traces of food in the blood, and not much of the latter, then you have hit in the belly; in such a case, let the beast lie quietly for some considerable time, and then track him when his wound has stiffened up.

There is then a detailed list of the effects of various sorts of hit. Condensed, and put into order, we see that: instant death follows on a hit low down behind the shoulders, or through the neck if the big veins or arteries are cut. The following are also fatal, in more or less time according to their place: in the loins, in the ribs near the shoulders, between the neck and shoulder, through the shoulders, in the neck at three fingers from the shoulder, frontally in the chest, and between the thighs near the vent. A hit between two joints of the spine will make the beast fall, but he will not die of it. Nor will he die from a hit far back in the flanks (in which case you will have a long chase after him), in the middle of the neck, in the buttocks, or high up in the shoulders.

Three methods are given where a company of archers is to hunt together. The first is the ordinary beat, with or without hounds or dogs, and differs in no way from what we should expect nowadays. But there must always be one dog present who can follow a blood-trail. The others are the use of a stalking-horse, and the employment of a cart as cover.

Perhaps 'stalking-horse' is not quite the correct term, since no close approach to the game is made by means of it. The idea is this. Two mounted men (not more, or the game will become suspicious) ride along slowly, one behind the other; the archers who are to do the shooting huddle together and walk in the cover of the horses' bodies, with their bows strung, until they get down-wind of the game. At this point the archers drop off, one by one, and remain posted in their several places, as shown them by one of the men on horseback, strung out along an arc of some length and well concealed. If there are any 'non-combatants', so to speak, these are also posted in hides, but not so well concealed as the archers. The horsemen then return the way they came; and when the game is between them and the archers, they ride towards it and put it up. The 'non-combatants' should now show themselves, so that the game avoids them and runs into the archers instead.

The method which employs a cart is said to be better than this. Deer have little fear of a cart; they see it frequently fetching timber from the forest. So rig one up with a lot of green branches, and let the archers get in and conceal themselves behind this screen. Then drive up into deer country. The whole point of the ruse is, however, that the wheels of the cart must squeak! Apparently the deer are attracted by the noise, and come to investigate. I am not quite sure of the translation here. Roi Modus says that, when they hear this noise, they '*musent voulentiers*'; and '*muser*' may mean either 'to wander about aimlessly', or 'to begin the rut'. Anyway, the noise is effective in bring-ing them within bowshot, and that is the idea. The modern method of mur-dering game from the shelter of a motor-car has apparently a long and highly respectable ancestry!

Several methods suitable for the solitary archer are then given. One can hunt '*a veue*', the still-hunt, either on foot or on horseback. There are two variations of the mounted method.

One can either walk close up to another man on horseback, and, when well-positioned, stop and draw; in which case the attention of the game will be attracted to the horseman: or one can ride the horse oneself. A peaceable animal is essential, one which will stop and stand still when required. Also, one must use a weakish bow, carried strung and with an arrow on the string in the left hand, reins in the right. When game is viewed, circle round it quickly, at a fair distance, moving only when it has its head down. Proceed in this way until you get within shot, select your beast, and let drive. Only, put your horse into such a position that you can shoot to the rear, not side-ways, nor to the front. To do this comfortably, see that your left stirrup-leather is a little shorter than the other, and make use of it to support yourself as you draw.

On foot, which is called shooting '*a guet*' (on the alert), and which I am unable to distinguish, by the description, from the method '*a veue*', the archer must go very early in the morning, alone, and up-wind. The best time is mid-

August to mid-September, when the rut will be on. If one goes earlier in the season than this, the game will be very hard to find. Work from one vantage-point to another, and make use of any overgrown rides that there may be. On no account must you be seen. Every scrap of cover, and every gust of wind, should be taken advantage of. If the beast can be seen, only move when his head is down. A bunch of green leaves held in the mouth will conceal the face. Wild, wet weather is the best time for this; deer are then afoot, and the archer has more chance of escaping detection. When you come within bow-shot, rise from your cover and loose; or, if your bow is both short and weak enough, you can shoot from one knee. Two fighting stags can be approached without any difficulty at all.

Stalking can be successfully done in high, open timber in a good game country. For this you must paint a representation of a hind on a large piece of cloth, and carry it in front of you extended on two poles. Use it as cover as you advance from tree to tree. When you get within range, stick the poles in the ground, and shoot over the top. The cloth has two eye-holes through which you look as you go.

A method of shooting by moonlight is also described. This you do in April and May, when the game is feeding in the fields. Note the trails by which they come to the fields from the woods, and make a hide at the woodland end of one of them. Go to this hide two or three hours before daybreak. There must be a good moon, and you must keep well down yourself. This is a very good method.

So much for deer; now for wild boar. The idea here is to shoot them while they are wallowing in the mud; 'au suel', at soil. This is a job for a solitary archer, and the best time for it is mid-October to the end of November. Find a wallow which is surrounded with bushes and small trees. In one of these make a hide some two feet off the ground, so that your scent will be above the boar's level. As you go to this hide for the actual shooting, be careful of the wind; otherwise pig at a distance will wind you and fail to put in an appearance where you want them. Besides pig, all sorts of creatures will arrive at a place like this.

Finally, in April an archer can get plenty of amusement shooting hares in their form, 'aux tasses'. The hares are then in the young corn; and you should go on horseback, with a varlet on foot leading a greyhound or two. When you have spotted a hare, place the hounds where she can see them, and then make a circuit on your horse. The hare will keep her attention riveted on the hounds, and you can approach from behind as close as you like. Use a weak bow, and don't stop the horse to shoot. Alternatively, you can go on foot, following close on a mounted man. On seeing a hare, he goes on while you stop and shoot.

This concludes the instruction on archery, and King Modus gives place to Queen Racio. She divides beasts into two classes: *'bestes doulces'* and *'bestes puantes'*, i.e. those which do not smell and those which do. The former are the stag (red deer) and his hind, the fallow buck, the roebuck, and the hare. These are nice beasts because they have no unpleasant smell, are of a jolly yellowish-brown and white colour, and do not bite. The others, those that stink, 'like the people at present in this world', are the wild boar and his sow, the wolf, the fox, and (I am sorry to say) the otter. All their alleged vices are given in detail; the boar, for example, representing the Ten Commandments of Antichrist, and the wolf the Seven Deadly Sins. It is all very entertaining, but has, I fear, little bearing on our subject.

The book was first printed by Anthoine Neyret, at Chambery, in 1486. Judging it as a whole, and by the above extracts in particular, there can be no doubt that the author had practised what he wrote. It is full of good woodcraft and common sense, and gives a very clear impression of what hunting was like in those far-off days.

'LE LIVRE DE CHASSE'

This is the ordinarily used name for the book on hunting written by Gaston III, Comte de Foix, nicknamed Phoebus. Its full title is *'Deduits de la chasse des Bestes sauvaiges et des Oyseaux de proie'*, and it was begun in 1387.

Gaston was a celebrated member of the great house of Foix; handsome, open, and jovial—hence the nickname; a great hunter, caring more for good form in his sport than for the bag. His book is a personal one. It formed the basis (and a good deal more) of *The Master of Game*, written by Edward, Duke of York, somewhere about 1410. The original manuscript is lost; the best remaining one is in the National Library in Paris. But, since we are concerned with the substance of these writings, and not with their beauty, I have found it more convenient to use the printed edition of 1510.

There is not really very much about archery. Indeed, I rather think that Gaston regarded the bow as something a little beneath his notice; more as the weapon of a poacher, or a person of low degree, than of a true hunter. It struck at a distance, and there was no danger to the user. Such was his philosophy; game must be taken dangerously. Whether it is more hazardous to confront a wild boar when on horseback and armed with a short sword, or on foot armed with a bow and arrows, is a matter on which I will not venture an opinion (although I have no doubt at all in which case I would rather be!);

The Great Hart (Red Deer)

The Great Hart (Red Deer)

The Doe (Red Deer)

The Fallow Buck

The Boar at soil

The Hare in her Form

31. Illustrations from *The Book of Roi Modus*
about one-third size

ussi peut on prendre bestes a trai∫
te aux arcz et aux arbalest∫re et a
larc de main que on appelle an∫
glois ou turquoy. Et s. se veneur
veult aller traire aux bestes et il veult a∫
uoir de main larc doit estre dif ou dautre
bors : et doit auoir de long de sune osche ou
la corde se met iusques a lautre vingt poul∫
cees : et doit auoir entre la corde et larc quãt
il est tendu tout ses cinq dois de sa paulme
de large . La corde doit estre de soye : car on
la peut faire plus gresse que dautre chose et
aussi elle est plus forte et dure plus que de
chanure ne de filet donne plus singlant et
grant coup. Larc ne doit pas estre trop fort
tant que cellup a qui il est ne se puisse bien
tyrer a son ayse sans soy trop deffraier en
guise que une beste se puisse veoir : et aussi
se tiendra il entoise plus longuement et la

main plus seure que sil estoit fort / Et ar
cuneffois une beste vient longuemet esc
tant lors conuient il quil ait sa entoise :
doit attendre ainsi iusques a tant que la ?
te soit pres pour tyrer. Et sil estoit trop f
il ne pourroit ainsi estre longuement / ma
se conuiendroit quant il tyreroit a ce rem
toit tant que sa beste se berroit. La flesc
doit estre de huyt poingnees de long de
boce de sa coche derriere iusques au bat?
de la flesche. Et elle doit auoir de large
bout des barbeaulx quatre dois : et doit ?
ser de chascune part et estre bien affille et
gu et doit auoir cinq doys de long . Et qu
il bouldra tyrer et mettre sa flesche en la ?
de pour traire il doit regarder que les pe
nons de la flesche aillent de plat contre ?
arc . Car quant il descocheroit et laitr
...ser sa saiette se les pennons estoient ?
uers larc ilz pourroient hurter a larc et?
fraiet quil nen tireroit la droit. Et sil se
chasser aux chiens il doit auoir tous ceu
qui sauent traire aux arcz a mettre au ?
soubz du vent tout de ranc au gect du
grosse pierre poingnal loing lung de la?
tre silz sont en cler pays : mais silz ne fo
en cler pays ilz doyuent estre plus pres ?
uant ung arbre chascun et non seurs esc
gnes derriere deuers larbre et les archi
doyuent estre plus pres deuant tous bes?
de vert : puis doit mettre ses deffences t?
au tour fors que la ou ses chiens et archi?
feront se plus pres quil pourra lung de ?
tie selon les gens quil aura . Et doyu?
parler lung a lautre et faire noise ainsi c?
me iay dit cy deuant . Puis doit aller ?
fer courre de dedans ses deffences le qu?
de ses chiens : et quant la beste vien:a a?
archiers les archiers doyuent des ce qu?
auront ouy laisser courre mettre se?
flesches en larc et aussi mettre seurs d?

32. Page from Gaston de Foix's *Livre de Chasse*
slightly reduced; printed edition of 1510

but evidently Gaston thought it was. He somewhat weakens his case, how-ever, by an open confession that he knows little about bows; and refers us to England for further information on the subject: 'They know all about it there.' He had certainly been out hunting with the bow, since he describes an accident which he once saw; but I do not think he was himself an archer.

Only one short chapter of his book is given to the bow; No. lxxi, entitled 'Cy deuise comment on peut traire aux bestes darbalestre et de larc a main'. Just as his own work was later plagiarized, so there can be no doubt that he copied shamelessly from Roi Modus, and inaccurately at that.

The bow is to be 'dif ou dautre boys', of yew or other wood. If for 'boys' we misread 'buys', then we have what is to me a very plausible explanation of the supposition, mentioned elsewhere in these notes, that bows used to be made of boxwood. It is to be twenty 'poulcees' long between nocks. I have tried very hard to discover what this measure really is, but without success. If we take it to mean 'thumb', then in my case, my thumb being 2¾ in. long from the big joint to the tip, the bow works out at only 4 ft. 7 in. This is im-possibly short, unless the good Gaston used a flat bow, which the woodcut in the printed edition does not bear out. If we take twenty-two units, as did Roi Modus, then at least we reach 5 ft.; but even that is too short for a bow of conventional cross-section. The only conclusion that can be reached is that Gaston was not good at figures, or that 'poulcee' does not mean thumb.

The arrow is to be eight 'poingnees' long from the nock to the points of the barbs. This is clearly the same unit as is used by Roi Modus, but two less of them. If Gaston really means that his arrows were only 24 in. long, then it is possible that his bow might have been as short as he says it was; but I think it more likely that again he is inaccurate. It is all very unsatisfactory.

The arrowhead is to be five fingers long, and four fingers wide at the barbs. An immense thing! And what size of feather would have been necessary to carry it? Let us leave Gaston; I am sure he was wise to say they knew more about it in England.

In the matter of actual hunting he is, of course, reliable. He copies, more or less word for word, all that Roi Modus says about the deductions to be drawn from the appearance of the blood, and the places where hits will, or will not, be effective. Also, he recommends a weak bow. Original points are:

Always try to get the game on your left side. If it comes on the right, you will have to turn your whole body to shoot, and will be seen.

If the beast is passing you, never aim between the four legs, or you will miss. Aim well in front.

If in company with another archer, it is dangerous to shoot at right-angles to a beast's flank, since the arrow may pass right through. 'It was by just such a chance that Sir Godfrey Harcourt was wounded in the arm.'

If you wound a beast, you will track him with hounds until you get him.

There is no advice to the lone archer; what there is deals with hound-work or the use of beaters. Evidently these methods now and then led to disputes as to the ownership of a particular beast that had been bagged. Gaston says that, in such cases, one must expect words to run high, 'but, at the end, Wine will bring peace'. Happy days!

A MINOR NOTE

For those who cannot get access to larger game, here is a note on hunting squirrels, taken from Nicholas Cox's *Gentleman's Recreation* (1697). A blunt arrow was used; and I rather think I can smell crossbow, but am not quite sure. It can hardly have been a very profitable game to anyone except the local fletcher; but no doubt it may have been amusing as an occasional diversion.

'Many must go together to Hunt them, and must carry Dogs with them: and the fittest place for the exercise of this sport, is in little and small slender Woods, such as may be shaken by the hand, Bows are requisite to remove them when they rest in the twists of Trees; for they will not be much terrified with all the hollowing, except they be struck now and then by one means or other. Well do they know what harbour a high Oak is unto them, and how secure they can lodge therein from Men and Dogs; wherefore since it is too troublesome to climb every Tree, that labour must be supplied with Bows and Bolts, that when the *Squirrel* resteth, presently he may be thumpt with the blow of an arrow: the Archer need not fear to do her much harm, except he hit her on the head; for by reason of a strong back-bone, and fleshy parts, she will abide as great a stroak as a Dog.'

SEASONS

Here is a table of the old seasons for hunting. In view of modern game laws and other restrictions this is only relevant in so far as it indicates those times when the flesh is in the best condition.

Hart (Red Deer)	..Nativity of St. John the	
Buck (Fallow) ..	Baptist to Holyrood Day	24th June to 14th Sept.
	or	
	Two weeks after Midsummer to Holyrood Day	8th July to 14th Sept.

Hind (Red Deer)	..Holyrood Day to Candle-	
Doe (Fallow)	.. mas	14th Sept. to 2nd Feb.
Roebuck	Easter to Michaelmas	22nd March
		25th April to 29th Sept.
Roe (Doe)	Michaelmas to Candlemas	29th Sept. to 2nd Feb.
Hare	Michaelmas to Candlemas	29th Sept. to 2nd Feb.
	or	
	Michaelmas to end of Feb.	29th Sept. to 28th Feb.
Boar	Nativity of Our Lady to	
	Candlemas	8th Sept. to 2nd Feb.
Coney (Rabbit)	All seasons	

'*Fencer Month*', during which no game might be killed, was from two weeks before Midsummer Day to two weeks after.

DISTRIBUTION OF DEER IN ENGLAND AND WALES

(The following information was given in an article by Mr. Gerald Johnstone, published in *The Field* in 1946.)

Red Deer

Exmoor, Brendon Hills, Quantock Hills, South of Taunton-Barnstaple railway line (in the big woods as far south as Tiverton and Chulmleigh).
Blackdown Hills.
Bodmin Moor.
Somerset-Dorset border.
New Forest (reduced to very low limits by poaching and war).
Lake District (Martindale Fell; also a large area in Westmorland, Lancashire, and north-west tip of the West Riding of Yorkshire; perhaps also in Cumberland).
Ashdown Forest (doubtful).
Savernake Forest.
Cotswolds (perhaps).

Fallow Deer

Most heavily-wooded parts of Kent, Surrey, Sussex, Hampshire, Wiltshire, Dorset; and the Wiltshire-Somerset and Dorset-Somerset borders.
North-west Dartmoor, south-east Devon, Bodmin Moor.
West Essex, Suffolk, north and south-west Norfolk.
Hertfordshire (greater part), Epping Forest, Berkshire, Nottinghamshire, Northamptonshire, Huntingdonshire, south-west Lincolnshire (Bourne area), Cannock Chase (and the thick woods on the Staffordshire side of the River Dove).

Shropshire, Herefordshire, Monmouthshire, Worcestershire, north Gloucestershire (and Gloucester-Oxford border).

Montgomery, Brecon (perhaps Radnor also), Forest of Dean (remnants may exist).

Northumberland and Durham (on Forestry Commission lands), Yorkshire (Allerston).

Roe Deer

Cumberland and Westmorland, including the Barrow district.

Eastern Northumberland, eastern Durham, Lancashire, Yorkshire.

Central Wales, including the forest areas of Carnarvon, Merioneth, Montgomery, Radnor, Brecon, Cardigan, and(?) Carmarthen.

Monmouth, Shropshire.

Devon (Haldon Hills), Dorset, south Wiltshire, Hampshire, Berkshire, Surrey, Sussex.

Exmoor, Blackdown Hills, Quantock Hills, Tiverton area.

Norfolk and Suffolk (Brandon, Harling, Thetford, Mildenhall area).

North-east Rutland, Bedfordshire, and Northamptonshire.

Sika Deer (Japanese)

Lancashire and Yorkshire (Ribblesdale and Pendle Forest area—but probably exterminated in the former).

Monmouth, Gloucester, Oxfordshire, Buckinghamshire, Berkshire.

Hertford, Essex.

Warwick, Northamptonshire, Huntingdon, Leicester.

Kent, Surrey, Sussex, Hampshire.

Wiltshire, Dorset, New Forest.

Chinese Water Deer

Bedfordshire, Buckinghamshire, Northamptonshire, and(?) Berkshire.

Muntjac (Barking Deer)

Bedfordshire, Buckinghamshire, Northamptonshire, Hertfordshire.

HUNTING WITH THE BOW

So there I will leave you. The experiences and triumphs of Dr. Pope and his friends are not yet ours. But already I have found that to have come sufficiently close to game to be able to use the bow, and to have drawn and actually loosed the arrow, has given me ten times as much care and thought, and infinitely greater satisfaction, hit or miss, than ever was to be got out of firearms. The wild thing is matched against the primitive weapon; and that seems fair and right.

Some day you, and I, will take the Great Hart by our own skill alone,
and with an arrow. And then the Little Gods of the Woods
will chuckle, and rub their hands, and say: 'Look,
Brothers. An Archer! The Old Times are
not altogether gone! Wish him
Good Hunting!'

ENVOI

'And nowe the Sunne is downe, therefore, if it please you, we will go home and drincke in my chamber.'

TOXOPHILUS.

We have come to the end. I wish, like the good Roger, that you could come to my chamber, and see and handle bows and archer's gear, and talk and talk, and, perhaps, even in these days, drink something also. The field-archers of to-day are so few and far apart, more's the pity.

But even if we cannot meet in the flesh, we can in spirit. If this book has held your attention at all; if it has stirred your imagination in the least; if it has roused in you some latent and unsuspected interest in an old and honourable weapon of the chase; then proceed, I beg you, to the logical conclusion:

Make yourself a Bow and Arrows,
and teach yourself to use them.
Therein you will discover
an enduring fascination
out of all proportion
to your pains.
Try it,
My Friend.

Farewell!

APPENDICES

APPENDIX I: OLD ENGLISH

Although archery, as an everyday thing, has been dead in England these three or four hundred years, it is still very much alive (if you can recognize it) in our present-day speech. It is curious that so many sayings, expressions, and proverbs should still survive, and be used by folk who have now little inkling as to their meaning or origin.

I have put down here as many as I could find, and the hunt for them has been most entertaining. There must be many more. Some are, perhaps, of rather doubtful authority, although to my way of thinking they have a right to be included. Wherever possible, the date has been given at which they are first recorded. Our English tongue is a tree of slow growth, and correspondingly enduring.

Before we begin on this, let us first take a look at the London Telephone Directory, and see what we find in those fat and ultra-modern volumes. In the issue before me now there is quite a goodly company. We begin with *Archer* and *Bowman*. There are two hundred and five archers, and one hundred and twenty-six bowmen. How many have kept up their forefather's tradition?

Of the Guilds which made the archers' tackle we find the following representatives. *Bowyers*, eighty-six (not counting the few Bowmakers, who have nothing in common with us, being builders); *Stringers*, sixty-eight; *Fletchers*, who made the arrows, three hundred and eighty-four; and *Arrowsmiths*, makers of broadheads and bodkin-points, thirty-one. There are also a few ready-made Bows and Arrows, but I do not think they are of our company. We seem rather short of arrowsmiths, and perhaps a little overweighted with fletchers; but setting aside these trifling discrepancies, we could, from London alone, if only John Stringer Esq. and William Bowman would revert to plain John the Stringer and Will o' the Bow, reconstitute quite a respectable nucleus of the tradesmen and archers of the old Tudor 'Artillerye'.

Of individual archers, whose names were once household words, we find *Hood*, *Loxley*, *Gilbert*, *Littlejohn*, and *Tuck*; but not Robin's other companions Scathelocke and Much. *Bell*, *Clough*, and *Cloudesley*, all three; *Asham* and

185

Askam, who certainly are of the same family as our old friend Ascham; and *Barlow*, the famous 'Duke of Shoreditch' created by Henry VIII.

How glorious if these could all appear once again like Chaucer's 'Squyer's Yeoman':

> And he was clad in cote and hode of grene,
> A shefe of pecocke arrowes bryght and shene
> Under his belt he bare ful thriftily
> Well coude he dresse his tackle yomanly;
> His arrowes drouped not with fethers lowe,
> And in hande he bare a myghty bowe.
>
> (*Canterbury Tales*, Prologue)

The sayings that follow are classified roughly by subject.

Of ARCHERS we have the following:

'*An archer is known by his aim, not by his arrows.*'

Nowadays we should say 'Fine feathers do not make fine birds', or perhaps 'Clothes do not make the man'.

'*Speak well of archers, for your father shot in a bow*' (recorded as 1721, but surely earlier).

A wholesome reminder to us not to be ashamed of our parentage. The medieval and later archer, the fighting man I mean, came always from the lower ranks of society, never from the nobility. The bow was essentially the weapon of the common man; and it was that which, before the coming of firearms, made the ordinary folk of England such a tough proposition for authority to tackle.

'*The man of God is better for having his bows and arrows about him*' (1659).

A plea, I take it, for common sense and a robust outlook among the clergy.

'*Every man will shoot at the foe, but few will gather up the shafts.*'

Gathering shafts is a difficult, tedious business. The ability of an arrow to hide itself must be experienced to be believed. Presumably, the meaning to be conveyed is that there are few men who can be relied upon to see a thing really through to the end themselves, without leaving the dull and uninteresting part to someone else.

'*He will shoot higher that shoots at the moon, than he who shoots at a dunghill, though he miss the mark.*'

High ideals, even if unattainable, are preferable to sordid ones.

186

OLD ENGLISH

Nicholas Breton wrote in 1600: 'From idle tales of Robin Hood, the blessed lord of Heaven deliver me!' and there are a number of other sayings of the same sort. The legendary Robin, with his impossible goings-on, had clearly become a nuisance; or, more likely, 'Tales of Robin Hood' had become a way of describing any nonsense. Strangely enough, there is not much concerning his archery. A very early example is:

'*Many talk of Robin Hood who never shot in his bow.*'

The original seems to be in Chaucer (*Troylus*, ii, 861) and dates from about 1374: 'They speken, but they bente never his bowe.' In other words, don't boast, or talk about things of which you know nothing.

'*As crooked as Robin Hood's bow.*'

The allusion is to the nature of yew wood. Yew is a difficult wood to make a bow of. One must follow, and not cut through, all the ups and downs of the grain; and these are many and various. The most difficult thing in the world is to get a piece of yew, a billet, which will make a straight, flawless longbow. Usually, if one can get a piece long enough to make a bow in one length at all, one has to work round knots and 'pins' leaving thicker places here and there, and one or other of the bow's limbs may have a disconcerting 'dog's leg' in it as well. None of these things matter provided that, when full drawn, the bow shows a true curve, or, in the old phrase, 'comes round compass'.

Thomas Fuller (*Worthies of England*, i, 116) refers to this also:

> England were but a fling,
> Save for the crooked stick and the grey-goose wing.

That is about all that we get of the good Robin, except for a very modern '*To overshoot Robin Hood*' or, even simpler, '*To overshoot the mark*', both used to denote exaggeration.

Leaving now fiction, and coming to fact, we find this downright assertion:

'*Every English archer beareth under his girdle twenty-four Scots.*'

So far from this being another insult to Scotland, we find that Ascham says, in *Toxophilus* (1545). 'The Scottes themselves ... gyve the whole prayse of shotynge honestlye to Englysshe men, saying thus: that every Englysshe archer beareth under hys gyrdle xxiiii Scottes.' The saying arose from the habit of archers of keeping arrows for immediate use under their belt, the quiver (if any) being used as a reserve. Twenty-four arrows made a 'sheaf', which was the unit of the official issue. Flodden was still fresh in men's minds, both Scots and English, at this time; and at Flodden the King of Scots had been killed by an arrow.

And now for something about the BOW itself.

'To draw the longbow' (1678).

Everyone knows this—and does it on occasion. I dare say the archers themselves were good talkers; they had good right to be at one time. But there is no question but that the ballad-mongers outdid them, to the point of absurdity. One knows that modern archers in America have shot somewhat over four hundred yards with the longbow used in the normal position; but I am quite sure that, with his heavy hunting tackle, Will Cloudesley himself would never have claimed to have shot that length (as is recounted in the old ballad called 'The names of the Three Archers'), much less to have split the wand at such a range. Nowadays, in this connection, we are apt to think less of archers, and more of fishers.

'To draw a bow at a venture.'

Another old friend; this time from that treasure of beautiful language, the Old Testament (1 Kings, xxii, 34). 'And a certain man drew a bow at a venture, and smote the King of Israel between the joints of the harness.' So Ahab died, killed by a stray shaft.

'There's many a good bow besides one in Chester.'

Perhaps nowadays we should say: 'There's many another good fish in the sea.' Cheshire bowmen were renowned for their skill and strength.

'I have a famous bow, but it is up at the Castle' (1641).

Said of someone who will undertake to do a thing without having the means of doing it.

'I have the bent of his bow' (1430).

Nowadays we should say that we had the measure of him; or, better perhaps, that we knew the cut of his jib.

'A bow long bent at last waxeth weak' (1546).

Ben Jonson wrote: 'The mind is like a bow, the stronger by being unbent.' It is, of course true that a bow should not be kept bent, or braced, for a moment longer than is absolutely necessary; and it is also true that a bow at rest, hung up on a wall, will increase somewhat in strength after a time.

'To outshoot a man in his own bow' (1585).

This, I suppose, is a way of saying that the man was outdone on his own

subject; or beaten on his own ground. Serve him right for lending his bow!
A bow is a very personal thing and dislikes being used by anyone but its
master. Everyone draws differently, and bows have enough to put up with
without being exposed to unnecessary trials.

'*Draw not thy bow before thy arrow be fixed.*'
Excellent advice.

'*The young are not always with their bow bent*' (1678).
Young people cannot be expected to be always serious. They must be
allowed their fling now and then.

'*The bow of Ulysses*' (Homer, *Odyssey*, xxi).
To draw this bow is to perform the impossible. The story is that Ulysses
had got it from one Iphitus, the son of Eurytus, King of Oechalia. The latter
had, some time before, had a shooting match with Heracles, better known as
Hercules, and been beaten by him. Not content with this, Heracles later on
murdered both Iphitus and Eurytus: and was, besides, a dirty archer, using
poisoned arrows. From the time that Iphitus gave Ulysses his father's bow it
seems that no one but the latter could draw it.

So much for bows; now a little about STRINGS.

'*To have two strings to one's bow*' (1477).
An old friend, which requires no attempted interpretation. In battle this
was sometimes done literally. In Moseley's *Essay on Archery*, a most tiresome
work (1792), there is, in Plate II, an engraving of a seal said to have been
found on the battlefield of Bannockburn. This shows an archer with two
strings fitted; one he is drawing, the other is left loose. I suppose that, if one
canted the upper limb of the bow slightly towards the right, one would make
sure that the loose string would hang free, and not mar the shot. Ascham
condemns the idea outright: 'In warre, if a stringe breake, the man is lost; and
is no man for his weapon is gone: and although he have two stringes put on
at once, yet he shall have small leisure and lesse roome to bend his bow;
therefore, God send us good stringers, both for warre and peace.'

Metaphorically, in Caxton's *Jason* (1477) we read: 'I will wel that euery
man be amerous and loue, but that he haue ij strenges on his bowe.' A
difficult and dangerous game, no doubt; as is pointed out very clearly
by Queen Elizabeth in a characteristically downright letter to James VI of
Scotland: 'I hope that you wyl remember, that who seaketh two stringes to
one bowe, he may shute strong, but never strait.' Elizabeth knew what she

was talking about, since both her father, Henry VIII, and his brother Arthur were keen and good archers; while she herself had had Ascham for her tutor.

'*High strung*.'

A bow is said to be high strung when the string stands well away from the handgrip, to a degree greater than usual. The whole bow is then under greater tension than is normally the case. So, now, we describe a state of high nervous tension.

'*To brace oneself up.*'

The opposite case to the one above. A bow is no good as long as the string is slack; nor is a person whose mind is in the same condition.

Of all the things which go to make up an archer's tackle, it is the ARROW which is the most familiar to the ordinary man to-day; not in the sense that he has ever seen one, for perhaps only one in a thousand has; but because it is familiar, in a conventionalized form, as a direction sign. Your man knows that it has a point at one end, and feathers (or something) at the other. Still, the conventional form is familiar, and quite a number of phrases concerning arrows are still current.

'*As straight as an arrow*' (1592).

If an arrow is not straight it is dangerous; it will 'gad' or 'flirt' in most unexpected directions. A good archer always looks over his shafts before he shoots.

'*He makes arrows of all sorts of wood*' (1732).

The old battle arrows used to be made of ash or aspen. Modern hunting arrows are of birch or bamboo. Target arrows of pine or fir. Nowadays we should be more likely to say that he had all sorts of irons in the fire, or, in a slightly different sense, that he can turn his hand to anything.

'*The arrow often hits the shooter*' (before 1500).

Physically speaking, it does not, unless it breaks at the loose; and then you may get a badly damaged hand. Anyway, it is a warning that if you lay traps for other people, or do them an unkind turn, you may be hoist with your own petard.

'*This arrow cometh never out of thine own bow*' (before 1590).

Surely this is not your own work?

'*Of a pig's tail you will never make a good shaft*' (1651).

Nor a silk purse out of a sow's ear.

OLD ENGLISH

A word spoken is an arrow let fly.'
And will hit something, or somebody—so be careful.

With arrows go BOLTS; and with bolts go QUARRELS. A bolt is the short, heavy shaft, usually with a knob for a head, used in the crossbow. The quarrel is a similar thing, but seems to have had a sharp, four-sided head. The name derives from the French word *carré*—square, or four-sided.

The crossbow was a perpetual thorn in the flesh of all English monarchs, who wished to preserve the use of the more efficient though more difficult longbow. For the crossbow was a machine; and it seems that men have always been willing to forsake the use of their own skill if only they could get a machine to take its place. The advantages of the crossbow were that it was much easier to aim and hit with than the longbow, and it could be carried already 'loaded' or wound up with a shaft on the string. The disadvantages were that it was slow and cumbersome, and shot neither so far nor so hard as the longbow. Also it was difficult to keep it dry; if it rained, and the string got wet, it could not be shot. I have never quite understood this, unless they used gut or rawhide for the string. A well-waxed flax string can stand any amount of rain. However, it must have been so, since the French lost the battle of Crecy partly for this reason. Inevitably, in spite of repeated laws against its use, the crossbow at last ousted the more difficult weapon, until it was itself slain by the coming of firearms.

It has left its mark in our speech in many forms:

To pick a quarrel.'
Presumably one picks an extra sharp or heavy one on meeting one's particular enemy. In the *Paston Letters*, Wm. Paston writes to John Paston (1449): 'The seyde parsone come to Cambryg sothyn, and hath pekyd a quarell to a Mastyr Recheforthe, a knyghtys son of Norforfolk. . . .' A later remark (1529) seems to confirm that the actual choosing of a quarrell before meeting one's adversary did give rise to the use of the saying in its figurative sense. 'yrste pycke a quarell, and fall oute with hym then' (Skelton, *Bowge of Court*).

To make a shaft or a bolt of it' (1600).
To make use of a thing somehow; or to 'have a go' at it. Shaft is synonymous with arrow. 'Ile make a shaft or a bolt on't, slid, tis but venturing' *Merry Wives of Windsor*, III, iv).

A fool's bolt is soon shot' (1225).
A very early one. Crossbows had not the same facility for rapid fire as

191

have magazine rifles. Hence, unless you were a fool, you did not loose off
before the proper time.

'*A fool's bolt may sometimes hit the mark* (1580).

So it may. 'Out of the mouths of babes and sucklings . . .' and so on. But
John Heywood (*Epigrams and Proverbs*, 1566) states the contrary case:

> 'A fooles bolt is soon shot, and fleeth oftimes fer,
> But the fooles bolt, and the marke, cum few times ner.'

So we may infer that a silly remark, or a foolish action, sometimes does, and
sometimes does not, turn out to be more sensible than it appears; which is
a very proper and profound conclusion.

'*I have shot my bolt*' (1577).

A crossbow took a long time to reload. So, when it had once been loosed
off, the man had done all he could for the moment—and was fair game for
the nimble, quick-firing longbow.

'*A bolt lost is not a bow broken.*'

Not a major catastrophe; it might have been worse.

'*This bolt never came out of your quiver!*' (1530).

You never invented that!

'*A bolt from the blue.*'

Archers in battle had the nasty habit, from their enemies' point of view,
of shooting upwards into the air, so that their arrows should fall vertically.
Such a one, coming out of the blue sky, must have been very disconcerting.
The expression now conveys a sense of unexpectedness as well.

'*Bolt-upright*' (1386).

This, also, is, perhaps, a little unexpected; but it is authentic, all the same,
and very old. In Chaucer's *Miller's Tale* (1386) there is the following:
'She was long as a Mast, and uprighte as a bolt.' The allusion is, of course, to
the extreme straightness which an arrow must have if it is to fly truly.

Of ARROWHEADS there is not much.

'*A barbed shaft.*'

A barbed head cannot be withdrawn from a wound. Some primitive tribes
make doubly sure of this by so arranging their arrows that the shaft, alone,
can come away easily, leaving the head in place. Very barbarous. So, figura-
tively, a remark with a sting in it sticks.

'*The Broad Arrow.*'

Although not part of the spoken word, this ancient sign cannot be left out of a catalogue such as this. It is the mark set on Crown property, including, oddly enough, certain persons detained during His Majesty's pleasure. You will see it particularly on warlike stores of all descriptions; guns, rifles, and such. In shape it is a very much conventionalized broadhead, looking more like the imprint of a crow's foot than anything else.

The exact origin of this mark, as applied to the King's property, is hard to discover. You can choose between two possibilities. In either case, the correct heraldic term for the Broad Arrow is 'Pheon'; and in the Book of St. Albans, that marvellous storehouse of terms of venery and the like, there is this: 'Feons be calde in armys brodearow hedys.' The pheon proper has the inner edges of the barbs wavy, or serrated; and it appears so in the Sidney arms, with the point downwards. Now a Sidney was Master of the Ordnance from 1693 to 1702. That is the first possible explanation of its present use.

The second is this: Fairholt (*Costume in England*, 1860) says that the pheon was a barbed javelin carried by the Sergeant-at-Arms in the King's presence, as early as Richard I. So it may have been the badge of the King's authority, or property in the twelfth century. Whichever you incline to, certain it is that it had been established by the reign of James II, for he himself gave orders to that effect.

When you have decided in your mind which explanation you like the better, you will find both of them dashed by what Viscount Dillon says (*Proc. Soc. Antiquaries of London*, Series 2, Vol. 17, 1899). He thinks that the mark had nothing to do with Sidney, nor with the King at all; but that it was merely a commercial sign, easy and convenient to place on cases of goods. In support of this he quotes two letters of Sir Thomas Gresham to the Council:

From Antwerp, 6th February 1553-4. 'Giving your Lordeshippes to undyrstand that at this daye I have resseved xxxvj barrells of gownepowder partte of the complement that was lent to the Regent, wyche I have shipped in an Inglishe Crayer Mr. Thomas Spache of Rye under this marke × In the margent, . . .'

From Seville, 30th November 1554. 'The cases have been sent off to-day . . . there is L cassys marked with the brode arrow and be nomeryd from No. I to No. L.'

The 'marke in the margent' is an elementary broad arrow. So, I fear, we must leave the matter. There seems to be no final or authoritative answer to the riddle how the mark first became the sign of Crown property.

The QUIVER, and the SHOOTING-GLOVE provide only one example each.

'To have a quiverful.'

The quiver is the case in which the archer keeps his spare shafts. The expression is used to describe parents with many children. Whether it is just a simple simile, or because a family of small children in a common bed, with their heads all peeping out in a row, does in a way remind one of a full quiver, I cannot tell you. It is a satisfactory comparison anyway.

'Lo, children are an heritage of the Lord: and the fruit of the womb is his reward. As arrows are in the hand of a mighty man; so are children of the youth. Happy is the man that hath his quiver full of them. . . .' (Psalm cxxvii.)

'To keep tab' on something.

To follow its progress; to keep your eye on it. This is not modern slang. If a bow is used much without some protection for the fingers which draw the string, these will get very sore. Archers, therefore, wear a shooting-glove, which takes the rub of the string. But as a glove is hot and cumbersome, very often a little piece of leather, slipped over two fingers, takes its place. This is called a 'tab'. An archer with his tab on is prepared for action.

Of MISCELLANEOUS GEAR, and the PRACTICE OF ARCHERY, there are quite a number of things which come to mind. Including these with the foregoing, it will be found, I think, that there is no part of archery or the tackle associated with it which is not represented in some saying or other.

'Out of bowshot.'

Out of range; out of one's reach. Literally, an average archer, using a good bow and heavy hunting (or battle) shafts, would be lucky to reach 250 yards. More likely, 200 yards would be his limit. Much greater distances, over 400 yards, have been reached in recent years; but only with special flight arrows, very light and carefully made. 'Out of earshot' is, I suppose, a play on the original.

'A Parthian shot.'

A shrewd remark made at the end of an argument; a parting shot.

The Parthians, who came from the country just south of the Caspian Sea, were most skilled archers and horsemen. Their favourite device was to retire rapidly, or pretend to do so. They would then turn round suddenly in their saddles and shoot their bows. For this manœuvre they would be using the short, composite bow of the East; the longbow cannot be shot from the back of a horse.

'*The Upshot.*'

Nowadays this is used generally to mean the final result of anything, a conclusion. This usage has become a little corrupted from the original. The upshot, in archers' language, does not necessarily mean the final result. When archers are shooting in competition the best shot made up to any given moment is the 'upshot'. It is the best shot, not always the final one.

'*To be a butt*' for somebody to ridicule, or vent their feelings on. The butt was the mound of earth at which archers used to shoot. 'The Butts' is a place still to be found in many English towns.

War arrows were not used for this practice shooting, but a special sort without barbs.

> . . . the very pinne of his heart,
> cleft with the blind Bowe-boyes but-shaft . . .
>
> (*Romeo and Juliet*, II, iv)

It is not, we must imagine, pleasant for the butt to be stuck full of shafts. And so a butt has come to mean a poor fellow who is the target for other people's wit, merriment, or malice.

'*Point-blank.*'

When shooting at the butts, a piece of white material was put up on it to serve as the mark. This mode of shooting was called 'shooting at the pricks'; the prick being the white mark, set at 'prick-height'.

Now an arrow has a high trajectory; its path is an arc, whose curvature is the more pronounced the longer the range. Sometimes, therefore, one has to aim above the mark (for long ranges), sometimes below (for short ranges). This requires much nice calculation.

But if one is at such a distance that the arrowhead has to be aimed neither above nor below the mark, but at it, then one is shooting '*point blanc*', the point rests on the white mark.

This directness, or lack of thought and calculation, leads to the modern usage, e.g. 'He refused point-blank'.

'*Underhand.*'

We have just seen that it is often necessary to aim above the mark. Take a bow (or a walking-stick), in your hand and do it. You will find that the target is wholly or partially concealed by your bowhand and arm. The target is beneath the hand, and you are about to shoot an 'underhand' shaft.

Whether this concealment has anything to do with the modern sense of underhand, meaning hidden, furtive, or mean, I will not venture to say; but it seems possible, and so I include it here.

For the sake of those who are not archers, the opposite of underhand is 'forehand'. The hand is then below the mark.

'To keep one's end up.'

Here is another doubtful one. In archery an 'end' is the sequence of arrows shot by competing archers before they go up to the target, turn round, and shoot the reverse end. The phrase might well mean, therefore, that one had shot well, and had not been defeated by one's opponent, which is the modern sense.

'A "Popinjay".'

The Popinjay, or Pepingoe, was the brightly coloured figure of a parrot, set on top of a pole as a mark for archers, principally crossbowmen. That the word does mean parrot can be gathered from what Hakluyt says in his *Voyages* (iii, 700): 'Likewise there bee popiniayes very great and gentle and some of them haue their foreheads yellow, and this sort do quickly learne to speake and speake much.'

Never having seen it, I have always thought this form of shooting must be very expensive in lost arrows, if the archers shoot from a distance; and very dangerous for the spectators if they shoot vertically. In Belgium the *tir à la perche* is still a popular pastime. The Société de St. Sébastien, in Bruges, is perhaps the best-known of these archery clubs.

'Rule of Thumb.'

When a bow is braced, ready for action, but not drawn, the string must stand off a proper distance from the inside, or 'belly', of the handgrip. The archer does not measure this accurately. He puts his fist on the belly, and stretches his thumb up towards the string, which it should just touch. This is quite accurate enough for all practical purposes.

Hence we use the expression to denote a casual, empirical, unscientific method of doing anything.

So—the tale is ended.

Some of these sayings are old friends; some may be new acquaintances. Some are dead, some are dying; and some are very much alive. If ever the time comes when all are gone clean from our understanding, it will be an evil day indeed.

APPENDIX II: A CALENDAR OF ENGLISH MILITARY ARCHERY

Here is a list of the more important dates in the history of English military archery. For those who may wish to read for themselves accounts of the events noted a reference relating to each is given. Many of the older accounts are exceedingly entertaining, but unfortunately not all are equally or readily accessible.

Date	Item	Reference
c. 449	The short bow arrives in England, brought by the Saxons, who 'troubled and subdued the Britaynes with nothing so much as with theyr bowe and shaftes, which weapon being straunge and not seene here before was wonderfull terrible unto them. . . .'	Toxophilus
c. 870	The Vikings come armed with bows and battleaxes	Trevelyan, History of England, 1926.
1066	Battle of Hastings. 'In the closing of the euening, when he (Harold) by the shote of an arrowe (which pierced his braine) was killed, the Englishmen fled away in the night season. . . .'	John Stow, Annales, 1631, and Trevelyan, loc. cit.
1169–1171	Conquest of Ireland	Hume, History of England, 1824
c. 1200	Robin Hood. Whether he was a mythical character or a real personage is still a matter for argument	Ritson, Robin Hood, 1795. Dictionary of National Biography, 1891 Archery News, Nov.– Dec. 1944

Date	Item	Reference
c. 1270	The longbow arrives in England, brought from Wales by Edward I. For the prowess of Welsh archers see	Trevelyan, loc. cit. Giraldus de Barri, called Cambrensis, *Itin. Cambriae,* C.3
1298	Battle of Falkirk. Edward I *v.* Wallace. 'The English archers chased the Scottish bowmen off the field. . . .'	Hume, loc. cit.
1314	Battle of Bannockburn. Edward II *v.* Bruce. 'The English failed properly to use their archers to advantage.'	Trevelyan, loc. cit.
1333	Battle of Halidon Hill. Edward III *v.* Sir Archibald Douglas. 'They were so galled by the English archers, that they were soon thrown into disorder. . . .'	Hume, loc. cit.
1340	Battle of Sluys. 'Then the Kyng set all his shyppes in order, the grettest before, well furnysshed with archers. . . .'	Froissart, Berners' Translation, 1812
1346	Battle of Crecy. Edward III *v.* Philip de Valois, King of France. 'Than thenglysshe archers stept forthe one pase, and lette fly their arrowes so holly, and so thycke, that it semed snowe. . . .'	Froissart, loc. cit.
1356	Battle of Poitiers. The Black Prince *v.* John, King of France. A classical example of the good tactical use of archers.	Stow, loc. cit.
1359	Battle of Nogent. Sir Eustace Dambreticourt *v.* The Lord Broquet de Fenestrayes. The French carry shields, 'pavesses', and are protected from the archers.	Froissart, loc. cit.

Date	Item	Reference
1364	Battle of Auray.	Froissart, loc. cit.

Sir John Chandos *v.* Charles of Blois. '... the frenchemen ... were well armed and pauisshed. Than tharchers ... cast away their bowes, and entred in among the frenchemen that bare the axes, and at ye first metyng they pulled out of some of the frenchemennes handes their axes, wherwith they fought after ryght handely.'

| 1415 | Battle of Agincourt. | Stow, loc. cit. |

Henry V *v.* the Constable d'Albert. '... the Frenchmen were slaine and wounded by the English Archers, and by the helpe of the stakes, which the Englishmen had fixed before them in the ground, whereby the horsemen were constrained to returne, or else to runne upon the stakes, where many of them were ouerthrowne and wounded, and many both horses and men slaine.'

| c. 1455 | Wars of the Roses. | Trevelyan, loc. cit. |
| 1513 | Battle of Flodden. | Stow, loc. cit. |

The Earl of Surrey *v.* the King of Scots, and the last important affray in which archers were used.

| 1545 | Publication of *Toxophilus*. | |
| 1547 | Battle of Pinkie. | Hume, loc. cit. |

The Duke of Somerset *v.* the Earl of Arran. Probably the final instance of the use of the Bow in battle.

| 1549 | Bishop Latymer's Sermon before | |

Henry VIII. 'The arte of shutynge ... is a gift of God, that he hath geven us to excell all other nacions

Date	Item	Reference
	withall. . . . In the reverence of God, let it be continued.'	
1590	An essay on the comparative value Bow and the Musket. '. . . for my part, I will neuer doubt to aduenture my life . . . amongst eight thousand Archers complet, . . . against twentie thousand of the best Harquebuziers and Mosquettiers, that are in Christendome.'	Sir John Smythe, 'Certain Discourses
1611	James I appoints a Commission to survey and restore all old archery grounds that have been encroached upon.	
1613	Defence of the Bow against firearms. The bow is the better because it strikes harder, can be shot more quickly and by more men at once, and the arrow strikes more parts of the body than the ball.	Sir John Hayward, Lives of the III Normans
1625	Publication of the Double Armed Man, to teach the combined use of bow and pike.	Wm. Neade
1662	End of the bow as a military weapon.	Statute, 14 Charles II

APPENDIX III: STATUTES OF THE REALM RELATING TO ARCHERY

(Extracted from the collection published by Parliament in the reign
of King George III)

1100–35	Law of Henry I, whereby an archer at practice who accidentally kills a man is not to be held for murder or manslaughter. The first official encouragement of archery, and to be found in *Archaionomia*, Laws of Henry I, Cambridge, 1644.
1252	Henry III's Assize of Arms. All males between 15 and 60 years of age shall keep arms including bows. See Stubbs's *Select Charters*, 1884.
1284	Statute of Winchester or Winton. Edward I confirms the provisions of the Assize of Arms.
1388	All servants and labourers are to have bows, and to practise with them on Sundays and holidays (12 Richard II).
1405	Regulations for the making of serviceable arrowheads (7 Hen. IV).
1416	Aspen wood to be used for arrows only, and not for pattens or clogs (4 Hen. V).
1464–5	Aspen that is not fit for arrows may be used for pattens (4 Edw. IV).
1472	Merchants are to bring into England 4 bowstaves with every ton of goods imported (12 Edw. IV).
1482–3	The price of yew bows is controlled at a maximum of 3s. 4d. (22 Edw. IV).
1483–4	Merchants are to import 10 good bowstaves with every butt of wine (1 Rich. III).
1487	Price of yew bows again set at 3s. 4d. (3 Hen. VII).
1503	To encourage the import of good bowstaves, Customs Duty will not be levied on staves longer than 6½ feet (19 Hen. VII).
1503	The use of crossbows forbidden to all except Lords and well-to-do freeholders (19 Hen. VII).

1511–12	To encourage the diminishing exercise of archery, every man up to 60 years old, and every man child, shall have and use long-bows; and bowyers shall be compelled to reside in such localities as may most require their services (3 Hen. VIII).
1511–12	The Statute of 19 Hen. VII is to be enforced (3 Hen. VIII).
1514–15	More legislation against crossbows (6 Hen. VIII).
1523	The acts against crossbows partially relaxed (14 Hen. VIII).
1533–4	—and now enforced again (25 Hen. VIII).
1541–2	—and again (33 Hen. VIII).
1541–2	The provisions of 3 Hen. VIII are confirmed, and rules for regular shooting practice laid down. Houses for 'unlawful games', played to the detriment of archery, are prohibited (33 Hen. VIII).
1557–8	Orders for the keeping of bows and arrows by all the population (4 and 5 Philip and Mary).
1566	Imported yew bows to be sold for not more than 6s. 8d. Bows of English yew for 2s. (8 Eliz.).
1571	The Statute of 12 Edw. IV is reaffirmed.
1623–4	Repeal of the arms provisions of the Statute of Winchester (21 James I).
1660	The duty on bowstaves to be £4 for 120 (12 Charles II).
1662	'An Act for ordering the Forces in the several Counties of the Kingdom.'
	The prescribed weapons are swords, pistols, muskets, and pikes. The bow is not mentioned, and as a military weapon is now dead (14 Charles II).

APPENDIX IV: THREE SONGS

ADAM BELL, CLYM OF THE CLOUGH, AND WILLIAM OF CLOUDESLEY

A very old traditional ballad, probably of date about 1200, but printed for the first time at the end of the fifteenth century. The version here given is taken from Thomas Percy's *Reliques of Ancient English Poetry*, 1775.

The subjects of the ballad were Outlaws in the Forest of Englewood, near Carlisle. They had been captured by the King, who had pardoned them at the request of the Queen, and is now curious to see how well they can shoot.

. . . . . .

The Kyng called hys best archars
To the buttes wyth hym to go;
I wyl se these felowes shote, he sayd,
In the north have wrought this wo.

The Kynges bowmen buskit them blyve,
And the quenes archers also;
So dyd these thre wyghtye yemen;
With them they thought to go.

There twyse, or thryse they shote about
For to assaye theyr hand;
There was no shote these yemen shot,
That any prycke might stand.

Then spake Wyllyam of Cloudesle,
By him that for me dyed,
I hold hym never no good archar,
That shoteth at buttes so wide.

At what a butte now wold ye shote,
I pray thee tell to me?
At such a but, Syr, he sayd,
As men use in my countre.

Wyllyam went into a fyeld,
With his two bretherene;
There they set up two hasell roddes
Full twenty score between.

I hold him an archar, said Cloudesle
That yonder wand cleveth in two
Here is none such, sayd the Kyng,
Nor none that can so do.

I shall assaye, Syr, sayd Cloudesle,
Or that I farther go.
Cloudesley with a bearyng arowe
Clave the wand in two.

Thou art the best archer, then said the king,
For sothe that ever I se.
And yet for your love, sayd Wyllyam,
I will do more maystery.

I have a son is seven yeare olde,
He is to me full deare;
I wyll hym tye to a stake;
All shall see, that be here.

And lay an apple upon hys head,
And go syxe score hym fro,
And I myself with a brode arow
Shall cleve the apple in two.

Now haste thee, then sayd the kyng,
By him that dyed on a tre,
But if thou do not, as thou hast sayed,
Hanged shalt thou be.

And thou touch his head or gowne,
In syght that men may se,
By all the sayntes that be in heaven,
I shall hang you all three.

That I have promised, said William,
That wyl I never forsake.
And there even before the kynge
In the earth he drove a stake:

And bound therto his eldest sonne,
And bad hym stand still thereat;
And turned the childes face him fro,
Because he should not sterte.

An apple upon his head he set,
And then his bowe he bent;
Syxe score paces they were out mete,
And thether Cloudesle went.

There he drewe out a fayre brode arrowe,
Hys bow was great and longe,
He set that arrowe in his bowe,
That was both stiffe and stronge.

He prayed the people, that wer there,
That they all still wold stand,
For he that shoteth for such a wager,
Behoveth a stedfast hand.

Much people prayed for Cloudesle,
That hys lyfe saved myght be,
And when he made hym redy to shote,
There was many weeping ee.

But Cloudesle cleft the apple in twaine,
His sonne he did not nee.
Ouer Gods forbode, sayde the kynge,
That thou sholde shote at me.

I geve thee eightene pence a day,
And mẏ bowe shalt thou bere,
And over all the north countre
I make the chyfe rydere.

And I thyrtene pence a day, said the quene,
By God, and by my say;
Come feche thy payment when thou wylt,
No man shall say the nay.

Wyllyam, I make the a gentleman
Of clothing, and of fe:
And thy two brethren, yemen of my chambre,
For they are so semely to se.

Your sonne, for he is tendre of age,
Of my wine seller he shall be;
And when he commeth to mans estate,
Shal better avaunced be.

And, Wyllym, bring to me your wife,
Me longeth her sore to se;
She shall be my chefe gentlewoman,
To governe my nurserye.

The yemen thanked them curteously.
To some byshop wyl we wend,
Of all the synnes, that we have done,
To be assoyled at his hand.

So forth be gone these good yemen,
As fast as they might he;
And after came and dwelled with the kynge,
And dyed good men all thre.

Thus endeth the lives of these good yemen;
God send them eternall blysse.
And all, that with a hand-bowe shoteth,
That of heven they never mysse. Amen.

THREE SONGS

EXTRACT FROM THE BALLAD OF CHEVY CHASE

This is also from the *Reliques*, and is said to be the original version written about the time of King Henry VI. It relates, however, to an earlier period, about the year 1388.

Percy was hunting in Douglas's forest without leave, and the Douglas had gone to turn him out. The account, legendary or not, is mixed up with events which did take place at the battle of Otterbourne.

.   .   .   .   .   .

The Ynglysshe men hade ther bowys yebent,
Ther hartes were good yenoughe;
The first of arros that the shote off,
Seven skore spear-men the sloughe.

Yet bydys the yerle Duglas uppon the bent,
A captayne good yenoughe,
And that was seen verament,
For he wrought him both woo and wouche.

The Dugglas pertyd his ost in thre,
Lyk a cheffe cheften of pryde,
With suar speares off mygghte tre
The cum in on every side.

Thrughe our Englysshe archery
Gave many a wunde full wyde;
Many a doughete the garde to dy,
Which ganyd them no pryde.

The Englysshe men let thear bowes be,
And pulde out brandes that wer bright;
It was a hevy fyght to se
Bright swordes on basnytes lyght.

.   .   .   .   .   .

APPENDICES

At last the Duglas and the Perse met,
Lyk to captaynes of myght and maine;
They swapt together tyll the both swat
With swordes, that wear of fyn myllan.

.   .   .   .   .   .

With that ther cam an arrowe hastely
Forthe off a mighty wane,
Hit hath strekene the yerle Duglas
In at the brest bane.

Thoroue lyvar and longes bathe
The sharp arrowe is gane,
That nevar after in all his lyffe days
He spake no wordes but ane,
That was, Fyghte ye, my merry men, whyllys
      ye may
For my lyffe days ben gan.

.   .   .   .   .   .

Off all that se a Skottishe knyght,
Was called Sir Hewe Mongon-byrry,
He sawe the Duglas to the deth was dyght;
He spended a spear a trusti tre;

He set uppone the lord Perse
A dynte, that was full soar:
With his suar spear of a myghte tre
Clean thorow the body he the Perse bore.

.   .   .   .   .   .

An archar of Northomberlonde
Say slaen was the lord Perse,
He bar a bende-bow in his hande,
Was made off trusti tre.

THREE SONGS

An arow, that a cloth yarde was lang,
To the hard stele halyde he;
A dynt, that was both sad and soar,
He sat on Sir Hewe Mongon-byrry.

The dynt it was both sad and soar,
That he of Mongon-byrry sete;
The swane fethars, that his arrowe bar,
With his hart blood wear wet.

THE AGINCOURT SONG

The more or less contemporary air (*c.* 1415) to which this was sung has
been published, with a modern accompaniment, by Curwen and Sons,
London, No. 71671.

Deo gratias Anglia redde pro victoria!

Owre kynge went forth to Normandy,
With grace and myght of chivalry;
The God for him wrought marvelously,
Wherefore Englonde may calle, and cry
    Deo gratias,
Deo gratias Anglia redde pro victoria!

He sette a sege, the sothe for to say,
To Harflue toune with ryal aray;
That toune he wan, and made a fray,
That Fraunce shall rywe tyl domes day.
    Deo gratias, etc.

Then went owre Kynge, with alle his oste,
Thorowe Fraunce for all the Frenshe boste;
He spared for drede of leste, ne most,
Tyl he come to Agincourt coste.
    Deo gratias, etc.

Than for sothe that knyght comely
In Agincourt feld he fought manly,
Thorow grace of God most myghty
He had both the felde, and the victory.
Deo gratias, etc.

Ther dukys, and erlys, lords and barons,
Were take, and slayne, and that wel sone,
And some were led into Lundone
With joy, and merthe, and grete renone.
Deo gratias, etc.

Nowe gracious God he save owre Kynge,
His peple, and all his wel wyllynge,
Gef him gode lyfe, and gode endynge,
That we with merthe mowe savely synge.
Deo gratias,
Deo gratias Anglia redde pro victoria!

BIBLIOGRAPHY

I n no sense is this a bibliographer's bibliography. It is not even a complete list of all the works on archery which have been published at one time or another. It represents simply those books which I have found it profitable or entertaining to study in compiling my own; together with some others which, although I have no personal acquaintance with them, I have been advised should be included as being worthy of the attention of the serious archer.

The omissions comprise works of minor or no value, ethnographical papers, and scientific studies. Those who wish to learn something about the archery of primitive man, and the inner mysteries of the apparently simple bow and arrow, should consult the excellent bibliography given in Paul H. Gordon's *The New Archery*. This will take them up to 1939; from there, a note to the *American Bowman-Review*, of McMinnville, Oregon, U.S.A., would probably bring them up to date, since most if not all of such work is done in the United States.

However, notwithstanding what is left out, if the reader can get access to and read all the books mentioned below (although some of the earlier ones are rare treasures and hard to come by), he can be assured that he will then have a very thorough and compendious knowledge of the art of archery as set forth through the centuries by those best qualified to inform him.

For the convenience of those who may be more interested in one aspect of the subject than another, I have divided the list into three parts—History, Archery, and Hunting and Woodcraft. It will be understood that the division is arbitrary, and that some books qualify for more than the one section in which they are listed.

HISTORY

14th Century. *Sir John Froissart's Chronicles*, translated from the original French at the command of King Henry VIII by John Bourchier, Lord Berners. Reprinted from Pynson's editions of 1523 and 1525. Printed for F. C. and J. Rivington and others, London, 1812.

BIBLIOGRAPHY

16th Century. *Raphael Holinshed's Chronicle.* Comprised in William Harrison's *Description of England in Shakspere's Youth,* edited from the first two editions of Holinshed's Chroncile A.D. 1577 and 1587 by F. J. Furnivall.
   Printed by N. Trubner, London, 1877–8.

1580   *Annales, or a General Chronicle of England.* John Stow.

1590   *Certain Discourses, written by Sir John Smythe, Knight, concerning the formes and effects of divers sorts of weapons, and other verie important matters Militarie, greatly mistaken by divers of our men of warre in these daies: and chiefly of the Mosquet, the Caliver and the Longbow.*
   Issued by R. Johnes, London.

1613   *The Lives of the Three Normans, Kings of England: William the First, William the Second, Henrie the First.* Sir John Hayward. Published by R. Barker, London.
   Reprinted in the Harleian Miscellany 1744 and 1808.

1765   *Reliques of Ancient English Poetry.* Thomas Percy.
   Edition by H. B. Wheatly, 1876–7.

1792   *An Essay on Archery, describing the Practice of that Art in all Ages and Nations.* W. M. Moseley. Printed at Worcester, and sold by J. Robson, London.

1824   *The History of England.* David Hume. Published by Jones and Co., London.

1841   *The Book of Archery.* G. A. Hansard. Published by Henry G. Bohn, London.

1917   *Shakespeare's England.* Oxford University Press.

1918   *A History of Everyday Things in England.* Marjorie and C. H. B. Quennell. Published by B. T. Batsford Ltd., London.

1929   *The Book of the Longbow.* Robert P. Elmer and Chas. Allen Smart. Published by Doubleday, Doran and Co., New York.

1936   *Bridleways through History.* Lady Apsley. Published by Hutchinson and Co., London.

1937   *History of England.* G. M. Trevelyan. Published by Longmans, Green and Co., Ltd., London.

1944   *English Social History.* G. M. Trevelyan. Published by Longmans, Green and Co., London.

BIBLIOGRAPHY

ARCHERY

1545   *Toxophilus, the schole of shootinge conteyned in two bookes.* Roger Ascham. Printed by Edw. Whytchurch, London.
      Marshe edition, London, 1557.
      Bennet's edition, 1761.
      Wrexham edition, London, 1778 and 1788.
      Arber edition, London, 1868.
      Constable edition, London, 1902.
      The Whole Works of Roger Ascham, edited by the Rev. Dr. Giles. Published by John Russell Smith, London, 1864.
      The Scholemaster, Toxophilus, and Selected English Works. Oxford University Press, 1904.

1625   *The Double Armed Man, etc.* William Neade. Printed for I. Grismand, London.

1634   *The Art of Archerie.* Gervais Markham. Printed for George Sawbridge, London.

1661   *The Compleat Gentleman.* Henry Peacham. Third impression, E. Tyler, London.

1697   *The Gentleman's Recreation.* Nicholas Cox. Printed by J. Dawks, London.

1801   *The English Bowman; or, Tracts on Archery.* T. Roberts. Printed by C. Roworth, London.

1822   *A Treatise on Archery; or, The Art of Shooting with the Long Bow.* Thomas Waring. Printed by T. and S. Bates, London, Fourth edition.

1831   *Sports and Pastimes of the People of England.* Joseph Strutt. Printed for Thomas Tegg, London, new edition.

1856   *The Theory and Practice of Archery.* Horace A. Ford. Published by J. Buchanan, London.
      Archery, its Theory and Practice, London, 1869, is the same; as also is the Toledo (Ohio) edition of 1880 published by R. D. Roff.

1864–   *The Archers' Register.* A yearbook, originally published by Horace
1914   Cox for the *Field* magazine.

1867   *A History of the Royal Toxophilite Society.* Printed for members by H. Abraham, Taunton.

1878   *The Witchery of Archery.* Maurice Thompson. Published by Charles Scribner's Sons, New York.
      Pinehurst edition, edited by Robert P. Elmer, 1928.

BIBLIOGRAPHY

1879   *How to train in Archery.* Will H. Thompson. Published by E. I. Horsman, New York.

1887   *Ford on Archery.* W. Butt. Published by Longmans, Green and Co., London.

1894   *Archery.* Badminton Library. Published by Longmans, Green and Co., London.

1901   *L'Art d'Archerie.* Henri Gallice. Limited edition, published by P. Renouard, Paris.
       Translation by Col. H. Walrond, published by Horace Cox, London, 1903.
       Reprint, published by Clement C. Parkes, Norristown, Pennsylvania.

1907   *A Summary of the History, Construction and Effects in Warfare of the Projectile-Throwing Engines of the Ancients, with a Treatise on the Structure, Power and Management of Turkish and other Oriental Bows of Medieval and Later Times.* Sir Ralph Payne-Gallwey. Published by Longmans, Green and Co., London.

1926   *Archery.* Dr. Robert P. Elmer. Published by Penn Publishing Co., Philadelphia.
       Revised editions 1933, 1939.

1927   *Bows and Arrows.* James Duff. Published by Macmillan Co., New York.
       Reprint 1932.

1929   *Modern Archery.* Arthur W. Lambert, Jr. Published by A. S. Barnes and Co., New York.

1939   *The New Archery.* Paul H. Gordon. Published by D. Appleton Century Co., New York.

1946   *Target Archery.* Dr. Robert P. Elmer. Published by Alfred A. Knopf, New York.

1947   *Modern Archery.* F. L. Bilson. Published by Paternoster Press, London.
       New edition 1949.

1949   *An Archer's Notes.* C. B. Edwards. Published by Frank Petty and Sons, Ltd., Leeds.

——   *The British Archer.* A magazine, published every two months, by P. Clover, 19 Military Road, Portsmouth.

BIBLIOGRAPHY

HUNTING AND WOODCRAFT

1338–48 *Le Livre du Roy Modus et de la Reine Racio.* Authorship not known for certain, but perhaps Henri de Vergy, Seigneur de la Fère, or Henri Ferrières. Manuscript.

1486 edition published at Chambéry by Anthoine Neyret.

1839 edition published at Paris by Elzéar Blaze.

1387 *Le Livre de Chasse*, by Gaston III, Phoebus, Comte de Foix. Manuscript.

Phebus des Deduits de la chasse des Bestes sauvaiges et des Oyseaux de proie. Printed edition by A. Verard, Paris, 1510.

La Chasse de Gaston Phoebus. Edition by Joseph Lavallée. Published by the Journal des Chasseurs, Paris, 1854.

1406–13 *The Mayster of Game.* Edward, second Duke of York. Manuscript. *The Master of Game.* Edition by A. and F. Baillie-Grohman with a foreword by Theodore Roosevelt.

Published by Ballantyne, Hanson and Co., London, 1904.

1925 *Hunting with the Bow and Arrow.* Saxton T. Pope. Published by G. P. Putnam's Sons, New York.

There is also a new edition of this.

1926 *The Adventurous Bowmen.* Saxton T. Pope. Published by G. P. Putnam's Sons, New York.

1926 *Lions in the Path.* Stewart Edward White. Published by Doubleday, Page and Co., New York.

1927 *Wilderness Hunting and Wildcraft.* Lt.-Col. Townsend Whelen. Published by S.A.T.P. Co., Marshallton, Delaware. This has nothing about archery in it. It is included here as one of the best of the many books from which the elements of woodcraft can be learned.

See also *Camping and Woodcraft* by Horace Kephart. Published first in 1917 by the Macmillan Co., New York, and in several reprints since.

INDEX

INDEX

INDEX

INDEX